www.inputoutput.de

Editors:
Florian Pfeffer Germany **Dieter Kretschmann** Germany

Contributing Editors:
Polly Bertram Switzerland **Sheila de Bretteville** USA **Irma Boom** Netherlands **Hans van Dijk** USA **Richard Doust** Great Britain
Debra Drodvillo USA **Gert Dumbar** Netherlands **Neil Grant** Great Britain **David Grossman** Israel **Steven Heller** USA **Ken Hiebert** USA
Werner Jeker Switzerland **Eckhard Jung** Germany **Bill Longhauser** USA **Sadik Karamustafa** Turkey **Hanny Kardinata** Indonesia
John Kortbawi Lebanon **Leila Musfy** Lebanon **Kali Nikitas** USA **Peter Rea** Great Britain **Louise Sandhaus** USA **Ahn Sang-Soo** Korea
Robyn Stacey Australia **Kan Tai-keung** China **Chris Treweek** Great Britain **Teal Triggs** Great Britain **Hans-Dieter Reichert** Great Britain
Chris Vermaas Netherlands **Omar Vulpinari** Italy

Welcome

In memory of
In Erinnerung an

Ingrid

>>>>>>>>>>>>>>>Preface >>Vorwort>>>>>>>>>>>>>>>>>>>>>>>>>>>>>>>>>>>>>>>

>>

>>>Florian Pfeffer>>>Dieter Kretschmann>>>>>>>>

:output is a book for the works of graphic design students. With the principle of »Show and Tell,« we present the works of students from all over the world. For us, the part of »Telling« is just as important as the part of »Showing.« We want not only to give a visual impression of the work, but also to tell about the way the works were approached, their process and the development of solutions.

»Show and Tell« *ist eine weit verbreitete Aufgabe für Schulkinder in den USA. Man bringt einen interessanten Gegenstand mit und erzählt den anderen, was es damit auf sich hat.*

:output ist ein Buch für Arbeiten von Grafik Design StudentInnen. Nach dem »Show and Tell«-Prinzip werden Arbeiten von Hochschulen aus der ganzen Welt vorgestellt. Dabei ist uns der Anteil des »Erzählens« ebenso wichtig wie der des »Zeigens«. Wir wollen nicht nur einen visuellen Eindruck vermitteln, sondern auch die Herangehensweise, den Arbeitsprozess und die Entwicklung von Lösungen darstellen.

:output is a global platform for »cross culture.« But, can cultural diversity be sustained in a merging world? With the worldwide distribution of images, texts and music, the tendencies of adaptation and interchangeability are becoming stronger and stronger. All the more important it is then to put an emphasis on the differences – and to sharpen one's view for individuality. That's why we do not want to only show works from countries with very strong traditions in design (that which is usually seen in design publications). We have a special interest in countries where design, as an economic and cultural factor, is just beginning to be perceived by the public and that, for this reason, is developed in very different ways for each culture. **At the :output calls for input: competition, designers from Australia, Austria, Canada, China, Denmark, Germany, Great Britain, France, Hong Kong, Hungary, Indonesia, Israel, Italy, Korea, Lebanon, Mexico, The Netherlands, Polen, Portugal, Russia, Sweden, Spain, Switzerland, Taiwan, Turkey and the USA finally meet.**

Jam|bo|ree: *das:*
eigtl. ziemlich laute (Fest)versammlung;
1. internationales Pfadfindertreffen.
2. Zusammenkunft zu einer
(Unterhaltungs-) Veranstaltung

:output ist eine globale Plattform für »cross culture«. Aber: Kann kulturelle Vielfalt in einer zusammenwachsenden Welt Bestand haben? Mit der weltweiten Verbreitung von Bildern, Texten und Musik verstärkt sich die Tendenz zu Anpassung und Austauschbarkeit. Um so wichtiger ist es, Unterschiede hervorzuheben und den Blick für das Individuelle zu schärfen. Wir wollen deshalb nicht nur Design aus den Ländern zeigen, die über eine lange Tradition auf diesem Gebiet verfügen und aus diesem Grund üblicherweise in Designpublikationen vertreten sind. Unser besonderes Interesse gilt Ländern, in denen Design als wirtschaftlicher und kultureller Faktor gerade erst wahrgenommen wird und sich entsprechend der jeweiligen Kultur völlig unterschiedlich darstellt und entwickelt. **In diesem Jahr trafen beim Wettbewerb :output calls for input: GestalterInnen aus Australien, Österreich, Kanada, China, Dänemark, Deutschland, England, Frankreich, Hong Kong, Ungarn, Indonesien, Israel, Italien, Korea, Mexiko, Libanon, Niederlande, Polen, Portugal, Russland, Schweden, Schweiz, Spanien, Taiwan, Türkei und USA aufeinander.**

:output is a visual »lost and found.« Graphic design from universities and colleges is different from that made in agencies and design studios for several reasons. It comes into being without a client. During education, the commercial aspect of design moves into the background. The themes selected are often of personal interest or have a social or political character. The possibility for the designer to act as author is also greater: What food producer would ever print posters promoting the vegan lifestyle (>> Nr. 27)? What publishing house would ever publish a diary of aliens on their first visit to Europe (>> Nr. 45)? What educational institution would ever print a handbook for serial killers (>> Nr. 122)? But there is also another huge difference: It isn't often that design made by students ever gets published and thus it is to a wider audience lost. We want to change that.
This year we have selected 145 works which await interested finders.

:output ist ein visuelles Fundbüro. Grafik-Design, das an Hochschulen entsteht, unterscheidet sich in mehrfacher Hinsicht von Arbeiten aus Agenturen und Design-Büros. Es entsteht ohne Auftraggeber. Während der Ausbildung steht der kommerzielle Aspekt von Design nicht im Vordergrund. Die Themenstellungen sind oftmals von persönlichen Interessen geprägt oder haben einen sozialen, gesellschaftlichen Charakter. Die Möglichkeiten für den Gestalter, als Autor tätig zu werden sind größer: Welcher Nahrungsmittelkonzern würde Plakate drucken lassen, die für einen veganischen Lebensstil werben (>> Nr. 27)? Welcher Verlag würde das Tagebuch der Außerirdischen über ihren ersten Europabesuch veröffentlichen (>> Nr. 45)? Welche Weiterbildungseinrichtung würde ein Lehrbuch für Serienmörder herausgeben (>> Nr. 122)? Es gibt aber noch einen weiteren wesentlichen Unterschied: Design aus Hochschulen wird für gewöhnlich nicht veröffentlicht. Dadurch geht es einem größeren Publikum verloren. Das wollen wir ändern. **In diesem Jahr sind 145 Arbeiten von uns ausgewählt worden und warten auf interessierte Finder.**

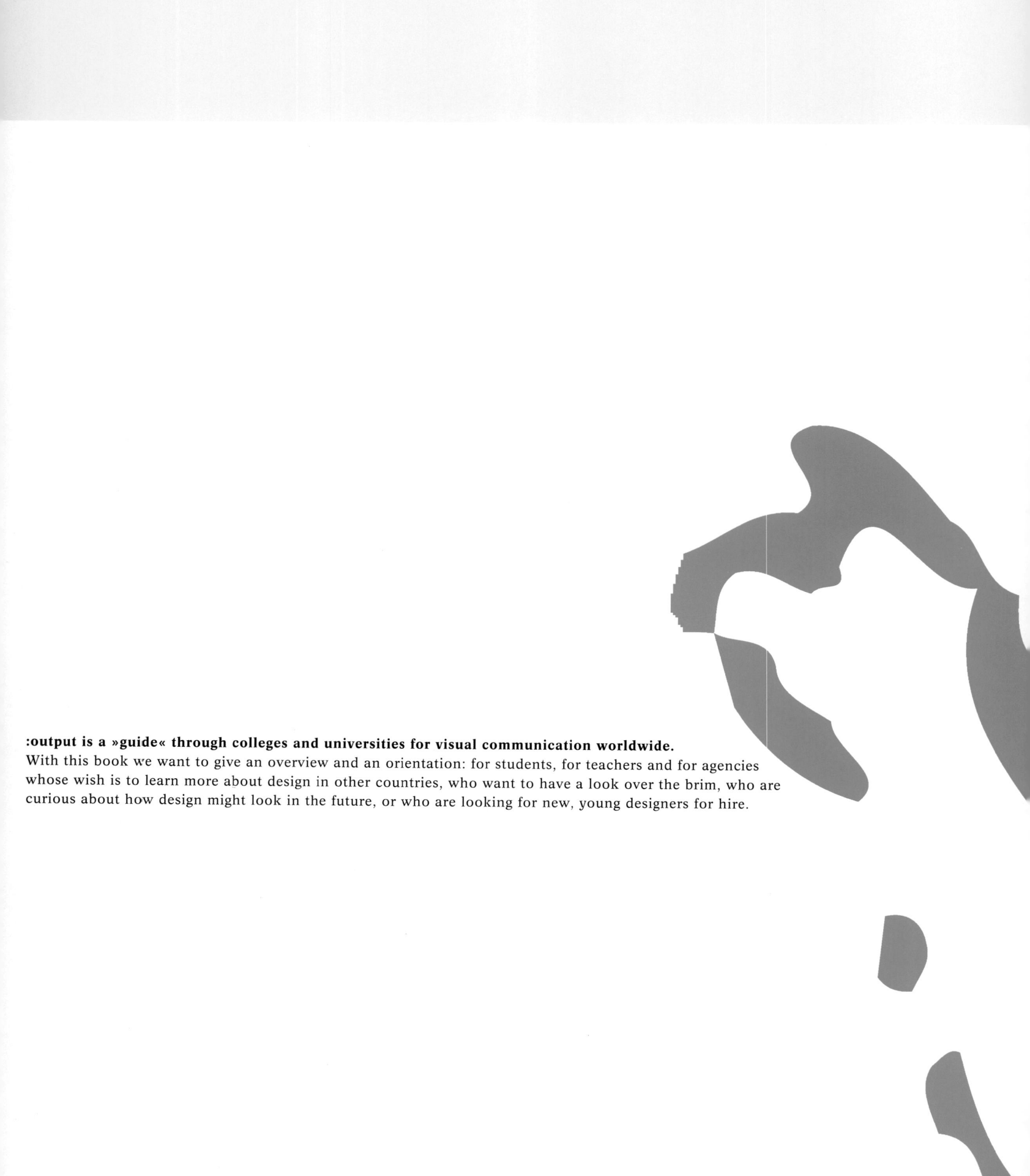

:output is a »guide« through colleges and universities for visual communication worldwide.
With this book we want to give an overview and an orientation: for students, for teachers and for agencies whose wish is to learn more about design in other countries, who want to have a look over the brim, who are curious about how design might look in the future, or who are looking for new, young designers for hire.

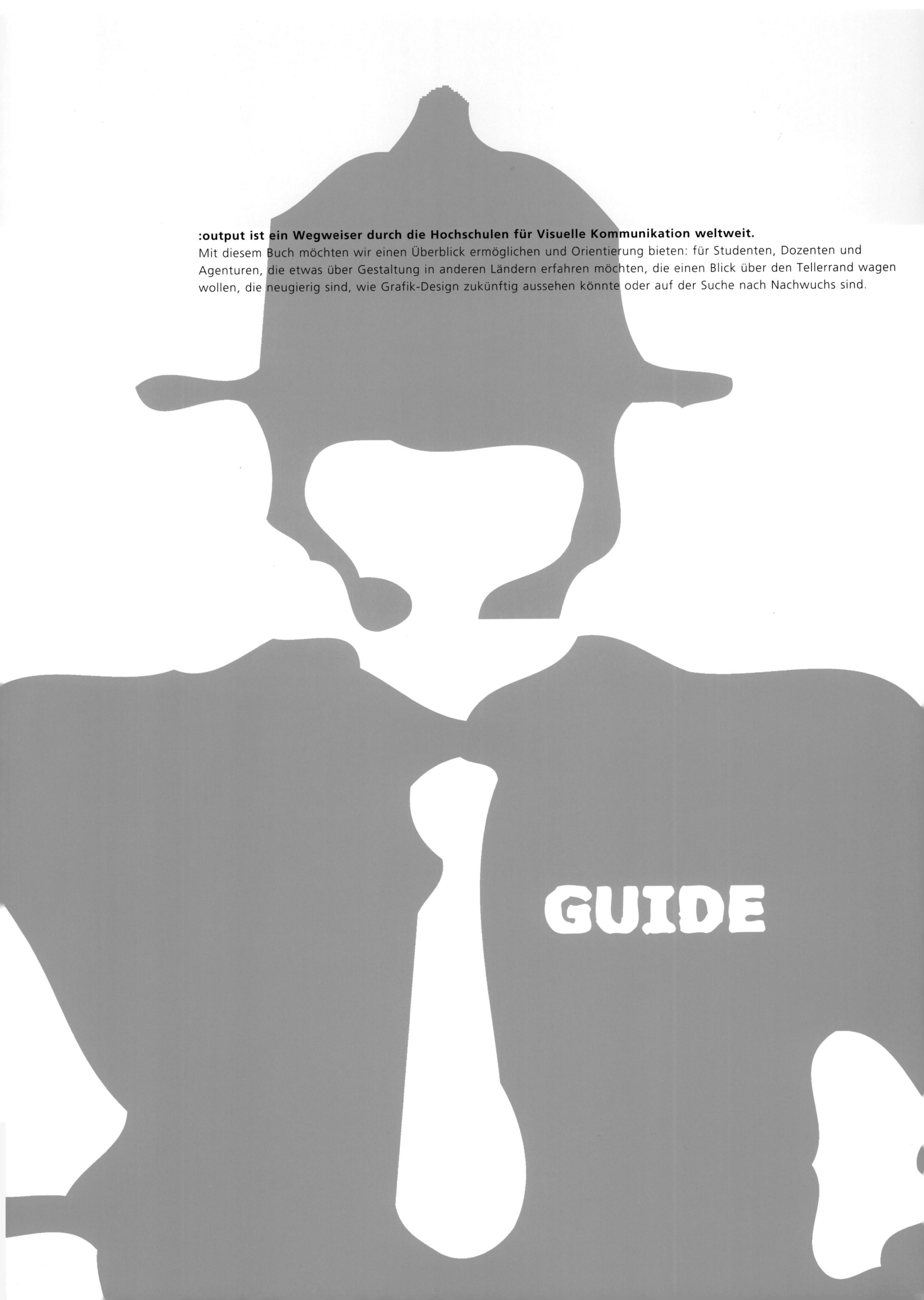

:output ist ein Wegweiser durch die Hochschulen für Visuelle Kommunikation weltweit.
Mit diesem Buch möchten wir einen Überblick ermöglichen und Orientierung bieten: für Studenten, Dozenten und Agenturen, die etwas über Gestaltung in anderen Ländern erfahren möchten, die einen Blick über den Tellerrand wagen wollen, die neugierig sind, wie Grafik-Design zukünftig aussehen könnte oder auf der Suche nach Nachwuchs sind.

GUIDE

:output is an international network for everyone who is active within graphic design education.
By the building of this network, we want to give the opportunity to exchange information, to work together, to critique or to help one another. Hundreds of students from more than two dozen countries have participated in this project. The colleges where they study, and not least of all their professors, are thereby bound together: through participation or as members of the jury (which is newly-composed every year). They also support :output as »contributing editors« – by giving their advice or by sending the best work of their students. Last of all, we hold the jury meeting in a different country every year (this year in Holland and 2001 in the USA) – in cooperation with partner institutions of the German Design Council.

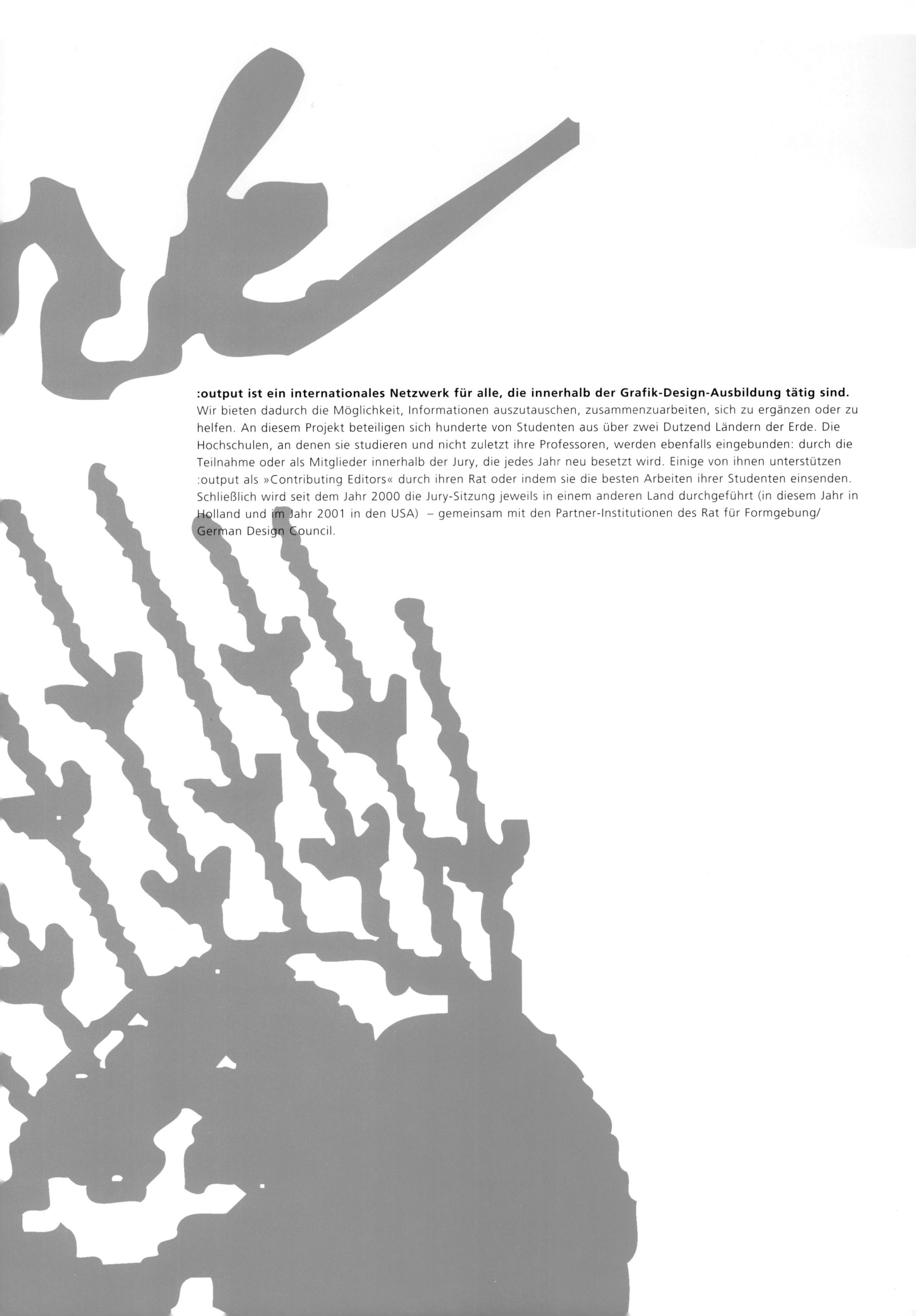

:output ist ein internationales Netzwerk für alle, die innerhalb der Grafik-Design-Ausbildung tätig sind.
Wir bieten dadurch die Möglichkeit, Informationen auszutauschen, zusammenzuarbeiten, sich zu ergänzen oder zu helfen. An diesem Projekt beteiligen sich hunderte von Studenten aus über zwei Dutzend Ländern der Erde. Die Hochschulen, an denen sie studieren und nicht zuletzt ihre Professoren, werden ebenfalls eingebunden: durch die Teilnahme oder als Mitglieder innerhalb der Jury, die jedes Jahr neu besetzt wird. Einige von ihnen unterstützen :output als »Contributing Editors« durch ihren Rat oder indem sie die besten Arbeiten ihrer Studenten einsenden. Schließlich wird seit dem Jahr 2000 die Jury-Sitzung jeweils in einem anderen Land durchgeführt (in diesem Jahr in Holland und im Jahr 2001 in den USA) – gemeinsam mit den Partner-Institutionen des Rat für Formgebung/German Design Council.

>>Advertising>>Werbung>>>>>>>
<<<<<<<<<<<<<Preface<<<<<<<<Vorwort<<<<<<<<<<<<<<<<<<<<<<<<<<<<<<<

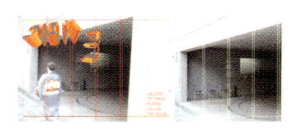

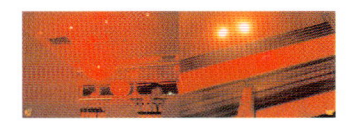

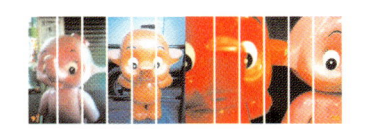

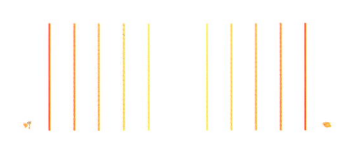

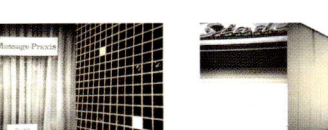

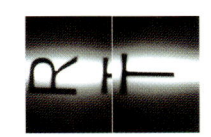

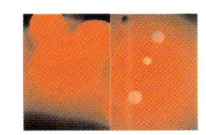

SIGN Kommunikation GmbH
Hanauer Landstr. 287-289
60314 Frankfurt am Main

tel ++49 (0)69/944 324-0
fax ++49 (0)69/944 324-50
www.sign.de

›verantwortung‹

Verantwortung ist uns Ausgangspunkt der Produktentwicklung. Ökologische Verantwortung heißt Reduktion auf das Wesentliche durch minimalen Materialeinsatz, meint Ressourcenschonung durch in Design und Material langlebige Produkte.

Ökonomische Verantwortung heißt Kostenreduktion durch beliebig veränderbare, also wiederverwendbare Messestände. Kulturelle Verantwortung aber bedeutet uns, die Tradition von Bauhaus und Ulmer Schule in zeitgemäßer Form fortzusetzen. Und damit die »Moral der Dinge« anzuerkennen.

Gern senden wir Ihnen weitere Informationen oder nennen Ihnen einen unserer Partner weltweit.

Burkhardt Leitner constructiv
Modulare Räume *Modular Spaces*
Am Bismarckturm 39
70192 Stuttgart
Tel +49 711.2 55 88-0
Fax +49 711.2 55 88-11
E-mail info@burkhardtleitner.de
www.burkhardtleitner.de

BURKHARDT LEITNER constructiv

Es gibt immer gute Gründe, Neues zu wagen. Mit uns.

www.interbrand.de

Creating and managing brand value
Interbrand Zintzmeyer & Lux GmbH

Interbrand Zintzmeyer & Lux
Zürich Köln Hamburg München

Charakter hat einen Namen: **Picto**

Infos unter Referenzangabe: RFF Picto
Wilkhahn, Postfach 2035, D-31844 Bad Münder
Telefon (05042) 999-179, Telefax 999-130
www.wilkhahn.com/Info@wilkhahn.de

Wilkhahn
Für Menschen mit Weitsicht

<<<<<<<<<<<<Advertising<<Werbung<<<<<<<<<<<<<<<<<<<<<<<<<<<<<
>>>>>>>>>>>>>>>>>>>>>>>>>>>>>>>>>>>>>>Works>>Arbeiten>>>>>>>>>>>>>>>

Stefanie Huber Student 1

↪ The images make the value of each stamp tangible.
✻ This page: Things that can be bought in Germany for 110 or 300 Pfennigs,
such as cottonwool tips, noodles, cauliflower, strawberries, hot dogs, etc.
✻ Opposite page: »two bananas + one orange« or »knife + fork + plate« or
»two clothes pegs + underwear« form the figures 1+1+0.

✻ Die Motive visualisieren den Wert der Briefmarke.
▸ Diese Seite: Dinge, die man für 110 oder 300 Pfennige kaufen kann:
Ohrenstäbchen, Nudeln, Blumenkohl, Erdbeeren, Hotdogs etc.
✻ Gegenüberliegende Seite: »Zwei Bananen + eine Orange« oder
»Messer + Gabel + Teller« oder »zwei Wäscheklammern + eine Unterhose«
formen die Ziffern 1+1+0.

Stamps Are Fun | Briefmarken, die Freude machen Title ✸ **2** Study Year ✸
FH Niederrhein College ④ **Germany** Country ✸ **Monika Hagenberg** Professor

David Cabianca Student

Stupidity Font Design Title ✳ **Typeface and Poster** Medium ✘
1 Study Year ❑ **Cranbrook Academy of Art** College ✣ **USA** Country ✣
Laurie Haycock Makela Professor

✣ »›Stupidity‹ was designed using Frederic Goudy's ›Californian‹ as a model. The name was chosen in deference to Mr. Goudy, who recognized the ›exuberance‹ of California's individuality: ›I have attempted also to preserve a certain regularity in the irregular forms while maintaining a severity in line and have made a letter which is individual and at times even presents willful traits that should enhance interest in the design.‹ ›Californian‹ is both grotesque and elegant because of the tightly contained novelty of each letter. ✧ As such, ›Stupidity‹ is a font which is destained to fail. It desires to be a text font and does not have the personality to be a display font. Knowing the rules and elements of design is no substitute for experience and talent: ›Knowledge creates its own stupidity.‹« ▼ »Für die Gestaltung der Schrift ›Stupidity‹ diente Frederic Goudy's Schrift ›Californian‹ als Vorlage. Der Name ›Stupidity‹ wurde in Respekt vor Goudy gewählt, der das Übermaß an Individualität in Kalifornien erkannt hat: ›Ich habe versucht eine gewisse Regelmäßigkeit auch in den unregelmäßigen Formen zu bewahren, während ich Strenge in der Linie beibehalten habe und Buchstaben entworfen habe, die individuell sind, manchmal mit eigensinnigem Charakter, die so Interesse an der Gestaltung erhöhen soll.‹ ›Californian‹ ist gleichsam bizarr und elegant, weil in jedem Buchstaben etwas Neues steckt. ✣ Die Schrift ›Stupidity‹ ist dazu bestimmt, zu versagen. Sie will als Fließtext funktionieren, hat aber nicht die Persönlichkeit für eine Display-Schrift. Das Wissen um die Regeln und Komponenten des Designs allein ist kein Ersatz für Erfahrung und Kreativität: ›Wissen schafft seine eigene Dummheit‹.«

Signage and Type in the Urban Environment | Beschilderung und Schrift im städtischen Raum Title ⓧ **Collage** Medium ➤ 4 Study Year ⑦ **American University of Beirut** College ✱ **Lebanon** Country Ⓜ **Leila Musfy** Professor

Rania Baltagi Student

3

♥ The collages show the use and appearance of type in signage, neon signs and posters on the streets of Beirut. By overlapping different layers of meaning and by using movement as form, they illustrate speed and urbanism.
🚊 Die Collagen zeigen den Umgang und die unterschiedlichen Erscheinungsformen von Typografie auf Schildern, Leuchtreklamen und Plakaten in den Straßen Beiruts. Durch die Überlagerung von Bedeutungsebenen und durch Bewegung veranschaulichen sie Urbanität und Geschwindigkeit.

Rūe 31 شارع ٣١

Teatri 90 Title ❋ Poster Medium ✳ Fabrica College ✝ Italy Country ❀ Omar Vulpinari Professor

♥ Omar Vulpinari Contributing Editor

4 ✳

Marco Morosini Student

Teatri 90 Milano 1-28 febbraio 1999 Palermo 12-25 aprile 1999

Teatri 90 festival, la scena ardita dei nuovi gruppi III edizione next generation italy. Comune di Milano, Settore cultura e musei, Settore sport e giovani Progetto giovani Comune di Palermo, Assessorato alla cultura Regione Lombardia, Provincia di Milano, Eti, Fondazione RomaEuropa, Teatro Franco Parenti, Teatro Litta, Teatro Out Off, Teatro Verdi, Centro Sociale Leoncavallo. Ideazione immagine di Fabrica, Centro di ricerca sulla comunicazione di Oliviero Toscani
Informazioni: Milano tel. 02.12345892156; Palermo 091.1235583

teatrinovanta

✓ »Teatri 90 is a festival for young international avant-garde theatre groups held every year in Milan and Palermo simultaneously. The groups playing are usually very young and very cutting-edge. Many belong to an extreme, hard core body art scene. For that reason, we used the metaphor of a pacifier pierced with nails.« ✳ »Teatri 90 ist ein Theaterfestival für junge, internationale Avantgarde-Theatergruppen, das jedes Jahr gleichzeitig in Mailand und Palermo stattfindet. Die Gruppen sind oftmals sehr jung. Viele von ihnen gehören einer extremen Hardcore-Körperkunstszene an. Aus diesem Grund haben wir die Metapher des mit Nägeln gepiercten Schnullers verwendet.«

Jennifer Wiefel, Erika Usselmann Students 5

Europe 2000 – Modern Architecture | Europa 2000 – Moderne Architektur Title
Stamps | Briefmarken Medium 2 Study Year FH Schwäbisch Gmünd College
Germany Country Michael Burke Professor

Cairo to Casablanca Title ❖ CD Packaging Medium 💬 School of Visual Arts, New York College
✝ USA Country ✳ Stefan Sagmeister Professor

❤ Steven Heller Contributing Editor

Claudia Atencia Student 6

🚫 »Cairo to Casablanca« is a compilation of music from different Arabic artists. The package is made to look as if it were a letter written by a traveler in Africa. It is written and painted with motifs relating to a journey through the desert. The CD becomes the centerpiece, a perfect »surprise« after unfolding the colourful panels. The stamps are originals from Egypt and the envelope is sealed with wax. 📷 Die CD »Cairo to Casablanca« ist ein Sampler mit Musik verschiedener arabischer Künstler. Die Hülle ist so gestaltet, als ob es sich um einen Brief handeln würde, der von einem Reisenden in Afrika geschrieben worden wäre. Die CD-Verpackung ist dieser Brief selbst, der vollkommen beschrieben und mit Motiven einer Reise durch die Wüste bemalt ist. 📷 Die CD ist in den Brief eingepackt und wird so zum zentralen Stück. Sie ist eine perfekte »Überraschung«, nachdem man den Brief aufgefaltet hat. Die Briefmarken sind original ägyptisch und der Brief wurde mit Wachs versiegelt.

Michael Lechner Student 7

Jazz Title ● Poster Medium ● 4 Study Year ● Minneapolis College of Art and Design College ●
USA Country ● John Falker Professor

Cass Lee Student

8

Be Active, Not Lazy | Sei aktiv und nicht faul Title ✱ Poster Medium ✱ 5 Study Year ★ Hong Kong Baptist University College 🌏 China Country ③ Wendy Wong Professor

要活躍！

These two posters are an appeal for regular blood donation. The figures are made with traditional Chinese cut-paper art and are combined with the character for »Blood.« The Rabbit and the headline above encourage people to take the initiative to donate blood. The Pig reminds one not to be lazy and to visit the blood bank regularly. ✻ Die beiden Plakate sind Aufrufe zum regelmäßigen Blutspenden. Die Motive sind in traditioneller, chinesischer Papierschneidekunst angefertigt und werden mit dem chinesischen Zeichen für Blut kombiniert. Der Hase und seine Headline animieren die Menschen dazu, aktiv zu werden und Blut zu spenden. Das Schwein erinnert daran, nicht faul zu werden und regelmässig zum Blut spenden zu gehen.

勿懶惰！

Claudia Nachtmann Student 9

Look Future Books Title ✖ Identity and book design for a publishing house |
Erscheinungsbild und Buchgestaltung für einen Verlag Project ✔ 5 Study Year
FH Nürnberg College ↦ Germany Country ✖ Peter Krüll Professor

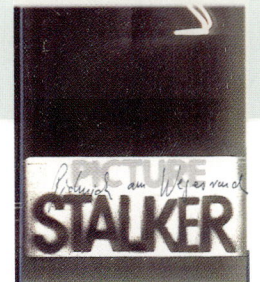

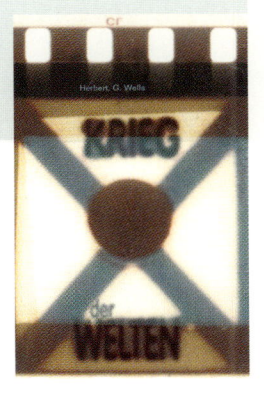

✽ Frames from the beginning and end of a 35mm film were used for the back covers. Found type was then also integrated into the design. Every book has its own character through individual colouring and type choice. The consistency lies in the colour fields on the back cover. ✽ Für die Gestaltung der Buchumschläge wurden Start- und Endbänder von 35mm-Kinofilmen verwendet. Die typografischen Fundstücke wurden in die Gestaltung mit einbezogen. Jedes Buch hat seinen eigenen Charakter in Farbgebung und Schriftwahl. Gemeinsamkeiten sind in der farblichen Unterteilung des Buchrückens zu finden.

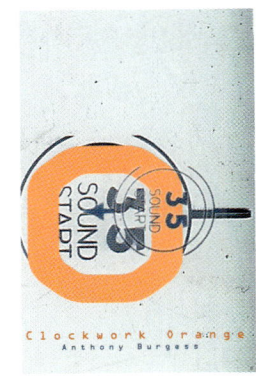

| 05 FEB | **REIFEPRÜFUNG** | 02 APR |

WAS MACHT EIN MÖBEL ZUM DESIGNKLASSIKER?

WWW.KUNSTMUSEUM-DUESSELDORF.DE

DI 11-18 UHR
MI 11-18 UHR
DO 11-18 UHR
FR 11-18 UHR
SA 11-18 UHR
SO 11-18 UHR

KUNSTMUSEUM DÜSSELDORF

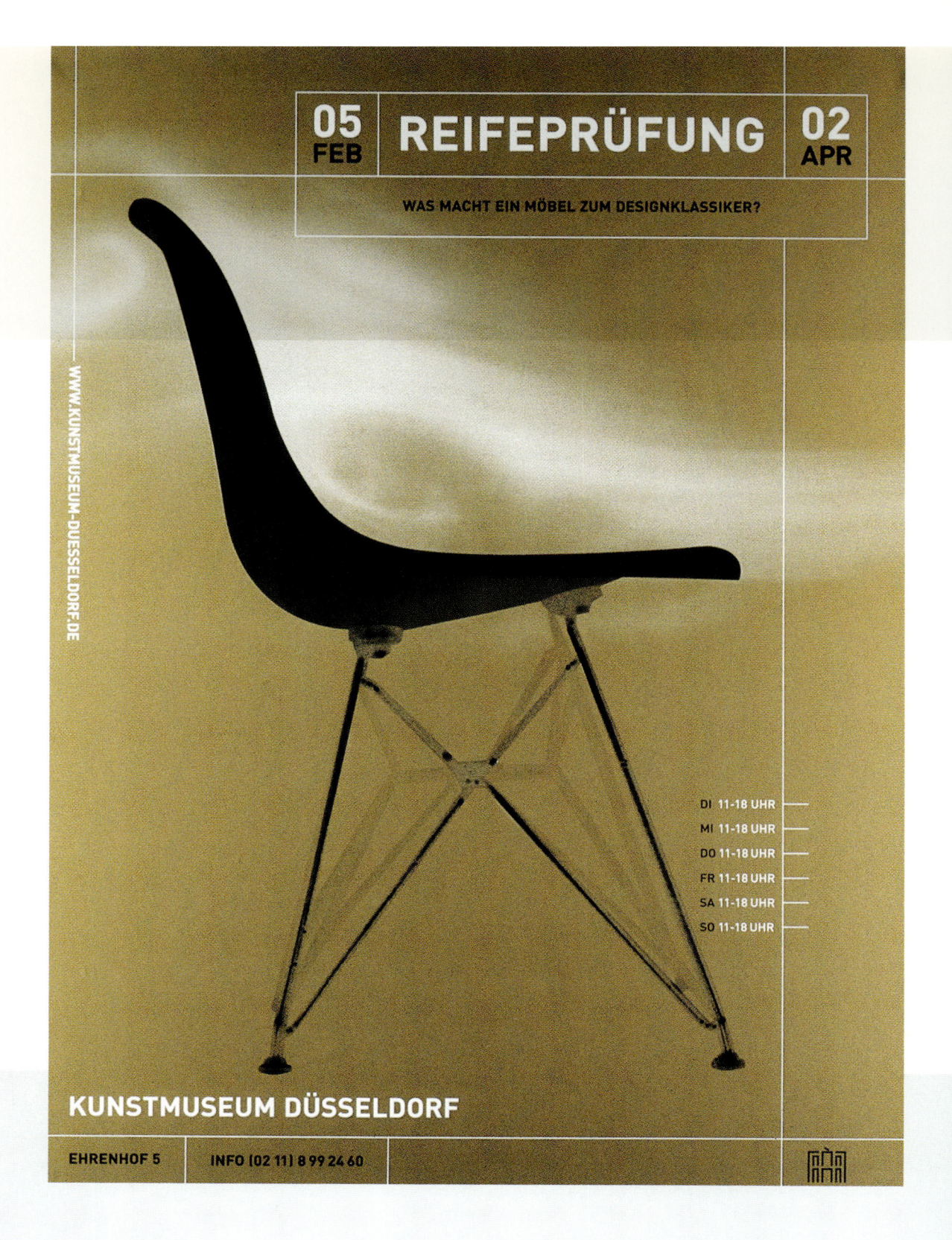

EHRENHOF 5   INFO (02 11) 8 99 24 60

◇ The exhibition »Graduation Exam« is a cooperative project between the Düsseldorf Museum of Arts and the design department of the College of Düsseldorf. The task was to conceive, design and carry out an exhibition for the museum's design collection. To present a design-exibition that is apart from the norm, the »test« concept was developed. Classic works of design were tested in a wind tunnel, by X-ray and with digital cameras. These procedures produced the image concepts for media used within the exhibition. The results collected during the »Test« were then represented typographically in the catalogue and the test-stations were displayed in the exhibition.

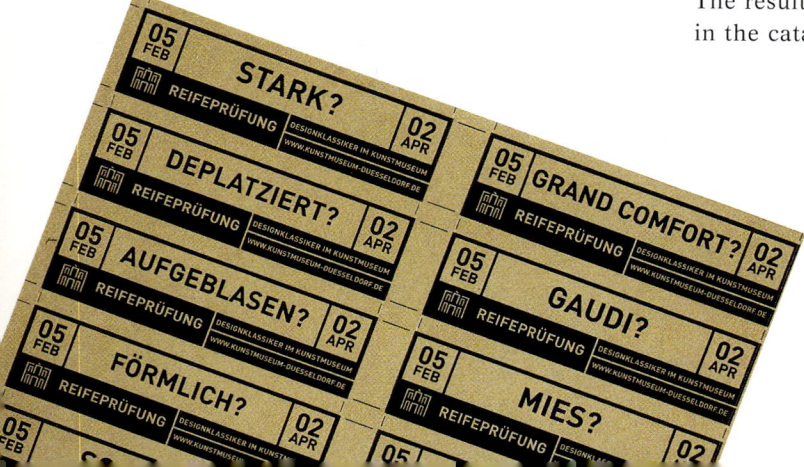

Graduation Exam | Reifeprüfung Title ✻ Exhibition Design Medium ✻
FH Düsseldorf College ■ Germany Country ♦ Philipp Teufel Professor

10

Susanne Erdmann, Kazem Heydari, Anja Kramps, Birgit Lehner, Aline Raab,
Sandra Schmutzenhofer, Ethel Strugalla, Minja Töniges, Britta Waldmann,
Simone Holzberg, Anke Dievernich, Nicola Brandt, Jana Behrendt,
Stephan Schmotz, Max Weber, Natascha Miteva-Efremova, Nils Schrader,
Ina Watermann, Daniela Koza, Nicole Liekenbröcker,
Susanne Meyer-Götz, Stephanie Westmeyer Students

•• Die Ausstellung »Reifeprüfung« ist ein gemeinsames Projekt des Kunstmuseums Düsseldorf und des Fachbereichs Design der FH Düsseldorf. Für die Designsammlung des Museums sollte eine Ausstellung über Designklassiker konzipiert, entworfen und realisiert werden. Um ein Konzept zu entwickeln, dass sich von den üblichen Ausstellungen über Design unterscheidet, wurde die Idee einer »Prüfung« entwickelt. Die Designklassiker wurden im Windkanal, mit Röntgenfotografie und digitalen Kameras getestet. Auf diese Weise ist ein Bildkonzept für alle Medien der Ausstellung entstanden. Die Fragen, die sich im Rahmen der »Prüfung« angesammelt haben, wurden im Katalog typografisch und in der Ausstellung mit Prüfstationen inszeniert.

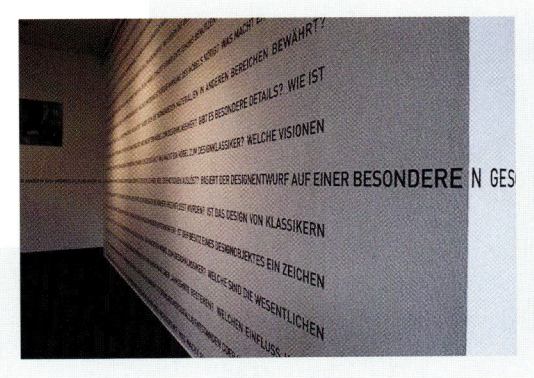

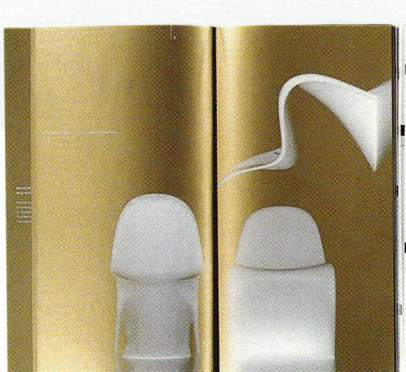

11

Daniel Holmes Student

Non-Places | Nicht-Plätze Title　**Poster** Medium
2 Study Year　**California Institute of Arts** College　**USA** Country
Jeff Keedy, Ed Fella Professors

✗ This poster discusses the construction of non-places, such as the highway, and their use of signage to mediate people and places – resulting in a loss of identity. ❊ Dieses Plakat thematisiert die Entstehung von Nicht-Plätzen, wie Autobahnen. Mit Hilfe von Schildersystemen werden dort Menschen und Orte miteinander verbunden, was zu einem Identitätsverlust führt.

12 Stefanie Hofmann Student

Skin | Haut Title ✳ Book Medium 4 Study Year
Merz Akademie Stuttgart College Germany Country Julio Rondo Professor

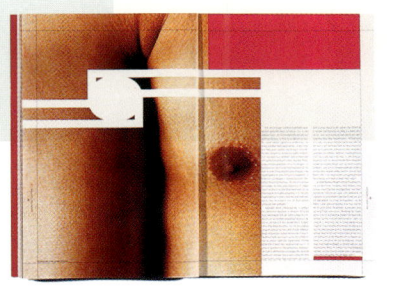

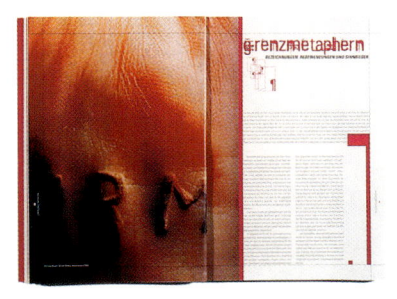

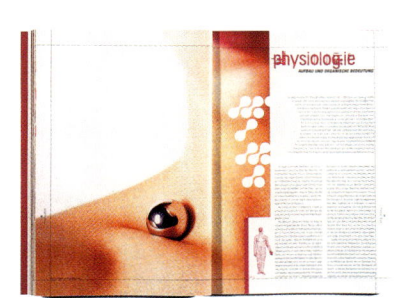

This book discusses the subject of »Skin« from linguistic, historic and organic perspectives. It displays traditional and modern ways of forming skin often as a reflection of cultural context – as well as modern artwork dealing with skin. ✶ Das Buch beschreibt das Thema »Haut« unter sprachlichen, historischen und organischen Gesichtspunkten. Es zeigt traditionelle und moderne Gestaltungsformen der Haut, oftmals ein Spiegelbild des jeweiligen kulturellen Umgangs, sowie aktuelle künstlerische Darstellungsformen in den neuen Medien.

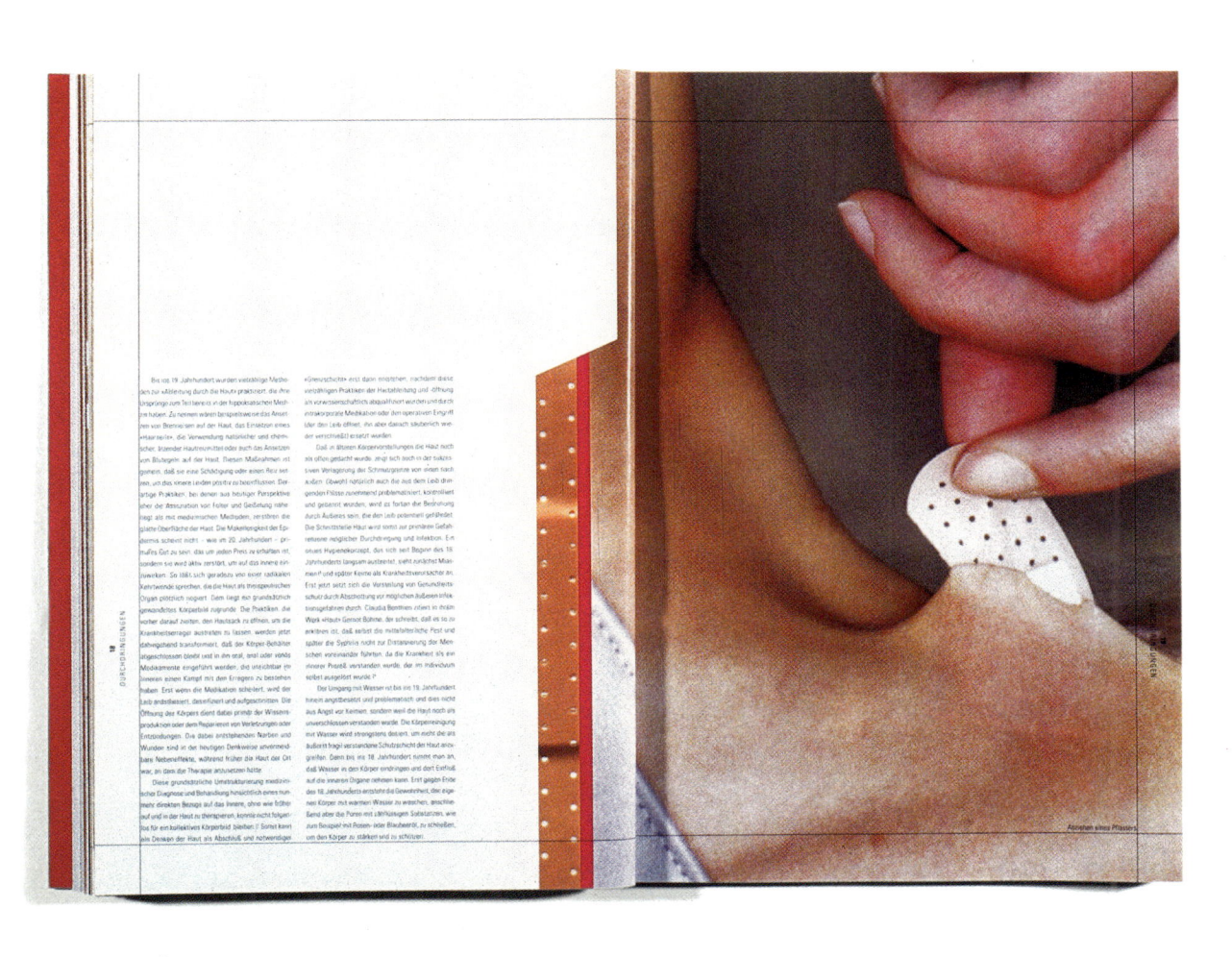

Trans Title ★ Magazine Medium ★ 4 Study Year ☆
FH Düsseldorf College ✤ Germany Country ☏ Prof. Weißmantel Professor

Anke Stache Student 13

The magazine »Trans« deals with a wide range of European issues. This bilingual magazine is published monthly. The languages are differentiated from one another by colour and the overflowing text is printed on separate sheets of transparent paper. The title »Trans« (German = English = French) corresponds to the overall concept – a connection between countries – and it also makes information more transparent for people from different cultural backgrounds. ⚜ Das Magazin »Trans« behandelt Themen aus Europa, die einen Blick über den eigenen Tellerrand zulassen. Es erscheint einmal im Monat und ist zweisprachig. Die Sprachen werden durch die Farbigkeit voneinander unterschieden und stehen bei größeren Textmengen auf getrennten (Transparent-) Papierbögen. Der Titel »Trans« (deutsch = englisch = französisch) illustriert das Gesamtkonzept des Magazins, das eine Verbindung zwischen Ländern herstellt und Informationen für Menschen aus unterschiedlichen Kulturen transparent macht.

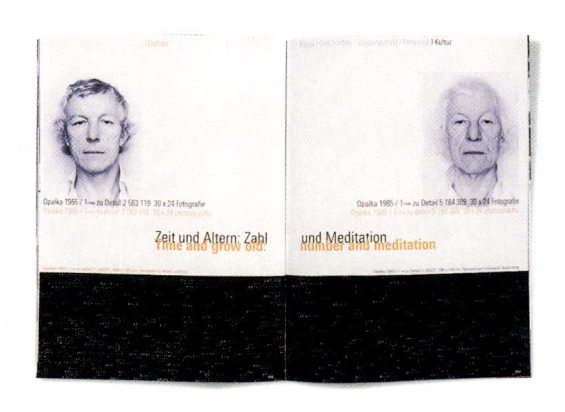

Cosima Böck Student

14

Motet Choir | Motetten Chor Title ✚ Folder | Faltblatt Medium
4 Study Year Staatliche Akademie der Bildenden Künste Stuttgart College
Germany Country Hans-Georg Pospischill Professor

»Motet Choir at Ulmer Münster. Singing in the minstrelry – we cordially invite you.«

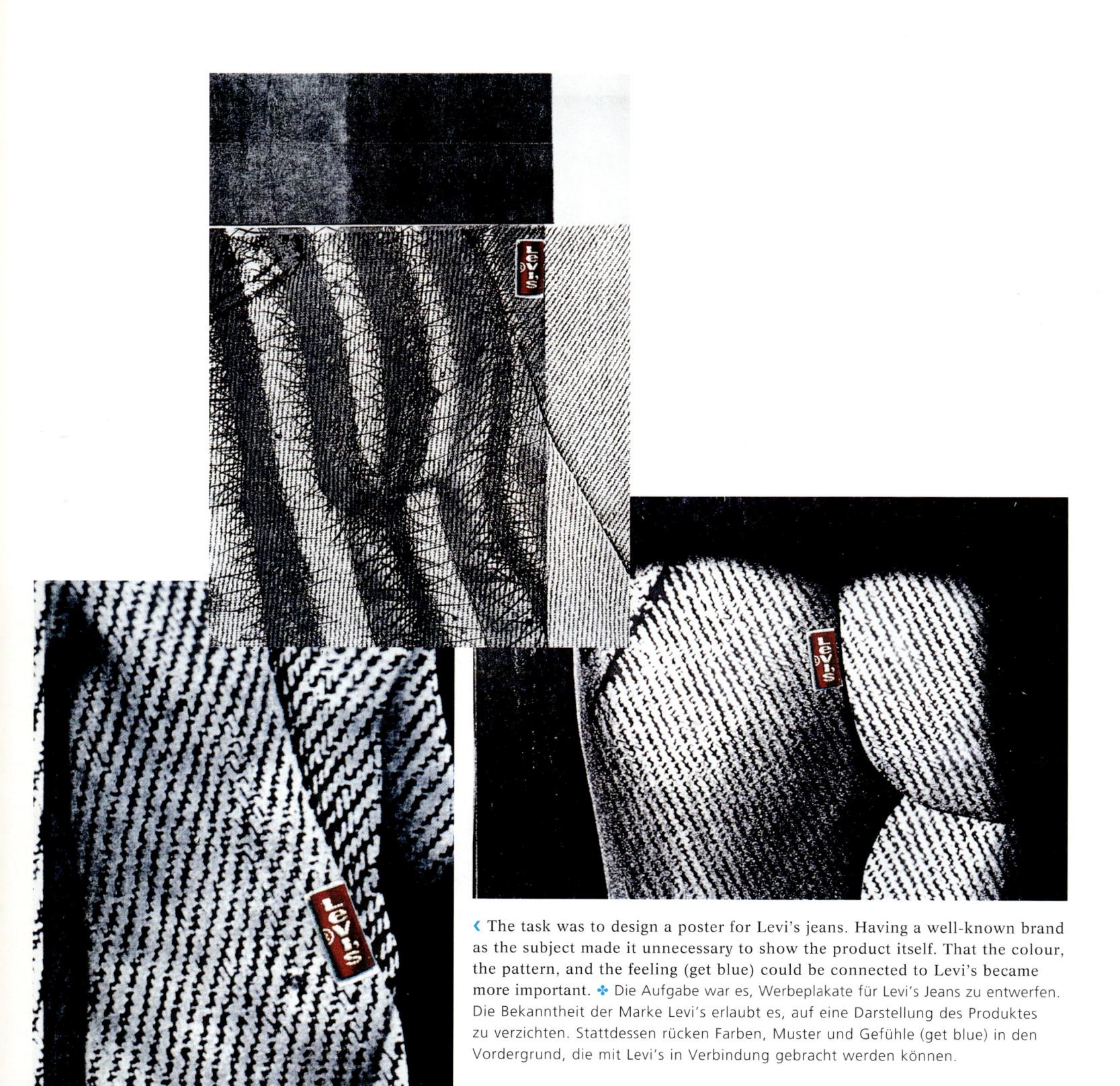

‹ The task was to design a poster for Levi's jeans. Having a well-known brand as the subject made it unnecessary to show the product itself. That the colour, the pattern, and the feeling (get blue) could be connected to Levi's became more important. ❖ Die Aufgabe war es, Werbeplakate für Levi's Jeans zu entwerfen. Die Bekanntheit der Marke Levi's erlaubt es, auf eine Darstellung des Produktes zu verzichten. Stattdessen rücken Farben, Muster und Gefühle (get blue) in den Vordergrund, die mit Levi's in Verbindung gebracht werden können.

Eva Heibl Student 15

Poster for Levi's Title ✢ 2 Study Year 〰 Universidad de Puebla College ✯ Mexico Country ✯ René Azcuy Professor

Marcus Meyer, Julia Baier **Students** **16**

Literary Week | Literarische Woche **Title** Poster **Medium** 4 **Study Year**
HfK Bremen **College** Germany **Country** Eckhard Jung **Professor**

25.–31.1.1999
Literarische Woche

23.

Bremen
Verleihung des
Bremer Literaturpreises
am 26.1.1999 um 12.00 Uhr
in der Oberen Halle des
Alten Rathauses zu Bremen

Rudolf-Alexander-Schröder-Stiftung   Schweizer Kulturstiftung Pro Helvetia

»Literary Week« is an event that takes place in Bremen once a year, introducing the literature from another country. In 1999, the focus was Switzerland, for which, above all, the four languages of Swiss literature needed to be expressed. Die »Literarische Woche« findet jährlich in Bremen statt und stellt jedes Mal Literatur aus einem anderen Land vor. 1999 war das Thema Schweiz, wobei vor allen Dingen die Viersprachigkeit der Schweizer Literatur zum Ausdruck kommen sollte.

Move Our Money ^{Title} Poster ^{Medium} 4 ^{Study Year}
Fabrica ^{College} Italy ^{Country} Stefan Sagmeister ^{Professor}

♥ Omar Vulpinari Contributing Editor

Paolo Palma ^{Student}

»Move Our Money« is a social-awareness campaign for the United States that pushes for a partial shift of public funds from military to public service organizations, such as hospitals and schools. The project was done during a three-day workshop with New York graphic designer Stefan Sagmeister. »Move Our Money« ist eine Kampagne für die Vereinigten Staaten, die dazu aufruft, öffentliche Gelder aus dem Militärhaushalt abzuziehen und Organisationen des Gemeinwohls wie Krankenhäusern oder Schulen zuzuführen. Dieses Projekt entstand während eines Workshops mit dem New Yorker Designer Stefan Sagmeister.

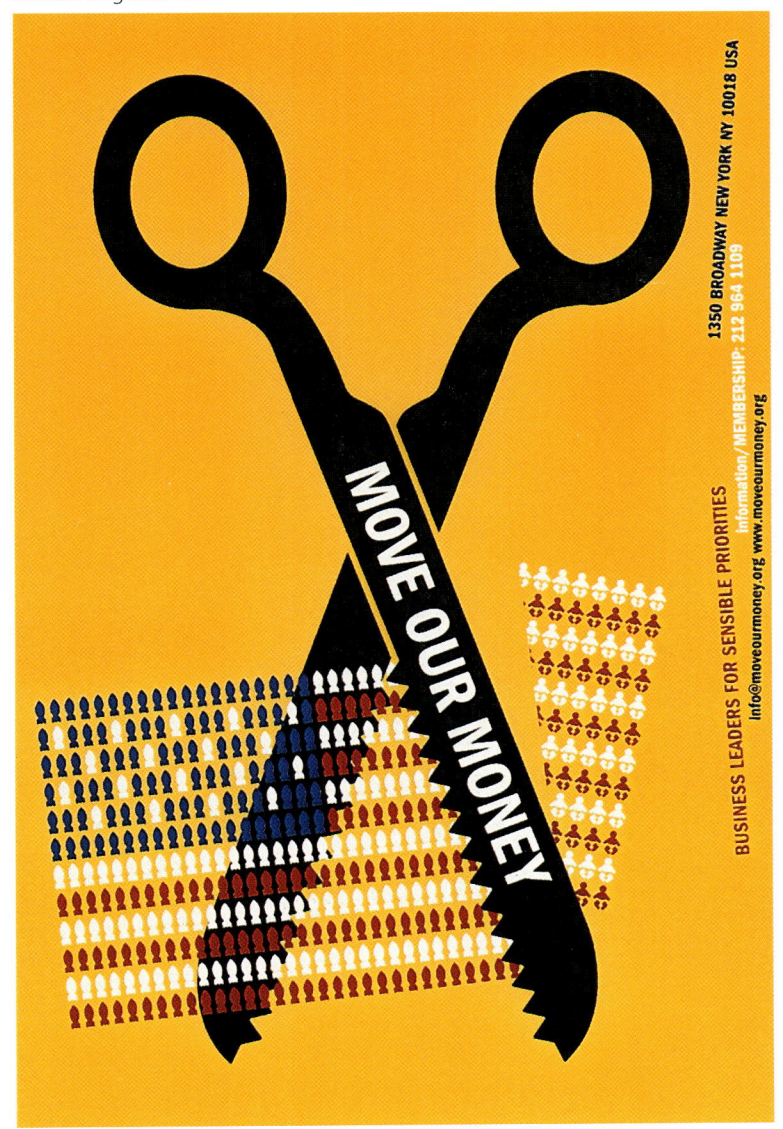

Qana, South Lebanon **Title** ✛ Political Campaign **Medium** ✛
4 **Study Year** ❣ Notre Dame University, Beirut **College** ❧ Lebanon **Country** ✩
John Kortbawi, Yara Khoury **Professors**

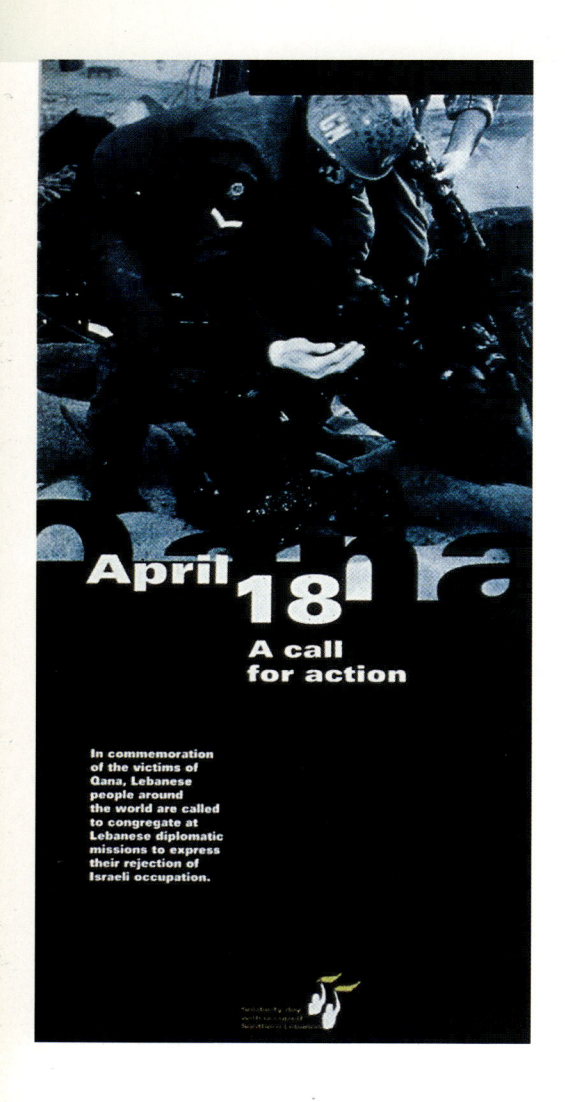

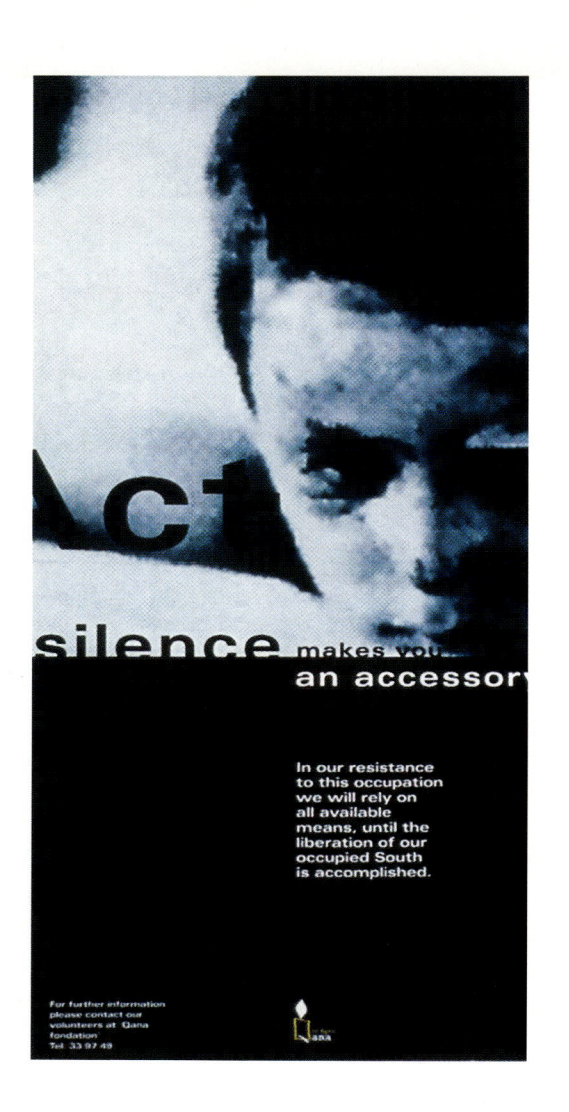

✳ »Qana, South Lebanon« is a campaign against the occupation of the South of Lebanon by the Israeli army. Its aim is to keep the memory of Qana alive, where more than 100 people were killed during a bomb attack while looking for shelter in the UN Headquarters. ✳ »Qana, Süd Libanon« ist eine Kampagne gegen die Besetzung des Südlibanons durch die israelische Armee. Sie will die Erinnerung an Qana am Leben halten, den Ort an dem 100 Menschen bei einem Bombenangriff ums Leben kamen, als sie Schutz im UN-Hauptquartier suchten.

♥ **John Kortbawi** Contributing Editor

Simona El-Khoury Student

18

✳

18 Apr
Qana

Pion Lee Student 19

Please Use the Footbridge | Bitte benutzen Sie die Fußgängerbrücke Title
Poster Medium 3 Study Year Hong Kong Baptist University College
China Country Wendy Wong Professor

👁 The traffic situation in Hong Kong makes crossing the street a dangerous undertaking for pedestrians. This poster series calls for the use of existing footbridges. The posters are made in the style of traditional Chinese woodcuts and play with the contrast between »Heaven and Hell,« i.e. »Life and Death.«
✱ Die Verkehrssituation in Hong Kong macht das Überqueren von Straßen für Fußgänger zu einem gefährlichen Unterfangen. Die Plakatserie ruft dazu auf, die bestehenden Fußgängerbrücken zu benutzen. Die Plakate sind im Stil der traditionellen chinesischen Holzschnitt-Technik angefertigt. Sie spielen mit den Gegensätzen von »Himmel und Hölle« bzw. »Leben und Tod«.

Visiting Artist Poster Title **4** Study Year
Minneapolis College of Art and Design College **USA** Country
Kali Nikitas Professor

Christiane Grauert Student **20**

♥ Kali Nikitas Contributing Editor

Jennifer Jenkins Student **21**

Motel Triptych | Motel Triptychon Title ✛ Photography Medium ✛ 4 Study Year
Minneapolis College of Art and Design College ✎ USA Country ☆
Vince Leo Professor

♥ Hans-Dieter Reichert Contributing Editor

Rasik Versani Student **22**

Gujarati Typeface Design Title ❖ 4 Study Year ❀
University of Reading College ⚜ Great Britain Country
✺ Gerard Unger, Chris Burke Professors

છ બ ઠ પ ન ચ ય વ ષ ર

મ ટ ક જ ઈ ઝ ઇ ક્ષ

ા ૢ ુિ ી િ ી .

ગી જા દિ પુ નૂ ક્લિ

❂ The aim of this project was to design a robust Gujarati typeface suitable for continuous reading at poor quality and at small typesizes – reducing the real space occupied by the letters while maintaining their real size.
▶▶ Ziel des Projektes war es, eine robuste Gujarati-Schrift zu entwerfen, die auch unter schlechten Bedingungen und in kleinen Größen noch sehr gut lesbar ist. Dazu wurde der von den einzelnen Buchstaben benötigte Platz reduziert, während die tatsächliche Größe beibehalten wurde.

Pustaka Sastra Kontemporer Title ✣ Book Cover Medium ✣
2 Study Year ❣ Universitas Pelita Harapan College ✎ Indonesia Country
✩ Yongky Safanayong Professor

Cecil Mariani Student ❋ **23**

♥ Hanny Kardinata Contributing Editor

◊ Contemporary illustrations and bright colours are used on the book covers to combat the idea that literature is »difficult.« The coloured stripe on the left side indicates the category of literature: blue for poetry, red for novels, yellow for short stories and green for foreign literature. ✎ Für die Buchumschläge wurden zeitgenössische Illustrationen und leuchtende Farben verwendet, um dem Vorurteil entgegenzuwirken, Literatur sei »schwierig«. Der farbige Streifen an der Seite zeigt an, um welche Kategorie von Literatur es sich handelt: Blau für Gedichte, Rot für Romane, Gelb für Kurzgeschichten und Grün für ausländische Literatur.

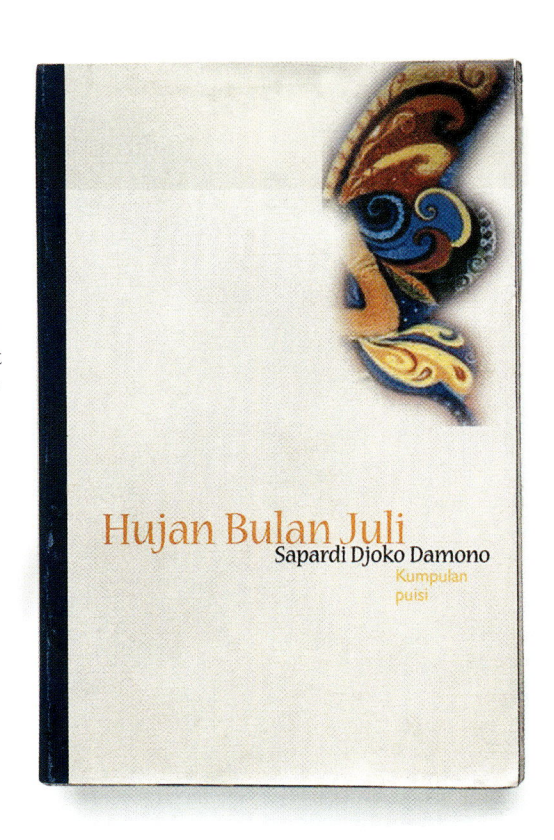

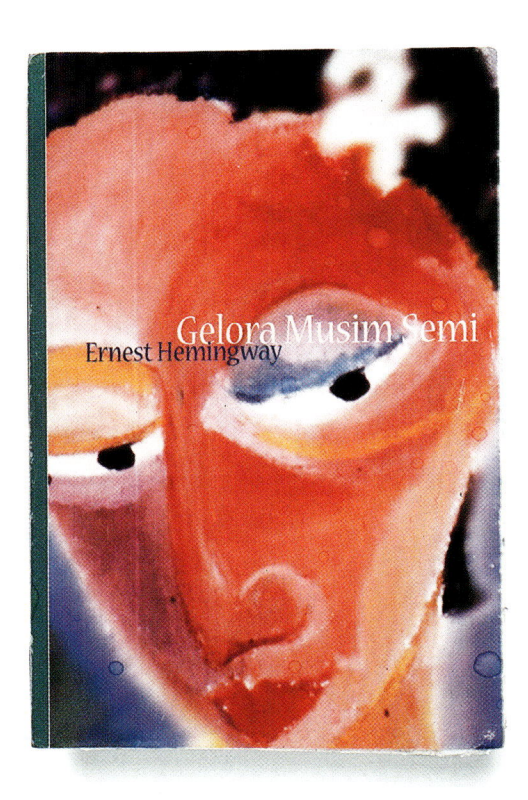

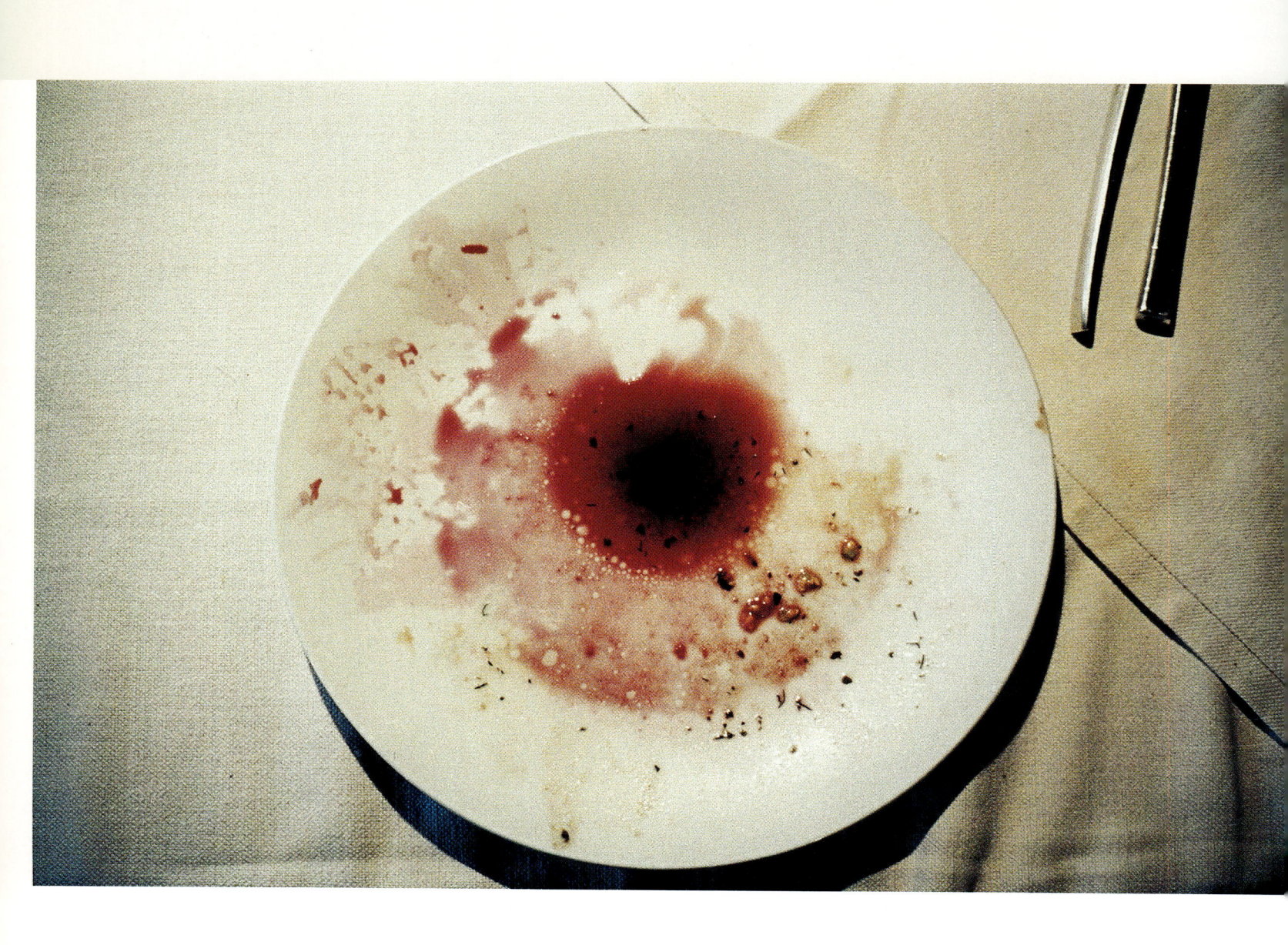

Eating + Drinking | Essen + Trinken Title **Photography** Medium **4** Study Year
HfK Bremen College **Germany** Country **Fritz Haase** Professor

Sabine Veerkamp Student 24

Carpe Diem – An attitude towards life | Carpe Diem – Eine Lebenshaltung Title
Photographic Documentary | Fotografische Dokumentation Medium
4 Study Year GH Kassel College Germany Country Christof Gassner, Bernard Stein, Nicolas Ott Professors

Stefani Konrad Student

25

»I always decide anew to stay true to the day with the help of and hand in hand with those moments, by wanting to seize them, think them over and preserve them.« (Peter Handke). Just take it as it comes, no matter if you are cleaning or reading; no matter if you are on the way somewhere or if you are talking with friends. Always be aware of what is in the moment. This work is the photographic documentation of a moment.

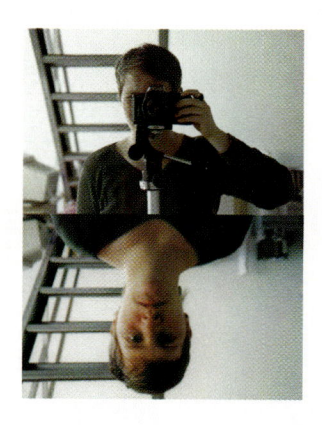

»Immer neu nehme ich mir vor, dem Tag mit der Hilfe, an der Hand jener Augenblicke treu zu bleiben (...), indem ich sie erfassen möchte, bedenken, bewahren.« (Peter Handke). Jeden Moment so zu nehmen wie er ist, sei es beim Putzen oder beim Lesen, auf dem Weg irgendwohin oder beim Gespräch mit Freunden. Bei der Sache zu sein, was immer das in diesem Moment auch ist. Die fotografische Dokumentation des Augenblicks wird zum Ziel der Arbeit.

Katrin Schlüsener Student 26

Various book covers for a novel by Max Frisch | Verschiedene Buchcover für einen Roman von Max Frisch Project 5 Study Year Staatliche Akademie der Bildenden Künste Stuttgart College Germany Country Günter Jacki Professor

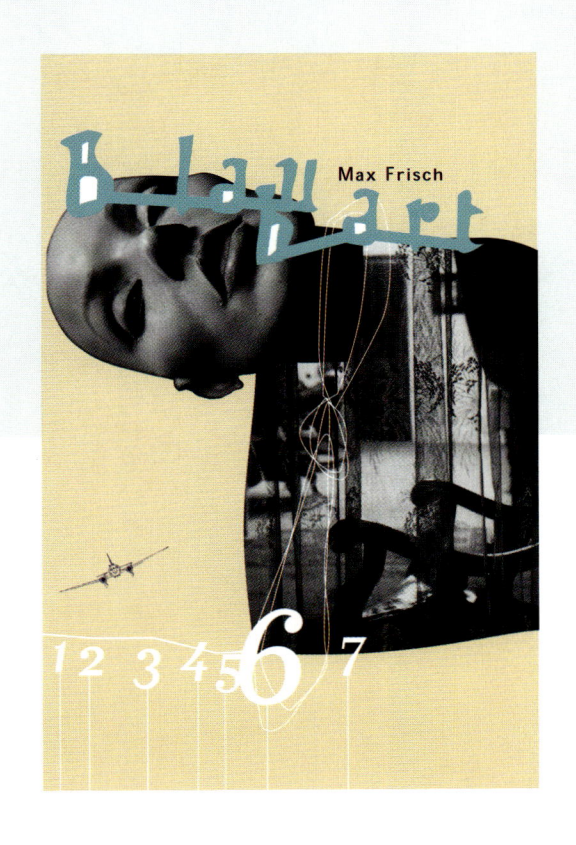

Kali Nikitas Contributing Editor

P.J. Chmiel Student 27

Vegan Campaign | Veganer Kampagne Title ✢ Poster Medium ✢ 4 Study Year
Minneapolis College of Art and Design College ✎ USA Country ✯ Jan Jancourt Professor

This series of posters promotes the vegan lifestyle by pointing out the results and dangers of intensive livestock farming. ✢ Die Plakatserie wirbt für einen veganischen Lebensstil, indem sie die Folgen von Massentierhaltung, Überzüchtung und Medikation von Tieren zeigt.

Keep the Harbour Clean | Haltet den Hafen sauber Title ✕ **Poster** Medium ∥
3 Study Year ■ **Hong Kong Baptist University** College ☐ **China** Country 🚌
Wendy Wong Professor

Joana Lai Student

◇ Images of dead fish and dolphins are rendered from rubbish. In this way, environmental pollution is put forward as the culprit for the death of marine life. The illustrations are made in the style of traditional Chinese watercolour painting in order to encourage the audience to rethink their traditional habits of thinking about refuse. ✷ Die Bilder der toten Fischen und Delfine sind aus Müll zusammengesetzt. Dadurch wird die Umweltverschmutzung durch den Menschen als Ursache für den Tod der Meeresbewohner hervorgehoben. Die Illustrationen sind im Stil traditioneller chinesischer Wasserfarbenmalerei angefertigt, um den Betrachter dazu anzuregen, seine althergebrachte Denkweise zum Thema Müll zu überdenken.

Change of Scenery | Tapetenwechsel Title ✦ Poster Medium ✦ 3 Study Year
Fachhochschule für Technik und Wirtschaft Berlin College · Germany Country
E. Bellot Professor

Julia Guther, Svenja Weber Students ✶ 29

ANDERE WÄNDE, ANDERE SITTEN ?

Deutsches Studentenwerk | Weberstrasse 55 | 53113 Bonn

DEINE AKTION
TAPETENWECHSEL
STUDIUM INTERNATIONAL
UNTERSTÜTZT DURCH DAS
DEUTSCHE STUDENTENWERK

*Different walls,
different customs?*

*Your action:
A change of scenery*

*International Studies
supported by the German
Student Association*

These posters were made for a contest put on by the German Student Association. They play with the petty fears and doubts one has when trying something new. ✤ Die Plakate sind im Rahmen eines Wettbewerbes des Deutschen Studentenwerkes entstanden. Sie spielen mit den kleinen Ängsten und Unsicherheiten, die einen überkommen, wenn man etwas Neues wagt.

AUF ZU NEUEN UFERN !

SPRUNG INS KALTE WASSER

DEINE AKTION
STUDIUM INTERNATIONAL
UNTERSTÜTZT DURCH DAS
DEUTSCHE STUDENTENWERK

Deutsches Studentenwerk | Weberstrasse 55 | 53113 Bonn

Off to new shores!

Your action:
Dive into the cold water.

I'm not going to just stay home with my soup.
No, I can't just stick around.

Your action:
Take a look over the brim.

ICH BLEIB IN MEINER SUPPE NICHT,
NEIN, IN MEINER SUPPE BLEIB ICH NICHT.

DEINE AKTION
SCHAU ÜBER DEN TELLERRAND
STUDIUM INTERNATIONAL
UNTERSTÜTZT DURCH DAS
DEUTSCHE STUDENTENWERK

Deutsches Studentenwerk | Weberstrasse 55 | 53113 Bonn

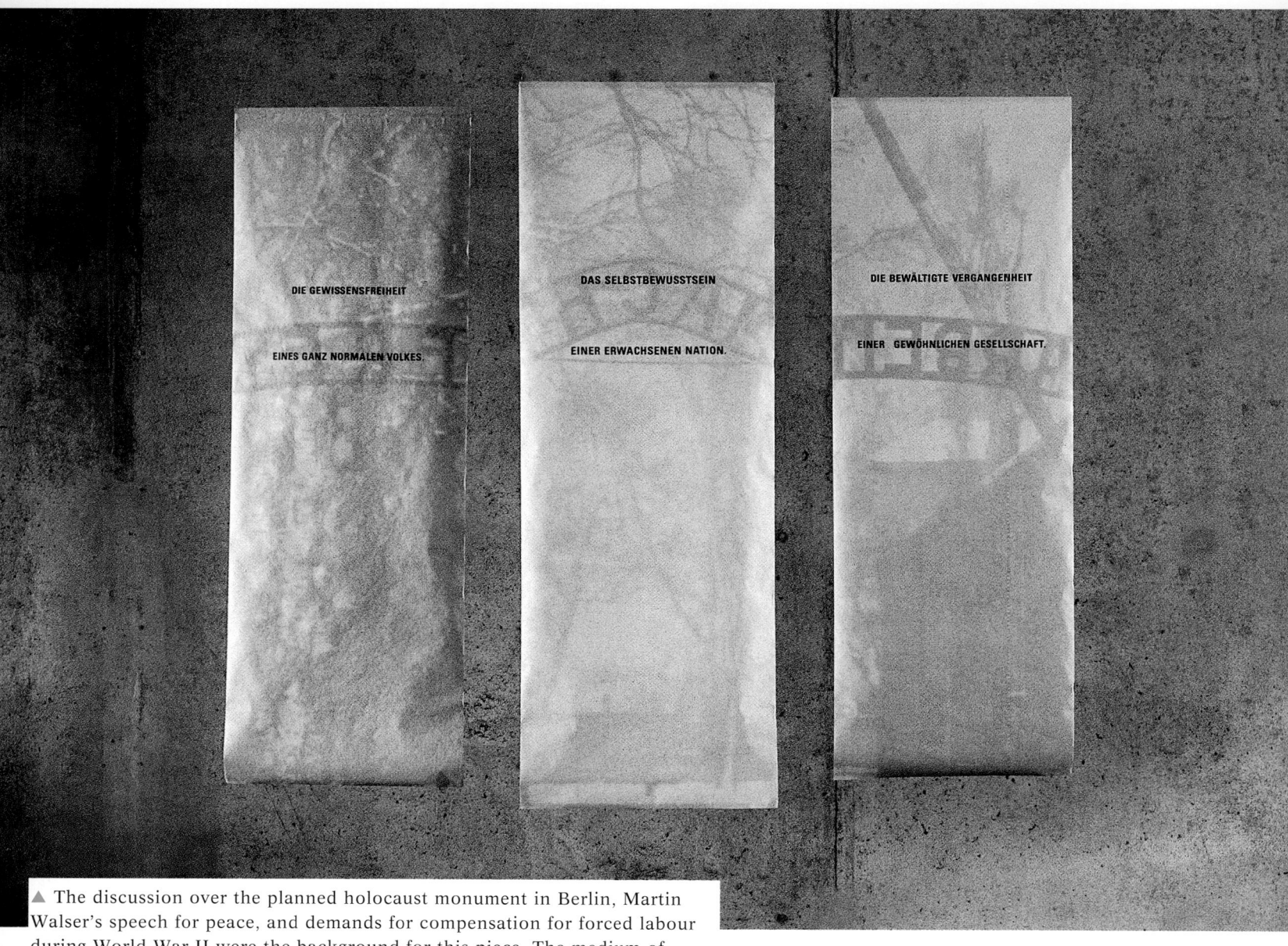

Flags | Fahnen Title ✳ **3** Study Year ◆ **FH Würzburg** College ◯ **Germany** Country
Ulrich Braun Professor

DIE GEWISSENSFREIHEIT

EINES GANZ NORMALEN VOLKES.

DAS SELBSTBEWUSSTSEIN

EINER ERWACHSENEN NATION.

DIE BEWÄLTIGTE VERGANGENHEIT

EINER GEWÖHNLICHEN GESELLSCHAFT.

▲ The discussion over the planned holocaust monument in Berlin, Martin Walser's speech for peace, and demands for compensation for forced labour during World War II were the background for this piece. The medium of the flag as a symbol for the nation-state presents the public in a special context. Apart from the type, the flags aren't as blank or as white as they'd like to be. The back of each flag is hardly discernible, but it's still there, faintly showing through. Because the flags hang away from the wall, it is possible to look behind them, thereby choosing your own point of view – though it's not necessarily obvious to do so.

Regina Schauerte, Thomas Klöß Students

30

*The freedom of conscience
of an average nation.*

*The self-confidence
of a mature nation.*

*A society that has
overcome its past.*

✕ Die Diskussionen um das geplante Holocaustdenkmal in Berlin, um die Friedensrede Martin Walsers und um die Forderungen ehemaliger Zwangsarbeiter/innen nach Entschädigungszahlungen bilden den Hintergrund, vor dem die Arbeit entstand. Das Medium Fahne stellt als Symbol des Nationalstaates Öffentlichkeit in einer besonderen Weise dar. Abgesehen von der Schrift sind die Fahnen dennoch nicht leer oder so weiß, wie sie es sein möchten: Die Rückseite ist kaum mehr zu erkennen, aber sie ist noch da, sie scheint sogar durch. Da die Fahnen nicht direkt an der Wand hängen, besteht für den Betrachter die Möglichkeit, dahinter zu sehen und einen eigenen Standpunkt zu wählen – auch wenn der scheinbar vorgegeben ist.

Stefanie Huber Student

31

At the Robbers' | Bei Räubers Title Illustration Medium
3 Study Year FH Niederrhein College Germany Country
Volker Lehnert Professor

✱ These illustrations for the story »At the Robbers'« by Heinrich Hannover depict the story of really naughty child riff-raffs. ✱ Die Illustrationen zum Text »Bei Räubers« von Heinrich Hannover erzählen die Geschichte der frechen Räuberkinder, die alles andere als brav sind.

Bye Mum | Tschüß Mutti Title ✢ Poster Medium ✢ 2 Study Year
Universität Essen College ✎ Germany Country ✯ Anna Berkenbusch Professor

Nadine Spachtholz Student

32

»The theme of the contest put on by the German Student Association was ›International Studies.‹ I'd found a washed-out Polaroid of a typical German shopowner in the flea market. She stood in front of her typical German shop, watching with concern as her son (in his mid-twenties) goes abroad. It's hard for both of them, but it must be so, for the sake of his education …
The student takes a photo of his mother with him abroad as a reminder of home.« ♥ »Das Plakat ist im Rahmen eines Wettbewerbes des Deutschen Studentenwerkes zum Thema ›Studium International‹ entstanden. Ich hatte das vergilbte Polaroid einer typisch deutschen Kramladenbesitzerin auf dem Flohmarkt gefunden. Sie steht vor ihrem typisch deutschen Kramladen und blickt mit Sorge ihrem ins Ausland gehenden Kind (Alter: Mitte 20) nach. Beiden fällt die Trennung sehr schwer, aber dem Studium zuliebe muss es wohl so sein …. Als Andenken an zu Hause nimmt der Student ein Foto seiner Mutter mit in die Fremde.«

»German students hardly ever leave their homeland. Only one in ten spends time studying abroad, although because the connectedness of the world is growing so rapidly, it's becoming more and more important to gather cultural experience and knowledge of foreign languages.
So, when will you have to say goodbye to your mum? (It won't be for long)«

„Tschüß Mutti"

Die deutschen Studenten sind Nesthocker. Nur jeder zehnte verbringt einen Teil seines Studiums im Ausland, obwohl die Bedeutung von interkulturellen Erfahrungen und Fremdsprachenkenntnissen in einer immer stärker vernetzten Welt wächst.
Also, wann sagst Du Deiner Mami adieu?
(Es muß ja nicht für immer sein.)

Anita Kolb Student   **33**

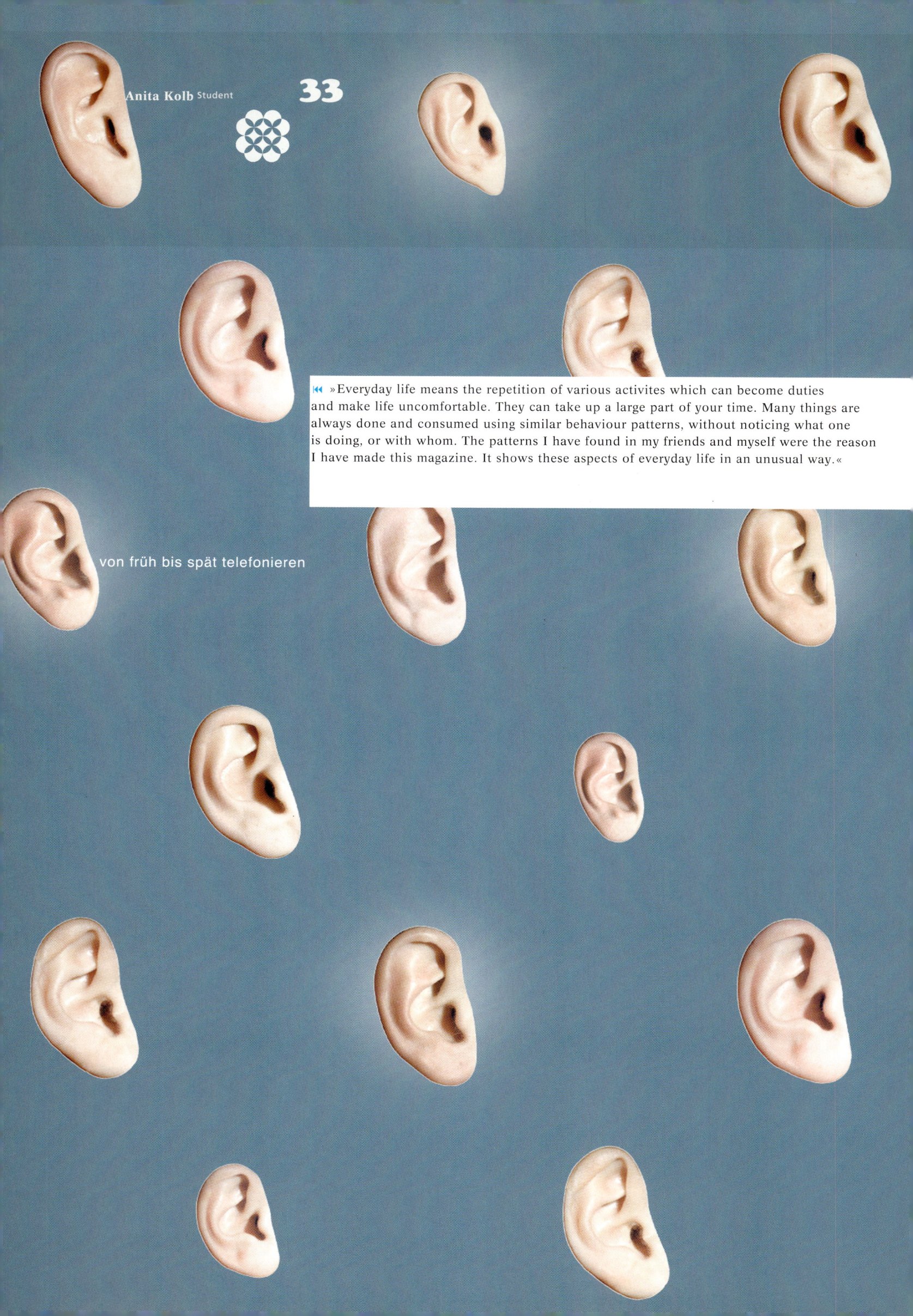

»Everyday life means the repetition of various activites which can become duties and make life uncomfortable. They can take up a large part of your time. Many things are always done and consumed using similar behaviour patterns, without noticing what one is doing, or with whom. The patterns I have found in my friends and myself were the reason I have made this magazine. It shows these aspects of everyday life in an unusual way.«

von früh bis spät telefonieren

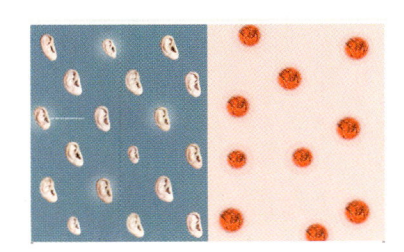

Empire | Imperium **Title** ✦ Magazine **Medium** ▲ 5 **Study Year**
⊠ FH Würzburg **College** ✎ Germany **Country** ♣ James Nitsch **Professor**

Calling ...
Telefonieren ...

Morals ...
Moral ...

Images ...
Bilder ...

Collecting ...
Sammeln ...

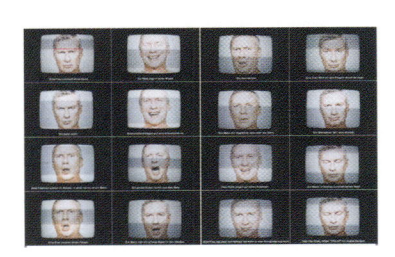

Watching TV ...
Fernsehen ...

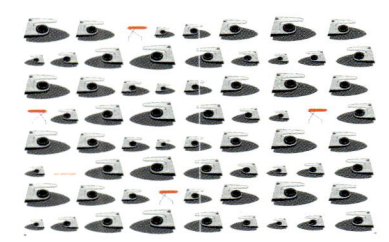

Ironing ...
Bügeln ...

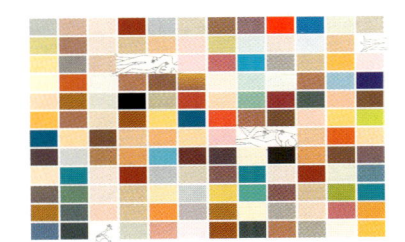

Love ...
Liebe ...

The daily washing-up ...
Jeden Tag abspülen ...

More than a car ...
Mehr als ein Auto ...

▲ »Alltag bedeutet die Wiederholung von verschiedenen Tätigkeiten. Viele dieser Tätigkeiten werden zur Pflicht und als lästig empfunden. Dennoch nehmen sie einen Großteil der Zeit in Anspruch. Viele Dinge werden mit den immer gleichen Verhaltensmustern benutzt und konsumiert, ohne sich bewusst zu machen, was man genau tut und mit wem man es zu tun hat. Die Muster, die ich bei mir selbst und bei anderen gesehen habe, habe ich zum Anlass genommen, eine Illustrierte entstehen zu lassen. Das Magazin zeigt verschiedene Beiträge zu Themen des Alltags aus ungewohnter Perspektive.«

Animation Open Day **Title** ✢ Poster **Medium** ✢ 2 **Study Year**
Royal College of Art, London **College** ✎ Great Britain **Country** ✦
Margaret Calvert **Professor**

Scott Williams, Henrik Kubel **Students**

34

*Poster for the Open Day
of the Animation Department
at the Royal College of Art*

*Plakat für den Tag der offenen Tür
im Animation Department
am Royal College of Art*

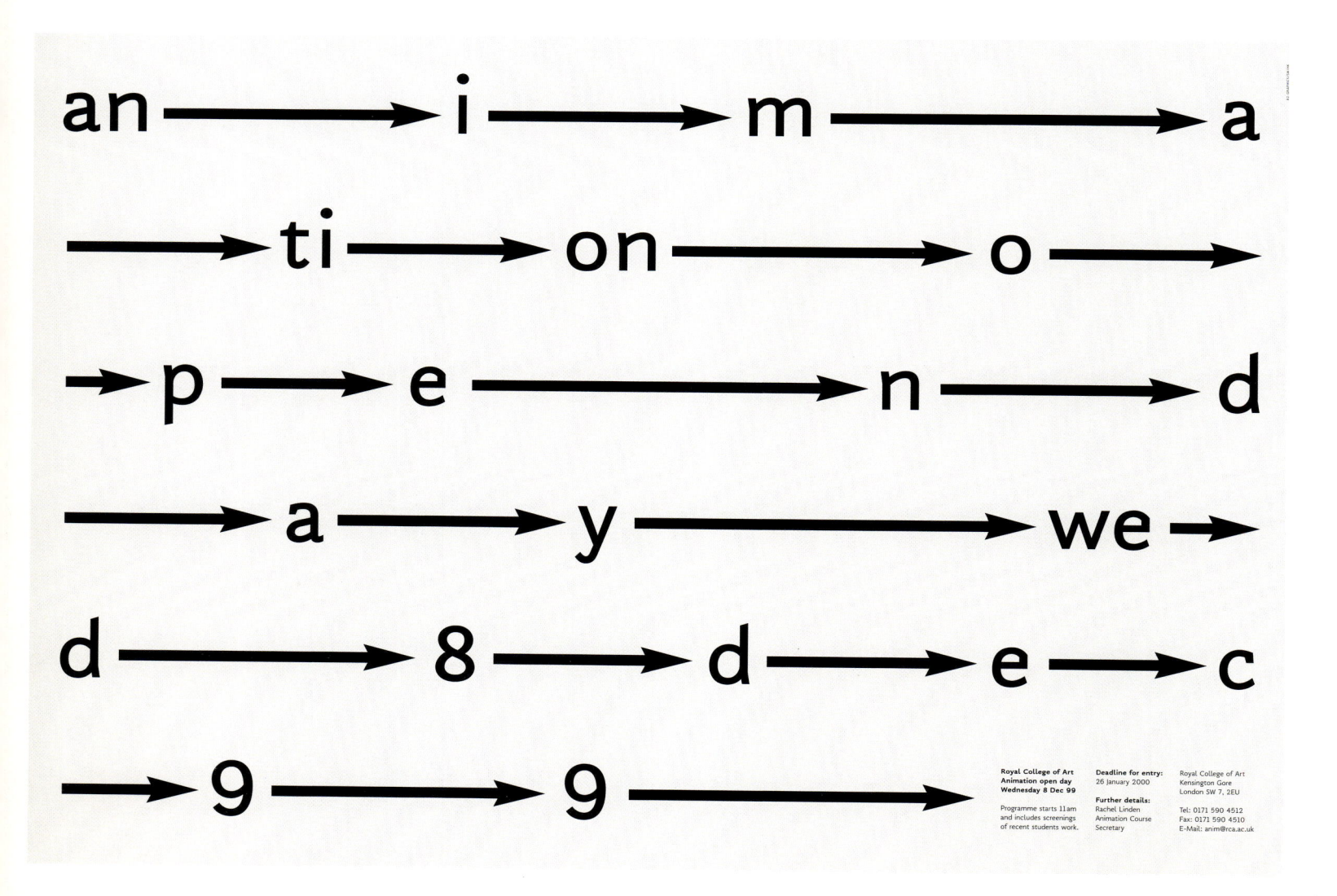

an ⟶ i ⟶ m ⟶ a
⟶ ti ⟶ on ⟶ o ⟶
⟶ p ⟶ e ⟶ n ⟶ d
⟶ a ⟶ y ⟶ we ⟶
d ⟶ 8 ⟶ d ⟶ e ⟶ c
⟶ 9 ⟶ 9 ⟶

**Royal College of Art
Animation open day
Wednesday 8 Dec 99**

Programme starts 11am
and includes screenings
of recent students work.

Deadline for entry:
26 January 2000

Further details:
Rachel Linden
Animation Course
Secretary

Royal College of Art
Kensington Gore
London SW 7, 2EU

Tel: 0171 590 4512
Fax: 0171 590 4510
E-Mail: anim@rca.ac.uk

Hatem Imam Student **35**

Lebanese Architecture Title ✢ **Stamp Series | Briefmarkenserie** Medium ✢
4 Study Year ✿ American University of Beirut College ✎ Lebanon Country ✩
Leila Musfy Professor

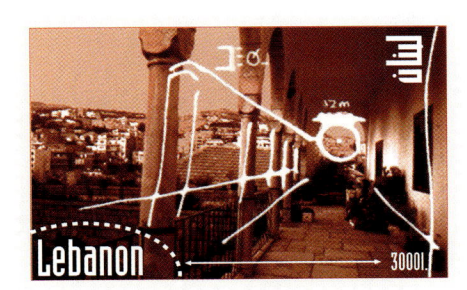

■ This postage stamp series graphically interprets the dialogue between the rough, rigid feel of typical Lebanese limestone and open, welcoming spaces. ⌣ Der Dialog zwischen der rohen Anmutung des für die libanesische Bauweise typischen Kalksteins und die offene, einladende Raumordnung wird in diesen Briefmarken grafisch interpretiert.

IMMER WIEDER ROSEL...

Nelli Zwirner Student **36**

Rosel, again and again | Immer wieder Rosel Title Exhibition | Ausstellung Medium
2 Study Year FH Augsburg College Germany Country Günther Woyte Professor

An object found at the flea market: her name is Rosel. Well, at least that is what is written on the slide cartridge filled with images of her. The rest remains a secret. She was probably photographed by her husband, but for what reason? Was it love or oppression? Passion or fetishism? Tenderness or brutality? Luck or perversion? Arousal or rage? Are these images funny or are they tragic? Ein Fundstück vom Flohmarkt: Rosel heißt die Frau. Das steht zumindest auf den Diamagazinen, die gefüllt sind mit ihren Bildern. Der Rest bleibt ein großes Geheimnis. Fotografiert hat sie höchstwahrscheinlich ihr Mann. Die Frage nach dem Warum bleibt jedoch offen. War es Liebe oder Unterdrückung? Leidenschaft oder Fetischismus? Zärtlichkeit oder Gewalt? Glück oder Perversion? Erregung oder Besessenheit? Sind diese Bilder lustig oder eher tragisch?

✺ Showing the photos is not meant as a joke or to disturb Rosel's privacy. It's moreso the inexhaustible value of the photo collection and its quality and authenticity that should be shown here. And, of course, it's in adoration of Rosel, for being model and muse for her husband. ✺ Bei der Ausstellung der Bilder von Rosel geht es nicht darum, in die Privatsphäre einer Person einzudringen und sie damit lächerlich zu machen. Vielmehr soll der unerschöpfliche Wert dieser Fotosammlung, ihre fotografische Qualität und Echtheit herausgestellt werden sowie der Person Rosel, die mit bewundernswerter Ausdauer ihrem Mann vor der Kamera posierte, ein Denkmal gesetzt werden.

❋ Repetition is the central theme of the exhibition: the large volume of photos, the never-changing pose, the permanent, almost penetrating, repetition of the photographic act. For this reason, the livingroom installed in the exhibition was plastered with pictures of Rosel, as was the museum shop selling Rosel souvenirs. The purpose of hanging the posters up all over the city is to incite paranoia – or to make Rosel a star. ❂ Die Wiederholung ist das zentrale Motiv der Ausstellung: Die Masse an Fotos, die immer gleiche Pose, die ständige, fast schon penetrante Wiederholung des Aktes des Fotografierens. Aus diesem Grund wurde das Ausstellungs-Wohnzimmer mit Rosel-Bildern zugepflastert, ebenso der Museums-Shop, in dem es Unmengen von Rosel-Souvenirs zu kaufen gibt. Die Plakatwände in der ganzen Stadt sollen einen Verfolgungswahn auslösen – oder Rosel zum Star machen.

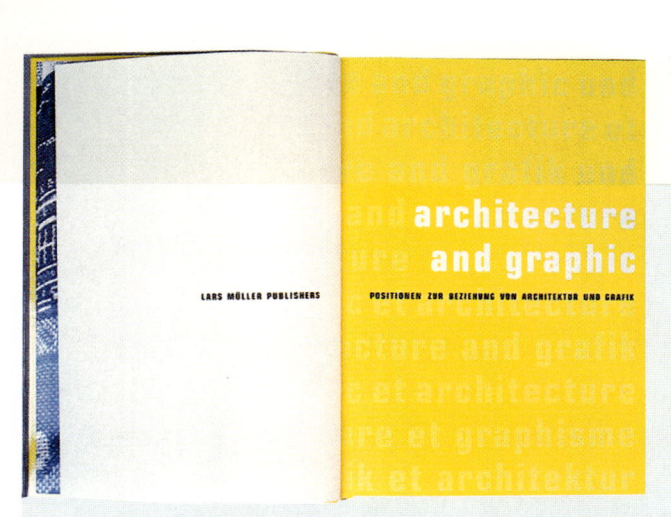

Architecture and Graphic Design **Title** ✛ **Book** Medium ✛ **5** Study Year
Hochschule für Grafik und Buchkunst Leipzig College ✎ **Germany** Country
Ruedi Baur Professor

Heike Burkhardt, Berit Kaiser, Anne Wichmann Students

37

The theme of the book is »Orientation and Disorientation.« It is divided into eight chapters containing text, independent student work and image selections. ▲ Das Buch beschäftigt sich mit dem Thema »Orientierung und Desorientierung«. Es ist in acht Kapitel mit Autorentexten, freien Studentenarbeiten und Bildteilen untergliedert.

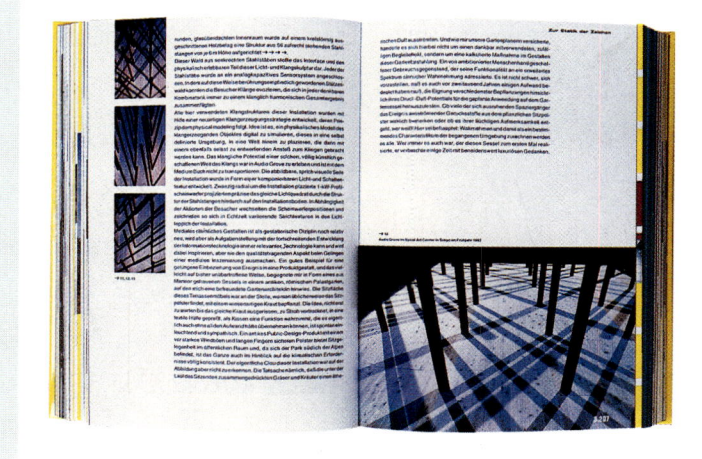

Elena Tolokonina Student

38

Vladimir Mersoev Theatre Title ✛ Identity System | Erscheinungsbild Project ✛ 5 Study Year ❣ Higher Academic School of Graphic Design Moscow College ✎ Russia Country ☆ Boris Trofimov Professor

Poster for three performances in St. Petersburg
Plakat für drei Aufführungen in St. Petersburg

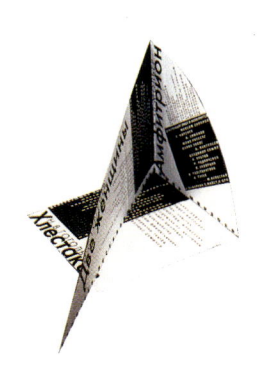

Folder with the theatre programme
Faltblatt mit dem Theaterprogramm

Nuyorican Soul ᵀⁱᵗˡᵉ ✚ CD Cover ᴹᵉᵈⁱᵘᵐ ✚ 3 ˢᵗᵘᵈʸ ʸᵉᵃʳ
University of Reading ᶜᵒˡˡᵉᵍᵉ Great Britain ᶜᵒᵘⁿᵗʳʸ
Hans-Dieter Reichert ᴾʳᵒᶠᵉˢˢᵒʳ

♥ Hans-Dieter Reichert ᶜᵒⁿᵗʳⁱᵇᵘᵗⁱⁿᵍ ᴱᵈⁱᵗᵒʳ

Paul Arnot ˢᵗᵘᵈᵉⁿᵗ ✱ **39**

Nuyorican Soul

01: Nuyorican Soul intro 1.24
02: I am the black gold of the sun 5.20
03: It's alright, I feel it 3.18
    lead vocals **Jocelyn Brown**
04: Maw Latin blues 6.20
05: Gotta a new life 4.27
06: Nautilus (Mawtilus) 7.12
07: Taita Caneme 4.59
08: Habriendo el dominante 6.08
09: Roy's Scat 3.08
    vibes and scat vocals by **Roy Ayers**
10: Sweet Tears 5.10
    vibes and scat vocals by **Roy Ayers**
11: Runaway 7.54
    lead vocals by **India**
12: Shoshana 7.14
13: Jazzy Jeff's Theme 2.53
14: You can do it (baby) 8.57
    lead vocal and guitar by **George Benson**

Roy Ayers, vibes; **George Benson**, guitar; **Edwin Birdsong**, bass; **Hilton Byrd**, alto saxophone; **Carlos Henrique**, percussion; **Luistro Quintruo**, flute, **David Sanchez**, drums; **Hue Ragaa**, trumpet; **Lonnie Liston Smith**, piano; **Fred Wesley**, trombone.

1997 Mercury Records Ltd. (London).
All rights reserved. Unauthorised copying, reproduction, hiring, lending, public performance and broadcasting prohibited.
1997 Mercury Records Ltd. (London). The copyright in this sound recording is owned by Mercury Records Ltd. (London).
Sleeve: original concept: P A STYLE
Design by: Paul Arnot

»Nuyorican Soul« could be described as an experimental fusion of New York flavour and a Latin American beat. The aim of the project was to reflect the nature of the music visually, using abstract shapes and colour.
»Nuyorican Soul« kann als experimentelle Fusion aus einem Hauch New York und lateinamerikanischem Beat umschrieben werden. Das Ziel dieses Projektes war es, die Natur der Musik durch abstrakte Formen und Farben zu visualisieren.

Hyun-Soo Kim Student

40

Jewel case Title ✦ CD Packaging Medium ✦
School of Visual Arts, New York College ✎ USA Country ☆
Stefan Sagmeister Professor

✽ This leaflet describes the beautiful scenery of Yuki Kuramoto's piano work. It shows continuous peaceful views parallel to Kuramoto's music and thoughts.

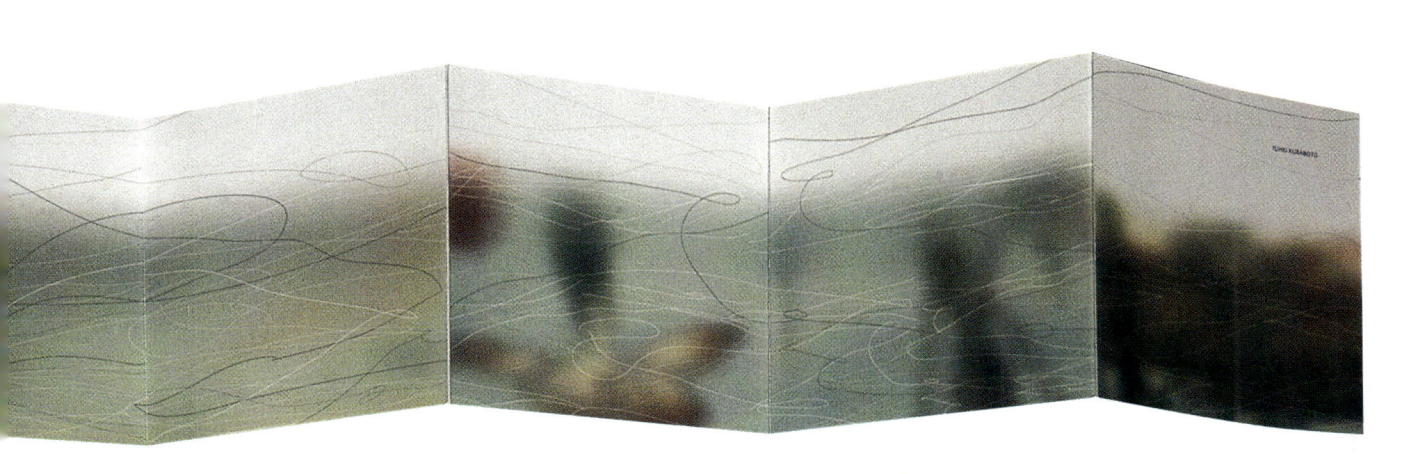

✤ Das Design beschreibt die wunderschöne Szenerie von Yuki Kuramotos Pianospiel. Das Faltblatt zeigt fortdauernde friedvolle Blicke vergleichbar der Musik und den Gedanken Kuramotos.

Neo-Chinese Opera Climax | Neo-Chinesischer Oper-Schlussakt Title
Poster Medium ✱ Hong Kong Baptist University College ✝ China Country
Wendy Wong Professor

Daniel Leung Student 41

⑤ This poster is a promotion for the Digital Graphic Communication Graduation Exhibition at the Hong Kong Baptist University. It gives a humorous touch to traditional Chinese opera images from the 1930s by using the look of modern computers. The work plays with the concept of the »Grand Display« of student work and the climactic closing scene that is usually found in the Chinese opera. ◆ Das Plakat wirbt für die Ausstellung der Abschlussarbeiten für digitale Kommunikation und Grafik an der Hong Kong Baptist University. Es gibt einen humorvollen Einblick in die Welt des tradtionellen chinesischen Theaters der dreißiger Jahre mittels einer modernen Computer-Optik. Die Arbeit vergleicht die Abschlussausstellung mit Szenen des großen Finales einer chinesischen Oper.

Katrin Degenkolb Student 42

Degustazione dell'Opera Title Book Medium 4 Study Year
FH Pforzheim College Germany Country Uli Kluss Professor

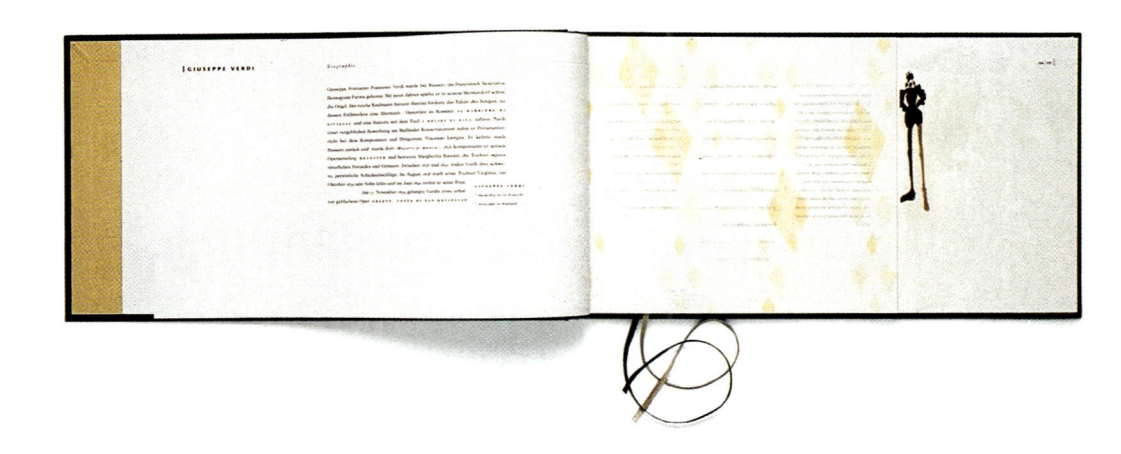

> This work is a visual appetizer made for music lovers as an easy entry into the world of opera. The operas »The Magic Flute,« »Rigoletto« and »Tosca« are each presented in individual books. The books contain background information for the piece, a libretto, illustrations and additional text. ❖ Diese Arbeit ist ein visueller Lustmacher zum Thema Oper, der dem musikinteressierten Menschen den Zugang zur Materie erleichtert. Es werden exemplarisch die Werke »Die Zauberflöte«, »Rigoletto« und »Tosca« in je einem Buch vorgestellt. Die Bände enthalten Hintergrundinformationen zu den jeweiligen Stücken, ein Libretto, Illustrationen und Textzusätze.

Quotations Title ❁ Folders | Ordner Medium △ 4 Study Year ✻
American University of Beirut College Lebanon Country ➪ Leila Musfy Professor

43

Carla Salem Student

This collection of »folders« in the form of book covers is concerned with the central theme of the human condition – of life and death.

Die Sammlung von »Ordnern« in Form von Umschlägen beschäftigt sich mit den zentralen Themen des menschlichen Lebens – von Leben und Tod.

Karen Buermann, Sibylle Lenz, Maike Taddicken, Natascha Schäfer Students

44

Micro- and Macrocosm of Reading | Mikro- und Makrokosmos des Lesens Title
Book and Video Medium * 5 Study Year * FH Hannover College † Germany Country
* Iris Maria vom Hof Professor

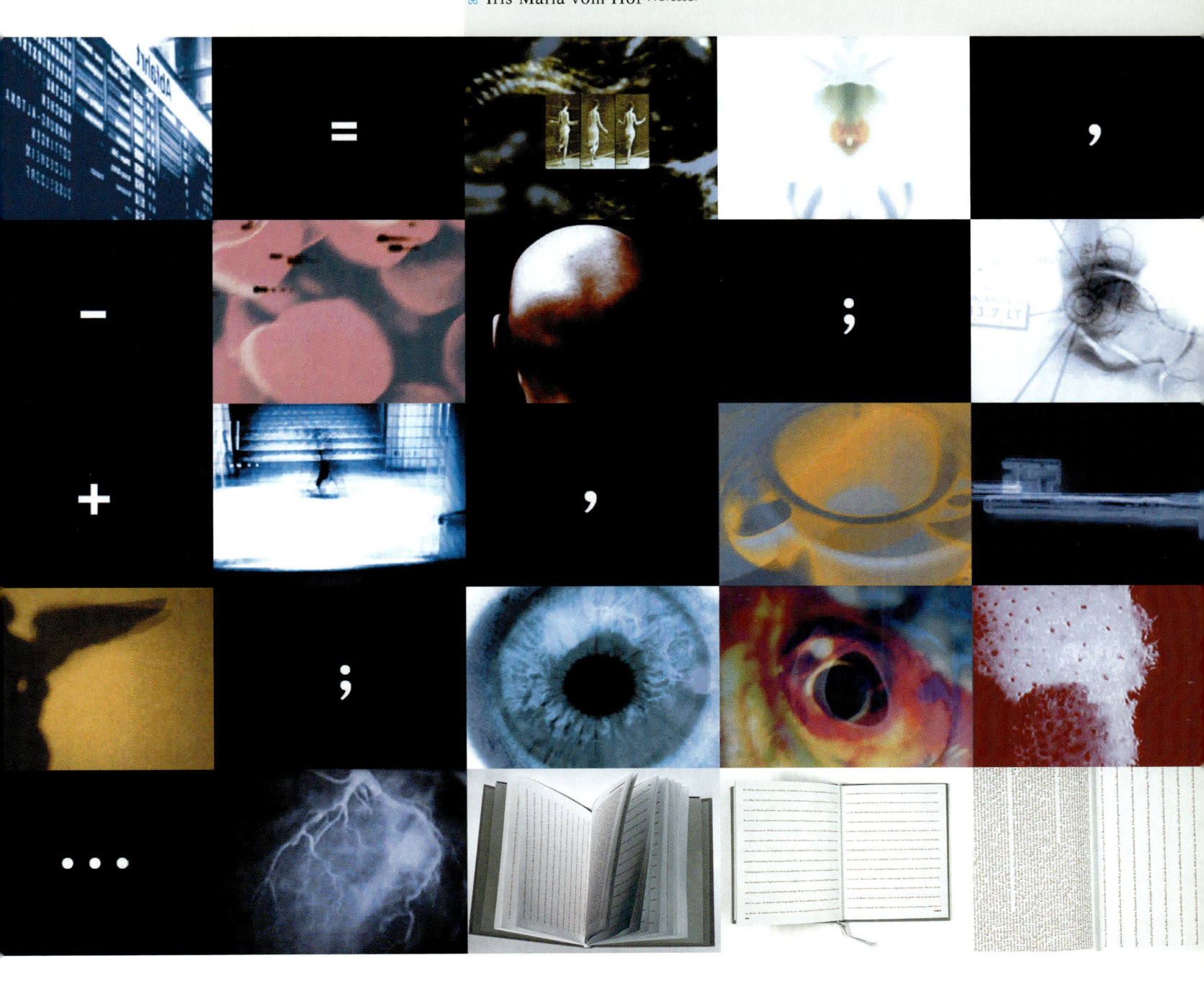

It is difficult to precisely define reading or the innumerable ways one reads. This work gets to the bottom of that mystery. The quality and variety of ways to experience reading are the sensual basis of the book and video »The Macrocosm of Reading.« »The Microcosm of Reading« is then a presentation of the world of letters. Eine genaue Definition, was Lesen ist und wie viele Möglichkeiten des Lesens existieren, fällt schwer. Das Geheimnis des Lesens zu ergründen, ist Thema dieser Arbeit. Die Erlebnisqualitäten und Erfahrungsweisen des Lesens bilden dabei die sinnliche Grundlage eines Buches und eines Videos – »Der Makrokosmos des Lesens« – und einer Darstellung der Buchstabenwelt – »Der Mikrokosmos des Lesens«.

The Fremd ⁺ Book Medium 5 Study Year ❘ Bergische Universität Wuppertal (Stipendium from the Centre National de l'Audiovisuel CNA, Luxembourg) College Germany Country ✳ Bazon Brock, Susan Lamér Professors

Thomas Zika Student

45

the fremd

The book project »The Fremd« is a fictitious photo diary made by aliens during their first visit to Europe. They see Europe with extraterrestrial objectivity. Our guests from outerspace let us peek into their visual explorer/tourist diary. ↪ Das Buchprojekt »The Fremd« ist das fiktive Fototagebuch der Außerirdischen bei ihrem ersten Europabesuch. Mit extraterrestrischer Objektivität soll Europa unter die Lupe genommen werden. Die Gäste aus dem Weltall gewähren Einblick in ein visuelles Forscher-/Touristen-Tagebuch.

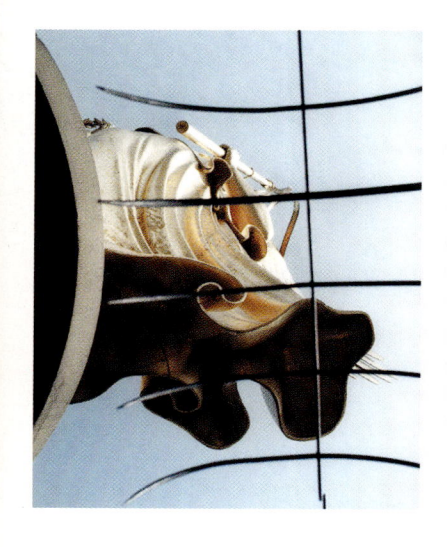

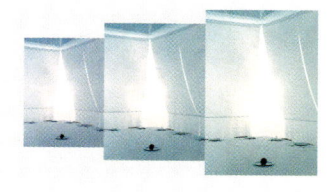

Kirstin Bauer Student 46

Thai Air Title ✛ Advertising Campaign | Werbekampagne Medium ✛ 5 Study Year
FH Nürnberg College ✎ Germany Country ✦ Prof. Stumpp Professor

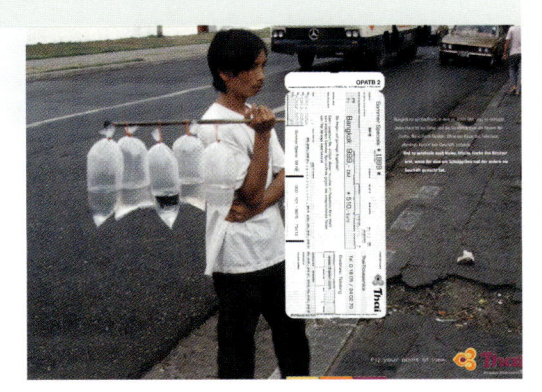

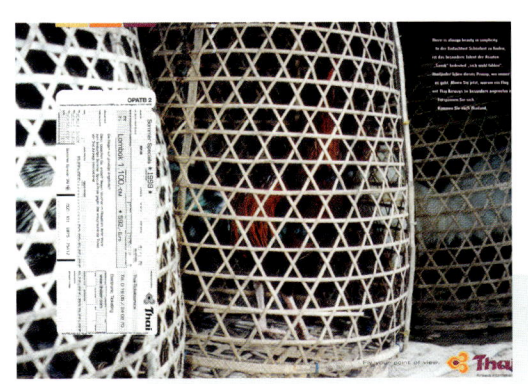

③ Ticket samples with various offers are stuck onto the advertisements (e.g. Bangkok DM 999,-). By peeling them off, new and surprising details of the photos are revealed. In die Anzeigen sind Muster-Tickets mit Angeboten für verschiedene Flugziele eingeklebt (z.B. Bangkok DM 999,-). Entfernt man diese Tickets, offenbart sich ein neues, überraschendes Detail des Fotos.

47

Maren Rache, Ole Kaleschke Students

E6 Project Room A 202 | E6 Projektraum A 202 Title ✓ Exhibition Catalogue | Ausstellungskatalog Medium ✶ 2 Study Year ✶ HfK Bremen College ⓘ Germany Country ✌ Wolfgang Jarchow Professor

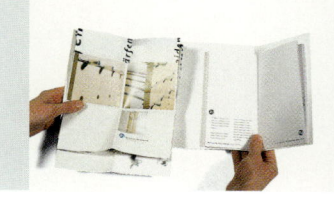

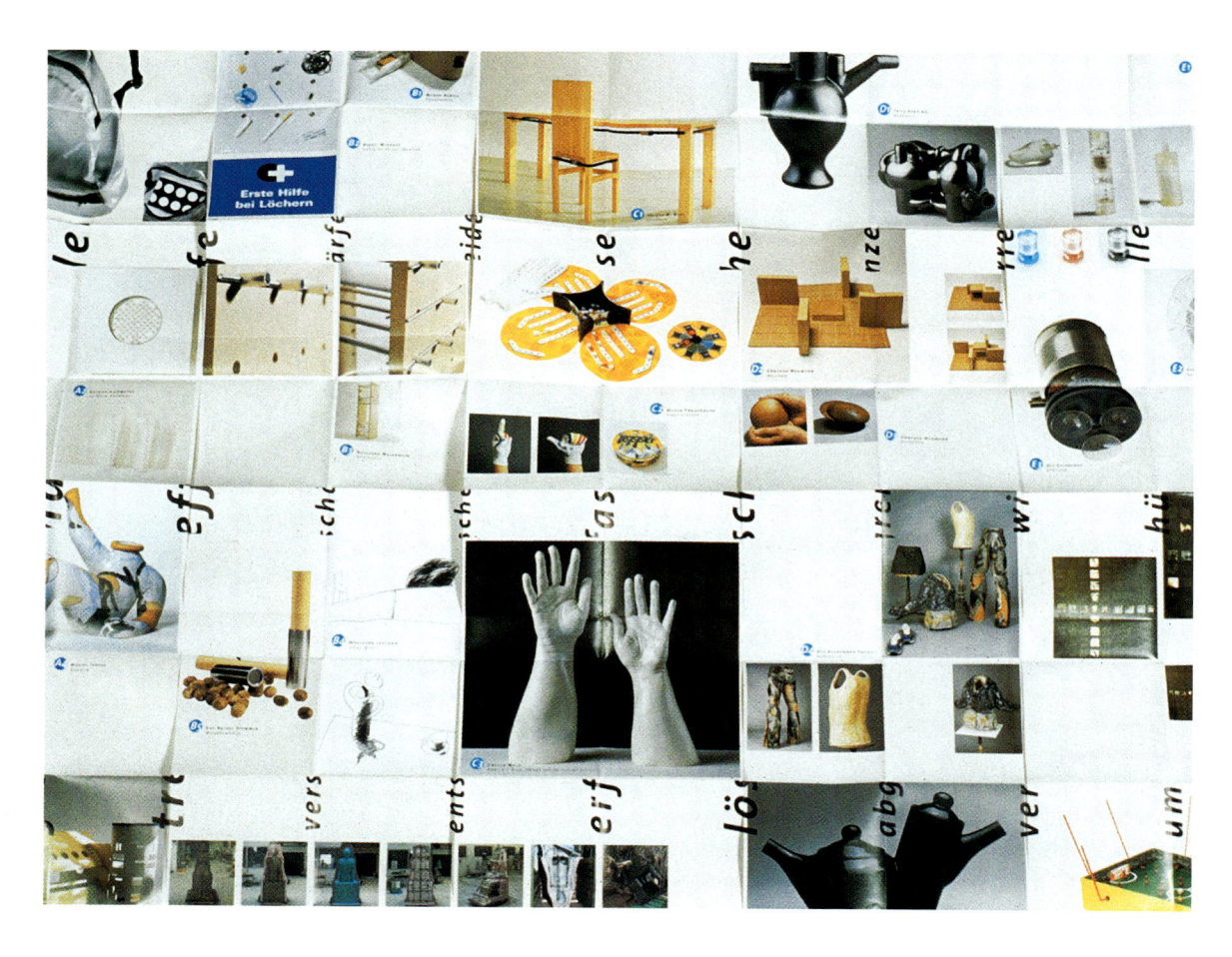

This catalogue was assembled for the »Gestures and Habits of Function« exhibition shown from November 5 to December 12, 1999, in the Bremen Design Center. It uses the style of a familiar navigation tool: the fold-out map. The map becomes part of the concept and signals the difficulty in approaching the displayed objects. It demands a response; its function wants to be understood. The blue points lead the reader across the map to the commentary in the legend. ➤ Der Katalog ist anlässlich der Ausstellung »Gestus und Habitus der Funktion« entstanden, die vom 5. November bis 12. Dezember 1999 im Design Zentrum Bremen gezeigt wurde. Er nimmt das Erscheinungsbild einer bekannten Orientierungshilfe auf – des Falk-Plans. Er wird damit Teil der Botschaft und signalisiert die Schwierigkeit der Annäherung an die gezeigten Objekte und beinhaltet die Forderung nach Auseinandersetzung: Funktionieren will verstanden werden. Der blaue Punkt führt als Lesehilfe den Betrachter über die Abbildungen im Kartenteil zu den Kommentaren der Legende.

Time® | Zeit® Title ✦ Minneapolis College of Art and Design College ✦ 1 Study Year
USA Country ✦ Emily Wilkinson Professor

Alejandro Quinto Student

48

✦ Time is something we are always short of. That's why TIME® products have been invented. Each tube contains one hour of time for a specific activity, such as sleeping, watching TV, eating pizza, having sex, shopping etc. They come in small packages that are durable and easy to carry. One should also be careful not to use the wrong combination of TIME® products at the same time (such as Sleeping and Pizza or Shopping and Sex).

✦ Zeit ist etwas, das wir nie haben. Das ist der Grund warum TIME® Produkte erfunden wurden. Jede Tube enthält eine Stunde Zeit für z.B. Schlafen, Fernsehen, Pizza essen, Sex, Shopping etc. Sie werden in widerstandsfähigen, leicht zu transportierenden kleinen Paketen geliefert. Man sollte aber vorsichtig bei zeitgleichen kombinieren der verschiedenen TIME® Produkte sein (wie Schlafen und Pizza essen oder Shopping und Sex).

The Dating Game Title　Board Game | Brettspiel Medium
Rhode Island School of Design College　USA Country　Hans van Dijk Professor

♥ Hans van Dijk Contributing Editor

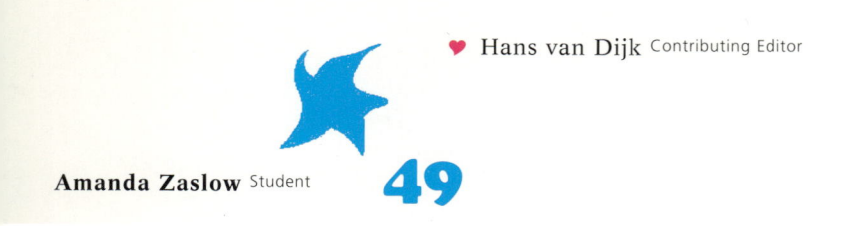

Amanda Zaslow Student　49

▲ »Mutiinga Myth – the Man Eater«: This myth is about the power struggle between men and women. In this particular story, the men take control away from the women after a violent struggle. The students' task was to retell this story in a contemporary context, using only visual means (except a short synopsis of the story). This solution is a board game called »The Dating Game.« Here, images of men and women, taken from the cinema, alternately express happiness or sadness. By throwing the dice, the players move around the board, landing on images of acceptance (happy faces) or rejection (sad faces) and sometimes receiving chance cards that award or subtract points. In this game there are no winners and the game never ends. The players endlessly win or lose the upperhand. »Mutiinga Myth – der Menschenfresser«: dieser Mythos behandelt das Ringen um Macht zwischen Mann und Frau. In dieser Geschichte nehmen die Männer nach einem ernsten und gewaltvollen Kampf den Frauen die Macht. Die Aufgabe der Studenten war es, die Geschichte in einem modernen Kontext nur mit visuellen Mitteln nachzuerzählen (außer einer kurzen Zusammenfassung der Geschichte). Das Ergebnis ist ein Brettspiel namens »The Dating Game«, »Das Verabredungsspiel«. In dem Spiel drücken Bilder von Männern und Frauen aus der Kinowelt Freude und Trauer aus. Durch würfeln wandert der Spieler über das Brett und landet auf Zustimmungsfeldern (glückliches Gesicht) oder auf Ablehnungsfeldern (trauriges Gesicht), oder er erhält Karten die Punkte zum Punktestand addieren oder abziehen. Es gibt keine Gewinner, und das Spiel hört niemals auf. Die Spieler gewinnen oder verlieren endlos an Macht.

Björn Börris Peters Student
50

Union Club, EuroVisions 2000 Title ✓ Magazine and Start-up Kit | Magazin und Startset
Medium ✳ Staatliche Akademie der Bildenden Künste Stuttgart College † Germany Country ▢
Hans-Georg Pospischill Professor

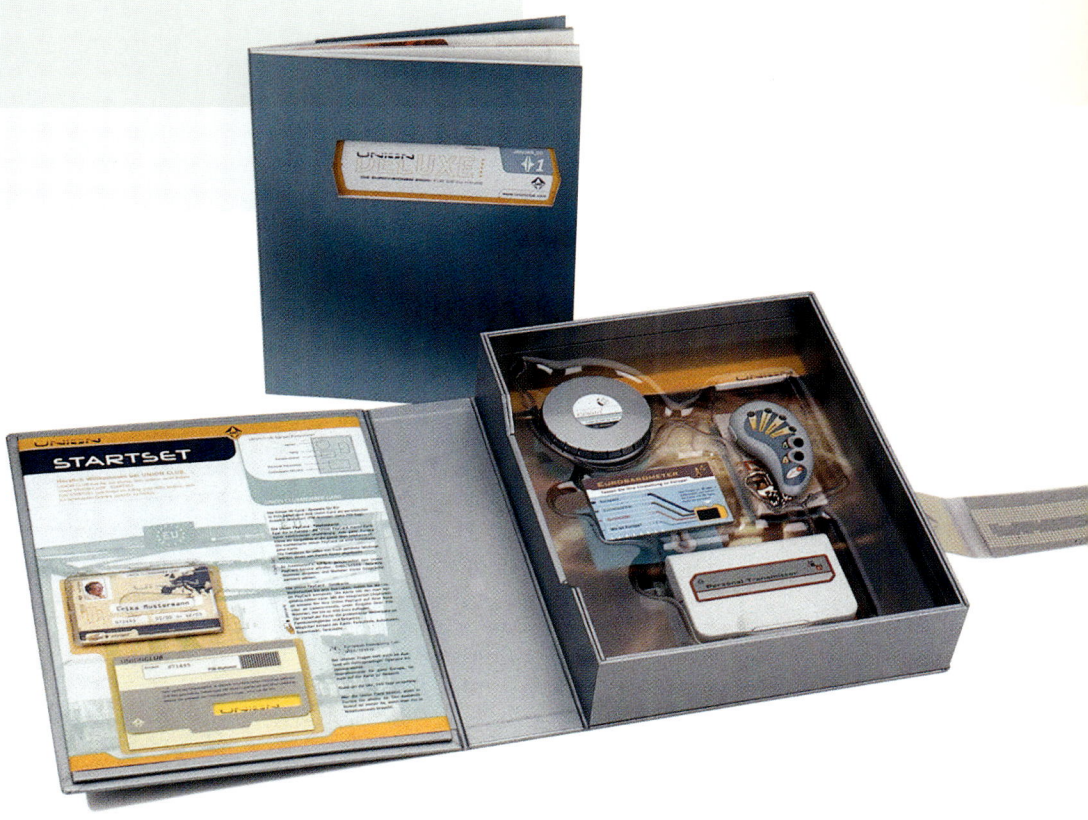

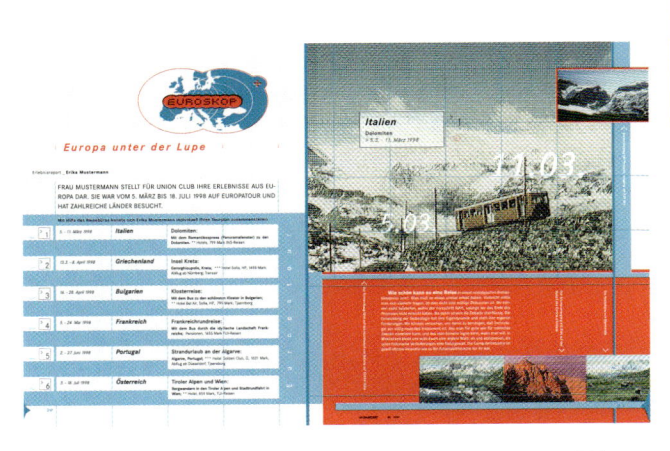

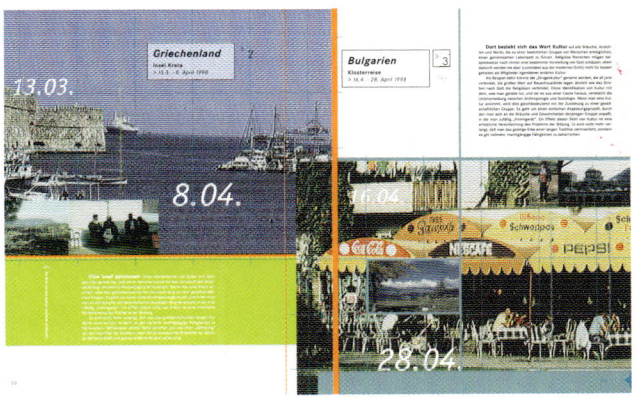

✳ The »Union Club« was founded to mobilize public support for the European Community. It provides background information and tries to persuade one to devote more personal energy to the cause. The start-up kit contains the »Clubmagazin Deluxe,« »Getty, the High-Tech Communication Aid,« »EpirinPlus«-drops for more energy, the »Personal Transmitter« for a better understanding and the »Eurobarometer« for testing one's own position towards Europe. ✿ Der »Union Club« setzt sich dafür ein, die breite Öffentlichkeit für die europäische Einigung zu mobilisieren. Er vermittelt den Bürgern die erforderlichen Hintergrundinformationen zum Verständnis der europäischen Integration und versucht, sie von der Notwendigkeit persönlichen Engagements zu überzeugen. Dabei helfen soll ein Startset bestehend aus dem »Clubmagazin Deluxe«, »Getty«, der High-Tech-Kommunikationshilfe zur verbesserten Kontaktaufnahme, »Epirin Plus«-Pastillen für mehr Energie, dem »Personal Transmitter« als Verständigungshilfe und dem »Eurobarometer« zum Test der eigenen Einstellung zu Europa.

Uta Krogmann Student

51

Kits Title ❋ Approach towards abstract ideas | Annäherung an abstrakte Begriffe Project ❋
4 Study Year ❋ FH Pforzheim College † Germany Country ❋ Uli Cluss Professor

★ *Luck: love, pleasure and calmness*
▢ *Glück: Liebe, Genuss und Gelassenheit*

❋ A kit is a collection of assorted objects for a specific purpose. For example, there are lunch kits, first-aid kits and toolkits. The concept of the work is to gather items for the kit that would make the user happy, wise or free. People aren't just hungry or thirsty, they need luck, beauty, knowledge, etc. Therefore the kits should also be made available in vending machines. ③ Ein Kit ist eine Zusammenstellung verschiedener Dinge zu einem bestimmten Zweck. Es gibt zum Beispiel Lunch-Kits, Erste-Hilfe-Kits oder Tool-Kits. Die Idee dieser Arbeit besteht darin, Kits zusammenzustellen, die den Benutzer glücklich, weise oder frei machen. Da die Menschen nicht nur Hunger oder Durst haben, sondern auch das Bedürfnis nach Glück, Schönheit, Weisheit usw., sollen diese Kits in Automaten zur Verfügung gestellt werden.

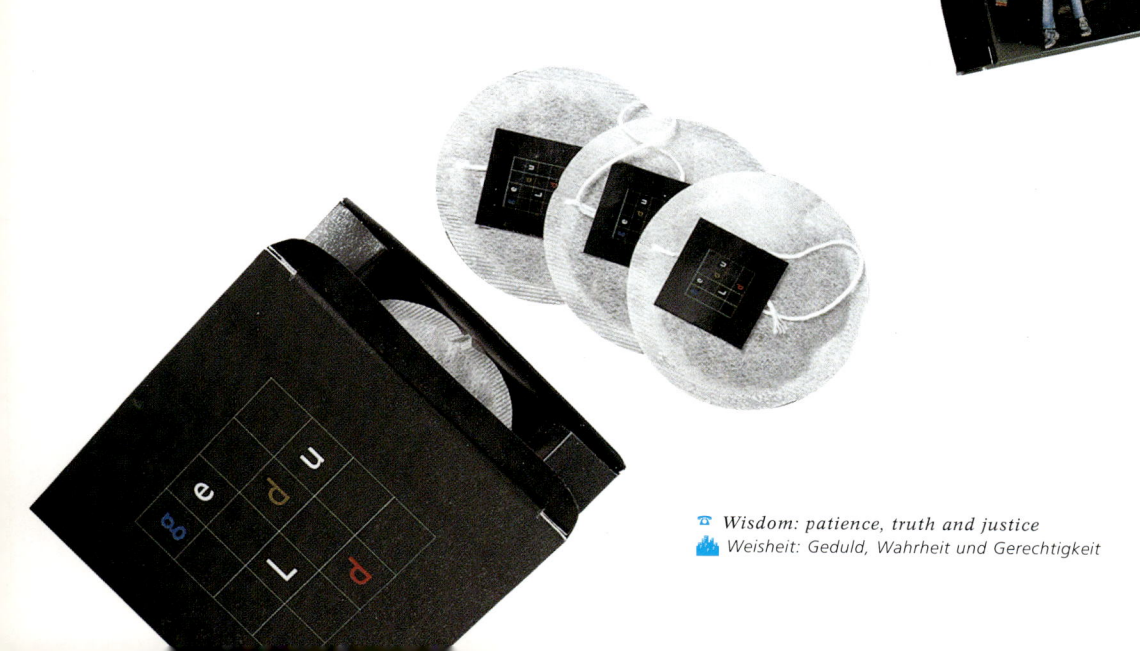

❋ *Vice: lies, envy and revenge*
▱ *Laster: Lüge, Neid und Rache*

π *Wisdom: patience, truth and justice*
▥ *Weisheit: Geduld, Wahrheit und Gerechtigkeit*

Memorial Park for Fallen Soldiers | Gedenkstätte für gefallene Soldaten Title
Vital – The Tel Aviv Center for Design Studies College † Israel Country
David Grossman Professor

David Grossman Contributing Editor

Avital Josef Yosef Student

52

» ... He follows me everywhere, at each hour of the day. I wake up with him in the morning and think of him before I go to sleep ... He is in every corner of the house, the garden, he is like a shadow that follows me. Wherever I go he is with me. In happiness, as in pain, he follows me and will keep doing so until the day I die. « (Tehila, mother of Avner, who was killed in a military training accident) The design focuses on the idea of shadows, the space between them and light, their movement throughout the day, the shapes and graphic elements which they form. The main objective is to link the dead soldiers and the youth – the upcoming generation. Children should visit the memorial every year and paint a metal plaque, each representing a deceased soldier. »... Er folgt mir überall hin, in jeder Stunde des Tages. Ich wache jeden Morgen mit ihm auf und denke an ihn bevor ich ins Bett gehe .... Er ist in jeder Ecke des Hauses, im Garten, er ist wie ein Schatten, der mir folgt. Wo auch immer ich hingehe, er ist bei mir. In Freude, wie im Schmerz, er folgt mir, und er wird es bis zu dem Tage tun, an dem ich sterbe.« (Tehila, Mutter von Avner, der durch einen Unfall während einer Militärübung getötet wurde). Das Designkonzept spielt mit der Idee von Schatten, dem Raum zwischen ihnen und dem Licht, ihrer Bewegung durch den Tag, den Formen und grafischen Elementen, die durch Schatten geformt werden. Das Hauptmotiv des Projekts ist es, die toten Soldaten mit der Nachfolgegeneration von jungen Menschen zu verbinden. Kinder sollen den Ort jedes Jahr besuchen, und eine Metallplakette anmalen, in Gedenken an einen verstorbenen Soldaten.

Slam Poetry *Title* ❋ Poetry Edition | Gedichtband *Project* 🏛 Höhere Schule für Gestaltung Zürich *College* ✝ Switzerland *Country* ❋ Leander Eisenmann *Professor*

Gisela Burkhalter Student

53

❋ The edition is screenprinted and the panels are held together with a rubberband. The illustrative elements are subjective reactions to the text – spontaneous operations while reading. Placed into the design, they become an element of it. Image segments line the bottoms of the single panels, combining to make a »wide-screen« picture. 🔹 Die Edition ist im Siebdruck hergestellt, wobei die einzelnen Tafeln durch ein Gummiband zusammengehalten werden. Die illustrativen Elemente sind subjektive Reaktionen auf den Text, spontane Eingriffe in das Manuskript während des Lesens, welche direkt in die Gestaltung einbezogen worden sind – und damit zum Gestaltungselement werden. Die einzelnen Tafeln sind mit einem Bildausschnitt unterlegt, die zusammengesetzt ein breitformatiges Bild ergeben.

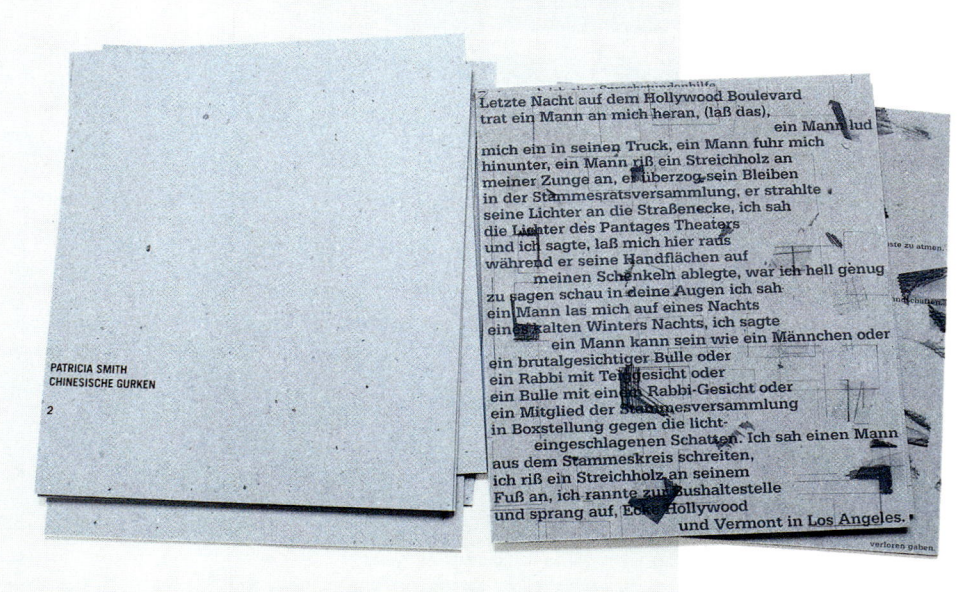

Carla Salem Student

Arabic Typography Title ✔ 4 Study Year ✷ American University of Beirut College ✝ Lebanon Country ❀ **Samir Sayegh** Professor

✷ The students' task was to write their own name in Arabic Calligraphic characters. ⌒ Aufgabe für die Studenten war es, den eigenen Namen in arabischer kalligraphischer Schreibweise zu gestalten.

Liban Post ᵀⁱᵗˡᵉ ✱ Identity System | Erscheinungsbild ᴹᵉᵈⁱᵘᵐ ✱ 4 ˢᵗᵘᵈʸ ʸᵉᵃʳ
✱ Notre Dame University, Beirut ᶜᵒˡˡᵉᵍᵉ ■ Lebanon ᶜᵒᵘⁿᵗʳʸ ✮ John Kortbawi,
Yara Khoury ᴾʳᵒᶠᵉˢˢᵒʳˢ

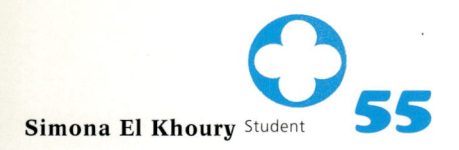

Simona El Khoury ˢᵗᵘᵈᵉⁿᵗ 55

collection

mail express service

☞ This identity system was developed for »Liban Post« to work in both English and Arabic. The arabesque pattern displays the line reading »Liban Post« in a calligraphic, Arabic style. ✽ Für die libanesische Post sollte ein Erscheinungsbild entwickelt werden, das sowohl in arabischer als auch in englischer Sprache anwendbar sein soll. Das arabeske Muster zeigt den Schriftzug »Liban Post« in arabischer, kalligraphischer Schreibweise.

Liban Post

Ingrid Haug Student

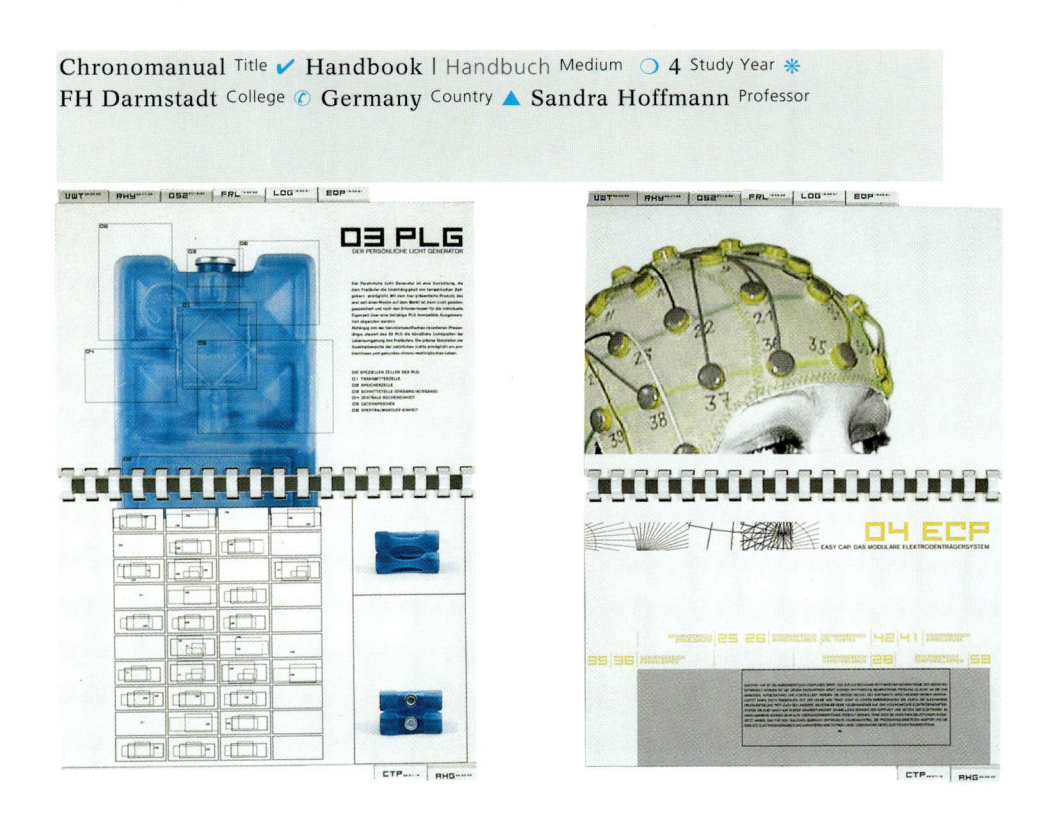

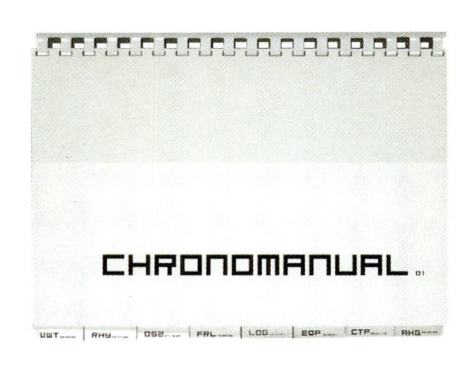

56

Chronomanual Title ✔ Handbook | Handbuch Medium ○ 4 Study Year ✲
FH Darmstadt College ⓒ Germany Country ▲ Sandra Hoffmann Professor

③ »Chronomanual« addresses those whose biorhythms deviate from the 24-hour cycle of Earth's rotation, such as »morning« or »evening« people. These people often suffer from sleeplessness and inability to concentrate. The manual goes through the basics of biorhythms and shows possible solutions to problems. Different mechanical aids are featured for different chronotypes; for example, a memory card that stores the user's individual time schedule, or glasses for shift-workers that, at dawn (after work), intensify specific colours of the spectrum releasing sleep hormones. ★ Das Chronomanual ist für alle Menschen gedacht, deren biologischer Rhythmus vom 24 Stunden-Zyklus der Erdrotation abweicht – also Morgen- oder Abendmenschen. Diese Menschen leiden oft an Schlafstörungen und Konzentrationsschwächen. Das Handbuch führt in die Grundlagen der biologischen Rhythmen ein und zeigt Möglichkeiten für Lösungen des Problems auf. Für verschiedene Chronotypen werden unterschiedliche Geräte vorgestellt, wie zum Beispiel eine Chipkarte, auf der die individuellen Zeitsysteme des Benutzers gespeichert werden oder eine Spektralbrille für Schichtarbeiter, die in der Morgendämmerung (also nach Feierabend) bestimmte Spektralfarben aktiviert und dadurch schlaffördernde Hormone freisetzt.

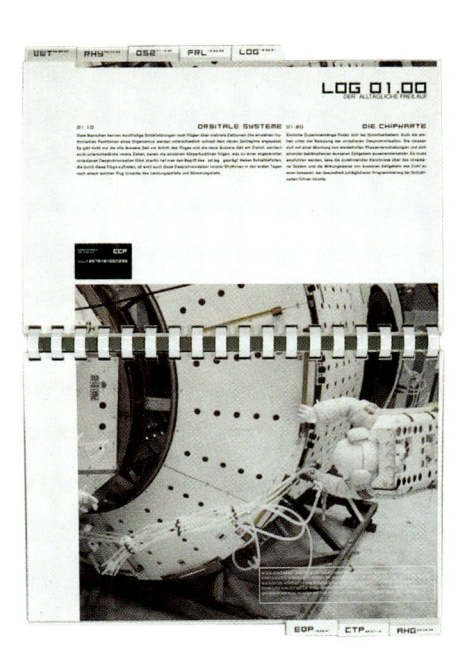

video view

Michael David Ochs, Ricarda Wallhäuser, Petra Schultze, Steffi Rall, Rena Chrysikopoulou, Norbert Bayer, Katharina Fiedler, Britta Lorch, Kirstin Leichtl, Julia Henning, Kristiane Krüger, Markus Baude, Petra Wierzchula, Nikolaus Birk Students

57

Video Interview Title Magazine Medium 3 – 5 Study Year
GH Kassel College Germany Country Daniela Haufe, Detlef Fiedler Professors

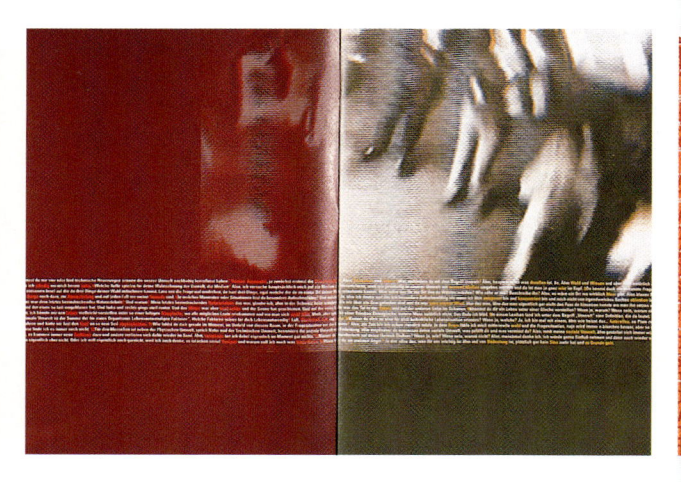

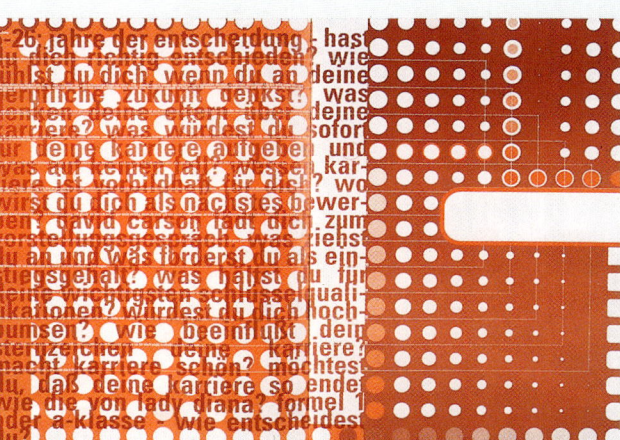

✺ The students' task was to choose one of fourteen themes, to compose a list of questions and an interview situation, to film it, and to design a magazine spread with the recorded imagery. ✤ Für die Zeitschrift standen 14 Themen zur Auswahl. Die Aufgabe jedes einzelnen Studenten bestand darin, zu seinem Thema Fragen sowie eine Interviewsituation zu entwickeln und diese mit einer Videokamera aufzunehmen. Aus den entstandenen Bildern sollte eine Doppelseite gestaltet werden.

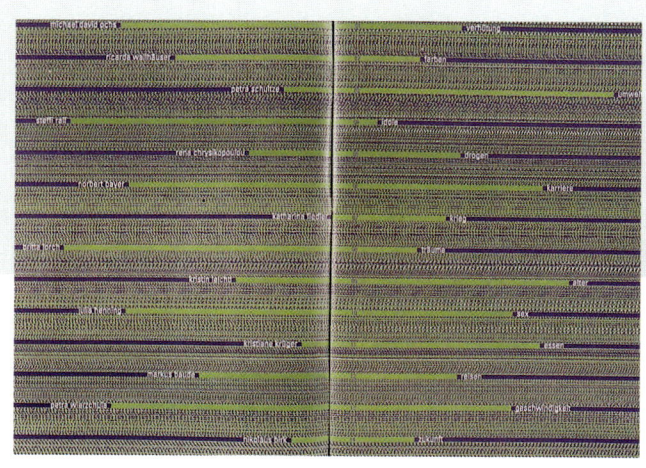

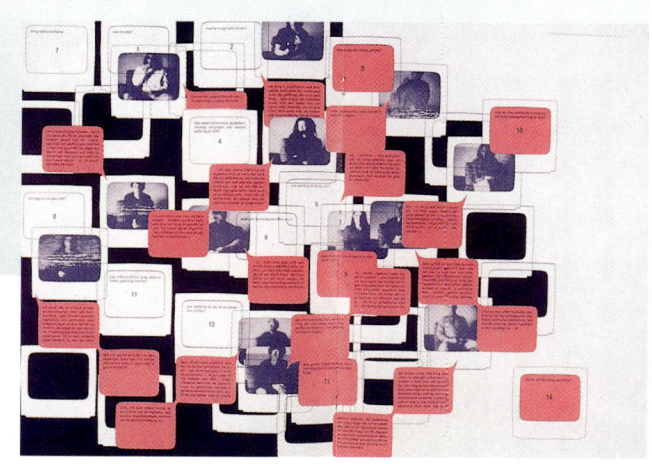

Elena Tolokonina Student

Brochure for the Design Masters Programme Project ✗ Booklet Medium ❼
5 Study Year ✓ Higher Academic School of Graphic Design Moscow College ）
Russia Country ✂ Boris Trofimov Professor

ᴀᴀ This booklet is a brochure presenting the Masters Programme at Moscow's Higher Academic School of Graphic Design. It's not an art school catalogue in the conventional sense, it shows with images the process of studying from a student's perspective. The booklet was made without using a computer.
✳ Das Booklet ist eine Broschüre über die Design-Meisterklasse an der Higher Academic School of Graphic Design in Moskau. Es ist kein Hochschul-Katalog im herkömmlichen Sinne, sondern beschreibt den Prozess des Studiums aus studentischer Sicht in visueller Form. Die Broschüre ist ohne Hilfe des Computers gemacht.

Coffe:in ᵀⁱᵗˡᵉ ✈ **Identity for a chain of coffee bars** | Erscheinungsbild für eine Kaffeebar-Kette ᴾʳᵒʲᵉᶜᵗ ⚓ 4 ˢᵗᵘᵈʸ ʸᵉᵃʳ ✳ **FH Mainz** ᶜᵒˡˡᵉᵍᵉ ▪ **Germany** ᶜᵒᵘⁿᵗʳʸ ✂ Olaf Leu ᴾʳᵒᶠᵉˢˢᵒʳ

Guido Böhm ˢᵗᵘᵈᵉⁿᵗ 59

✹ The logo is set in a typeface (coffe:in Mono) that was made especially for the coffe:in company. Monospace typefaces have their origin in computer printers, train station and airport timetable displays, etc. They are a symbol of modernity and speed, characterizing the atmosphere in the coffe:in bars. The coffee bar has its own magazine along with other print products and packaging. ✤ Das Logo ist in einer eigens für die coffe:in-Company entwickelten Schrift gesetzt (coffe:in Mono). Monospace Schriften haben ihren Ursprung in Computerdrucken, Bahn- und Flughafenanzeigetafeln usw. Sie sind Zeichen von Modernität und Schnelligkeit. Sie charakterisieren so die Atmosphäre in den coffe:in Bars. Neben Drucksachen und Produktverpackungen gibt es eine eigene Zeitschrift für die Kaffee-Bar.

Alexandra Ostrovskaya, Elena Isaeva Student

60

Kvas Title ✼ **Packaging for a Drink** | Produktverpackung für ein Getränk Medium
5 Study Year ✼ **Higher Academic School of Graphic Design Moscow** College
Russia Country ✼ **Boris Trofimov** Professor

This packaging came out of a project for the »Ostankino Factory for Non-Alcoholic Drinks.« »Kvas« is a light Russian drink that is normally made from scratch. The rough look of the rope emphasizes this home-made character. By using various elements which combine to make new images, the bottles become collectors' items. Die Verpackung entstand in einem Projekt für die »Ostankino Factory for Non-Alcoholic Drinks«. »Kvas« ist ein leichtes, russisches – üblicherweise hausgemachtes – Getränk. Die rauhe Anmutung der Seile unterstützt seinen selbstgemachten Charakter. Durch die verschiedenen, seriellen Motive, die man untereinander zu neuen Bildern kombinieren kann, werden die Flaschen zu Sammlerobjekten.

Noriko Yuasa Student **61**

Second Language | Zweite Sprache Title ⦿ **Pillow** | Kissen Medium
Minneapolis College of Art and Design College ✴ **USA** Country ✴ **Joe Monnens** Professor

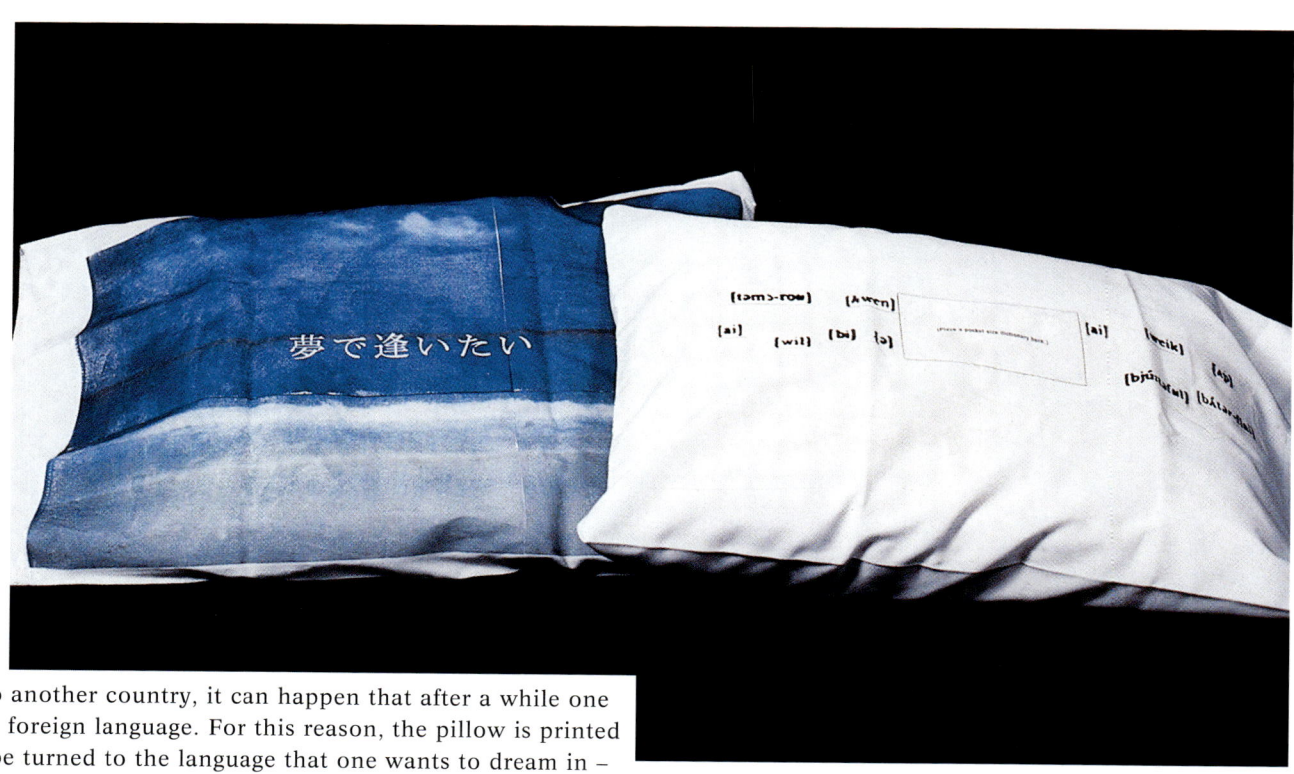

✴ When one travels to another country, it can happen that after a while one starts to dream in that foreign language. For this reason, the pillow is printed on both sides. It can be turned to the language that one wants to dream in – Japanese or English. ✴ Wenn man in ein anderes Land reist, kann es vorkommen, dass man nach einer gewissen Zeit beginnt, in der fremden Sprache zu träumen. Das Kissen ist für solche Fälle auf beiden Seiten bedruckt und kann gewendet werden – je nachdem in welcher Sprache man nachts träumen möchte: Japanisch oder Englisch.

Song Roman Title ❋ Typeface | Schrift Medium ❋ 5 Study Year ❋
Yale School of Art College ❋ USA Country

Li Wei Student ❋ 62

喜欢吃中国菜的西方人甚多，了解中国艺术的西方人甚少；同样，用西方电器开西方车的中国人太多，了解西方艺术的中国人也是太少。西方人对中国文化的认识阶段似乎总停留在中国的古代，在科技信息日益发达的今天，双方在对当代文化艺术的相互认识上差异如此之大，误会如此之深，不能不说是一大遗憾。庆幸的是，真知胜于偏见，我们现在都已开始承认、研究和缩短着这种差异，并努力寻求着了解和沟通。为此，我们已经开始广泛地以各种方式进行深入的交流。由中国优秀中青年艺术家组成的中国油画家代表团受到美国国际艺术研究会和加拿大亚太国际艺术公司的邀请，飞越重洋，将把十二位中国当代油画家的作品呈献给美国、加拿大的同行和朋友。这是中国艺术家走出国门最大的一次集体行动，也是中西方在当代艺术上更进

Westerners know more about Chinese food than they do about Chinese art. Similarly, the Chinese understand Western electronics and cars far more than they do Western art. Part of the problem is that the western mind still believes Chinese art and culture have remained in the ancient past. This is a regrettable situation for both sides. With so many differences and misconceptions still existing, it is difficult for our two cultures to truly understand each other. But we believe that real knowledge is superior to prejudice, especially in these developed, scientific times. And so we have tried to understand and connect by admitting the problem, researching solutions and developing methods to shorten our difference. This art exhibition is one way in which our efforts will help to

❤ »This Roman typeface was designed to accompany an existing Chinese typeface ›Song,‹ thus, it was named ›Song Roman.‹ More and more bilingual situation occur in today's visual communications, and I have been troubled for a long time by unsuccessfully designed Roman letterforms that are originally made from parts of Chinese characters. As an attempt to bring together the inherently different forms of Chinese characters and Roman letters, my goal was to achieve an overall balance of colour and texture between the two.« ☎ »Diese lateinische Schrift wurde entworfen, um gemeinsam mit der bereits existierenden chinesischen Schrift ›Song‹ verwendet zu werden. Aus diesem Grund trägt die Schrift den Namen ›Song Roman‹. Die heutige Kommunikation erfordert mehr und mehr zweisprachige Gestaltungskonzepte. Ich wurde lange Zeit von schlecht gestalteten lateinischen Schriften geplagt, die aus Elementen chinesischer Schriftzeichen aufgebaut waren. Ich habe mit meinem Entwurf versucht, die unterschiedlichen Formen chinesischer und lateinischer Schriftzeichen miteinander zu vereinen. Ziel war es, eine gleichmäßige Verteilung der Farben und Formen zwischen den beiden zu erzeugen.«

宋 songroman

abcdefghijklmnopqrstuvwxyz,.

So-Hyon Choe Student

63

Reflected Images | Spiegelbilder Title ✱ **Photography** Medium → **6** Study Year
HdK Berlin College ✱ **Germany** Country **Holger Matthies** Professor

Contact Title | Poster Medium 5 Study Year Hong-Ik University College
Korea Country → Ahn Sang-Soo Professor

Sohn Ik-Weon Student

64

♥ Ahn Sang-Soo Contributing Editor

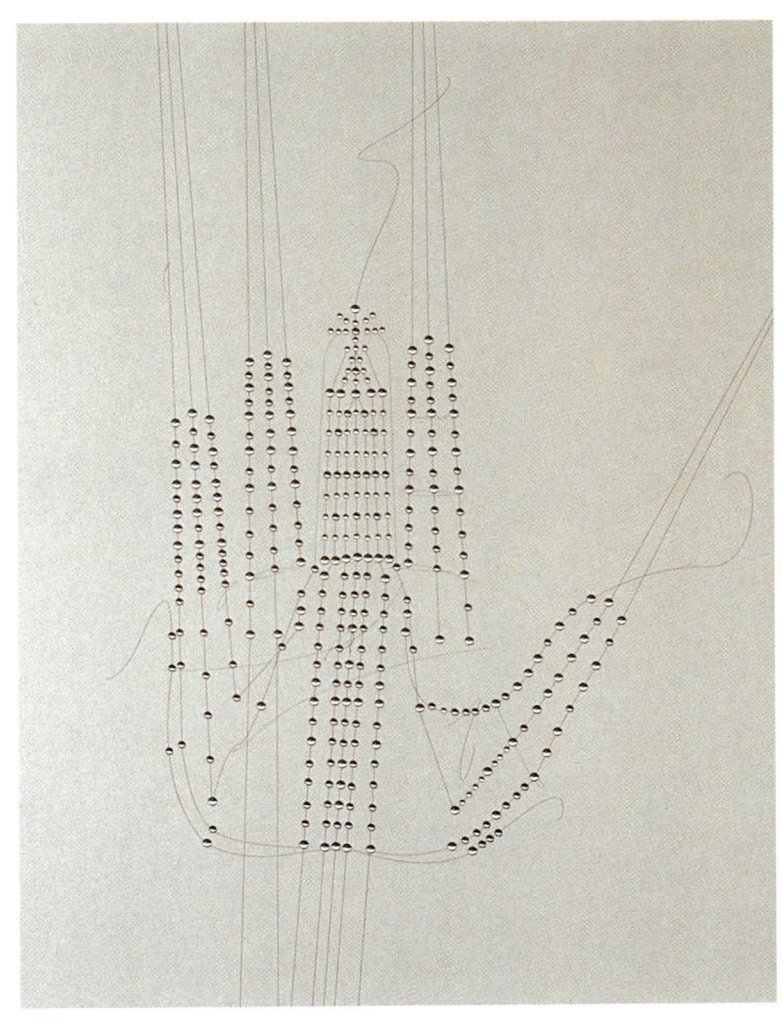

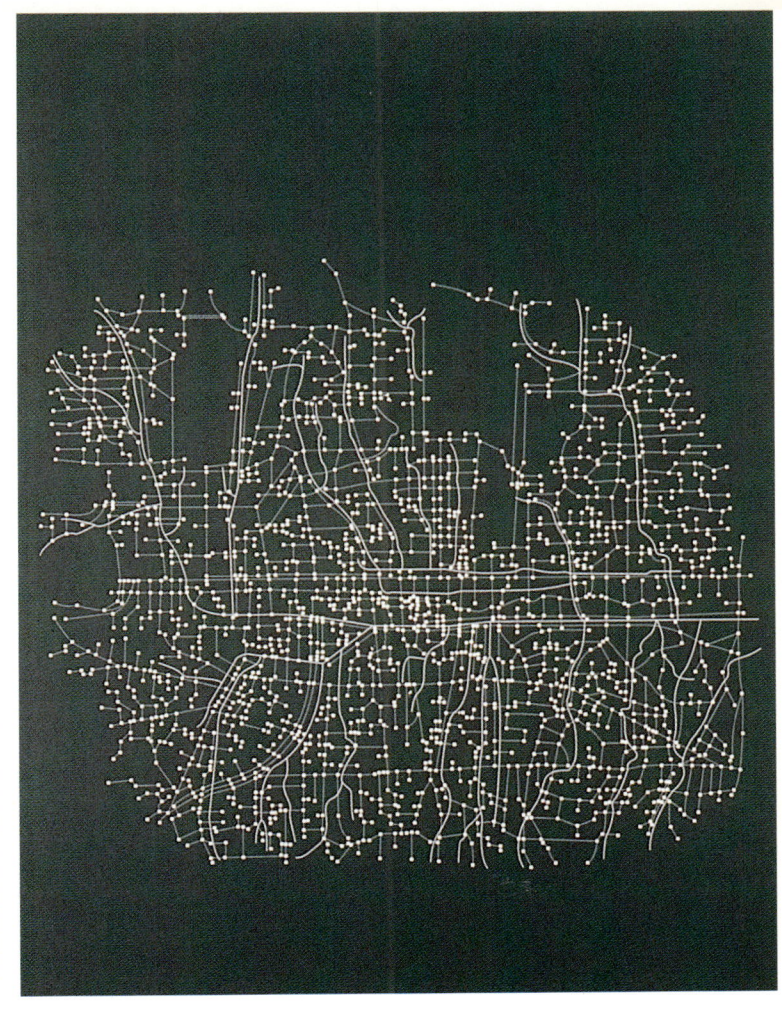

→ *Inhumane Universe* ♦ *Unmenschliches Universum*   ＊ *City* ✳ *Stadt*

◇ Two from a series of four posters about the connection between man and nature. → Zwei aus einer Serie von vier Plakaten über die Zusammenhänge von Mensch und Natur.

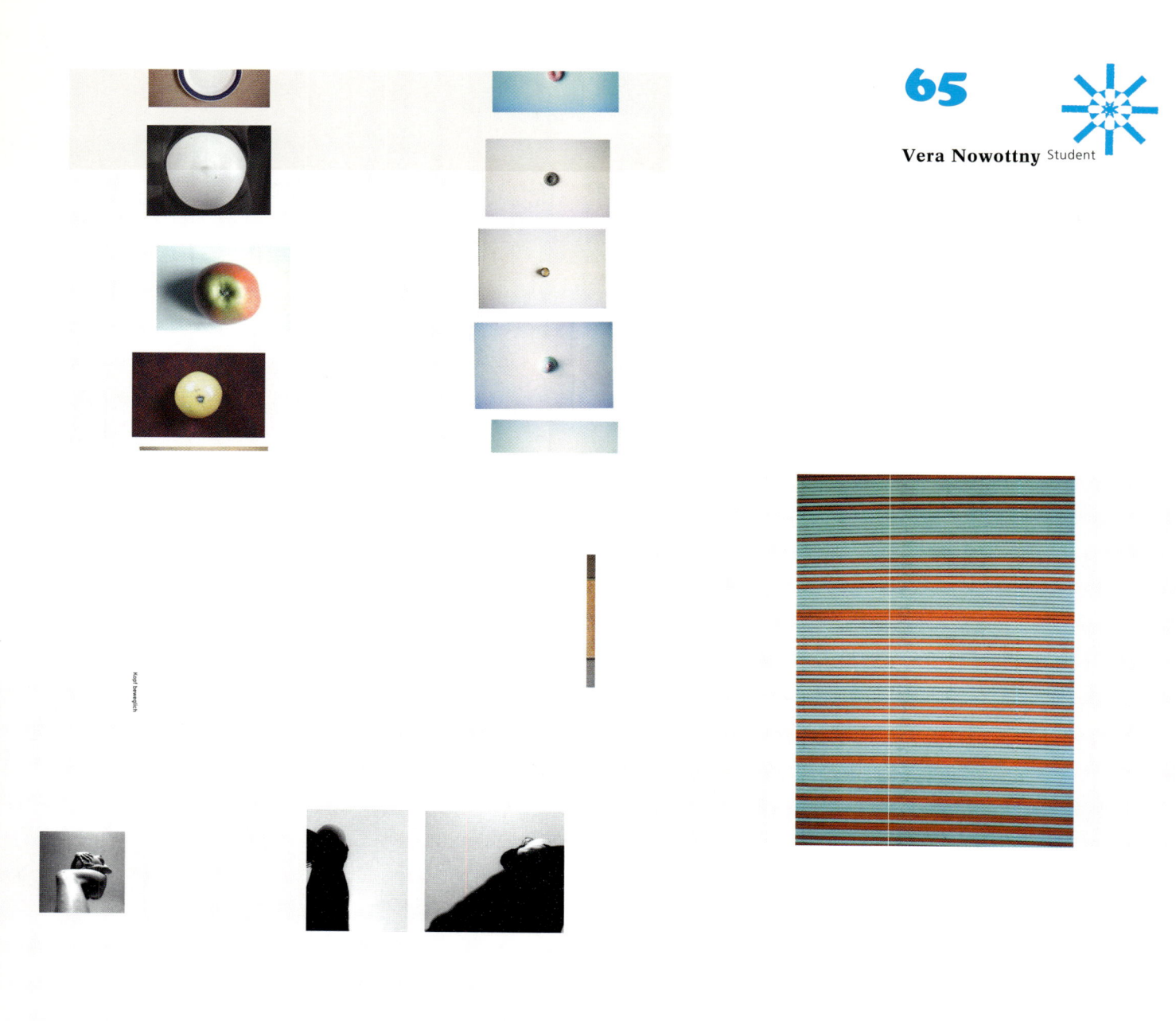

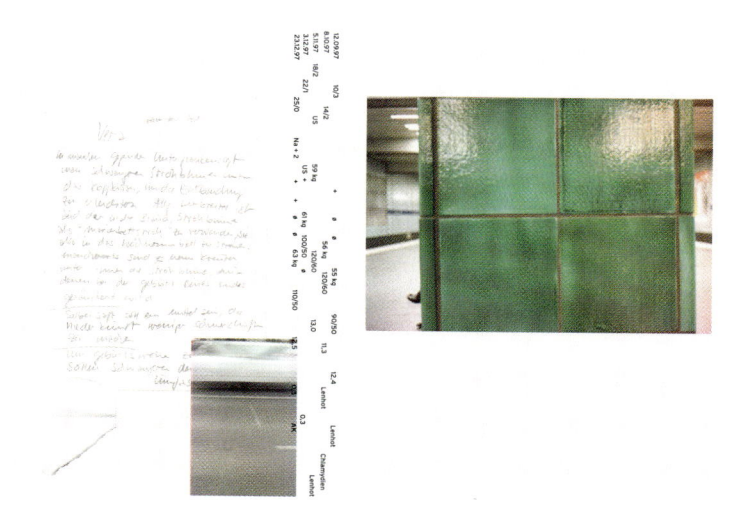

Side Views | Seitenansichten Title Book Medium 6 Study Year FH Würzburg College
Germany Country Karlheinz Hornung, Frieder Grindler Professors

65

Vera Nowottny Student

»The book is a photographic discussion of a specific time period. I am the only continiuous thread throughout the book. My physical condition strongly influences both the theme and my way of seeing and taking photographs. The book is dedicated to my daughter Linda.« »Das Buch ist eine fotografische Auseinandersetzung mit dem Zeitraum. Der rote Faden, der durch das Buch führt, bin ich selbst. Mein derzeitiger körperlicher Zustand prägte die Thematik und beeinflusste die Fotografie und Sehweise. Gewidmet ist das Buch meiner Tochter Linda.«

Tanya Pike Student

66

♥ Robyn Stacey Contributing Editor

R.L. The People's Game Title ⊜ Book Medium ✳ 4 Study Year ⑩
University of Western Sydney College ➪ Australia Country ⊱ Robyn Stacey Professor

Class, community, tradition, identity, culture, capitalism and politics ... »The People's Game« represents 100 years of social harmony and conflict within Australia. Rugby was made by the people, for the poeple and is kept alive by the tradition and culture which came from the people. However, with the arrival of corporate giants and recognition of the sports' popularity and profitability, the game has been bought from the people without them even knowing it was for sale. As a documentary and cultural study, the book provides a broad overview of League's history through a compilation of social commentary. Klasse, Gemeinschaft, Tradition, Identität, Kultur, Kapitalismus und Politik ... »Das Spiel des Volkes« repräsentiert 100 Jahre sozialer Einheit und sozialer Konflikte in Australien. Rugby wurde von den Menschen, für die Menschen gemacht und wird von der Tradition und Kultur der Menschen am Leben gehalten. Mit der Beteiligung von großen Unternehmen, die den wirtschaftlichen Wert und die Popularität des Sports für sich nutzen, wurde das Spiel den Menschen jedoch abgekauft – ohne dass sie bemerkt hätten, dass es zum Verkauf stand. Das Buch gibt als Dokumentation und kulturelle Studie einen umfassenden Überblick zur Geschichte der Rugby-Liga in Form einer Sammlung sozialer Kommentare.

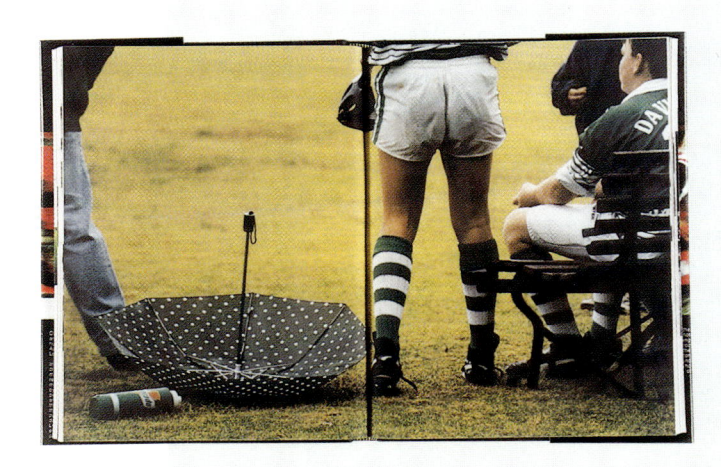

Ziad El Khoury Student

67

Adam & Eve Title   Folder and Inserts | Mappe und Einlagen Medium
4 Study Year   American University of Beirut College   Lebanon Country
Leila Musfy Professor

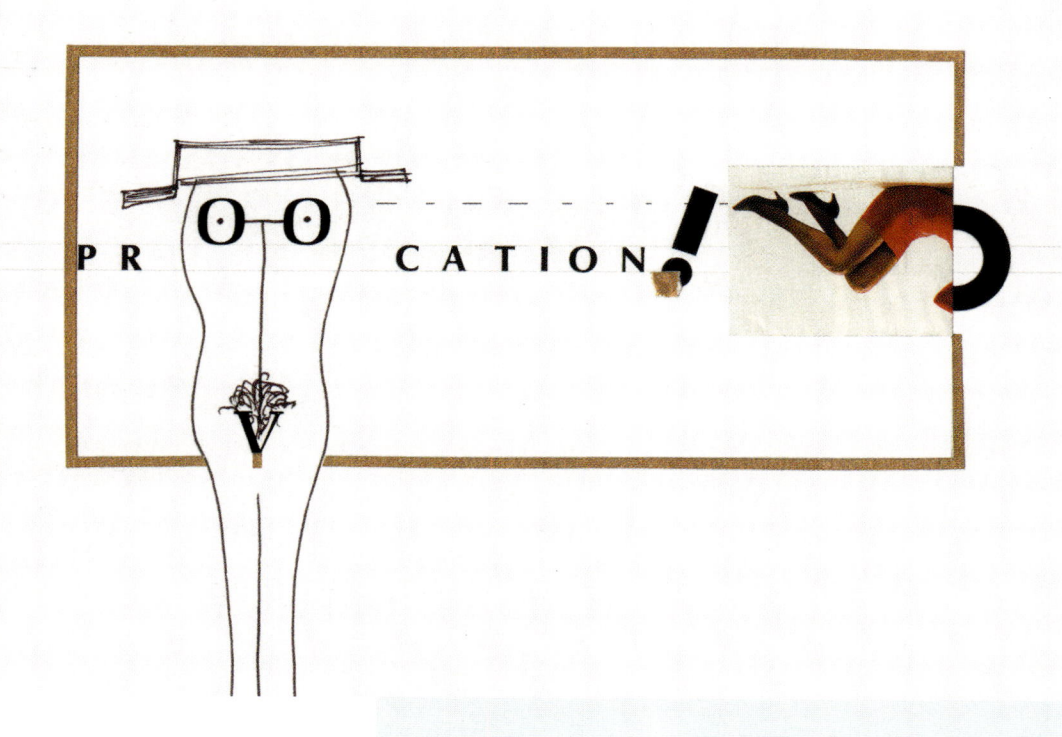

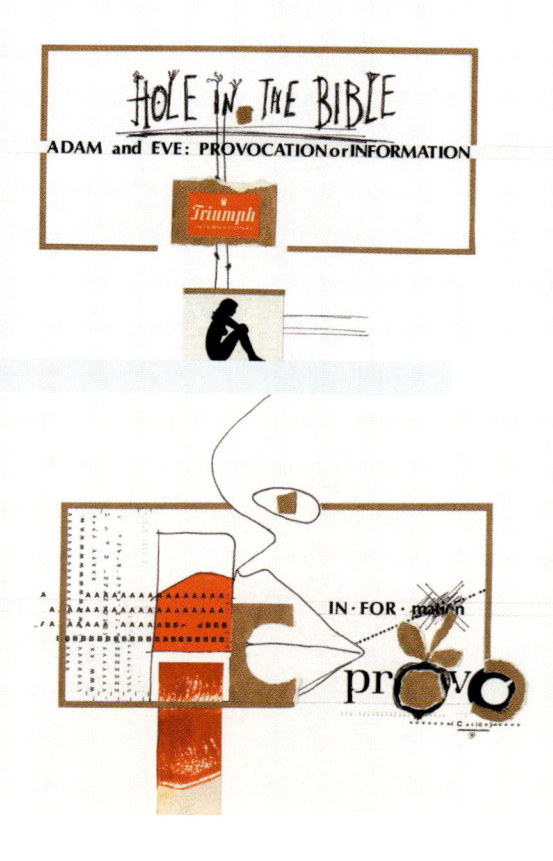

Illustrated Book | Illustriertes Buch Title | 2 Study Year
Universität für angewandte Kunst Wien College ◆ Austria Country ◆
Walter Lürzer Professor

Christina Gschwantner Student

68

Once upon a time there was a small giant ...

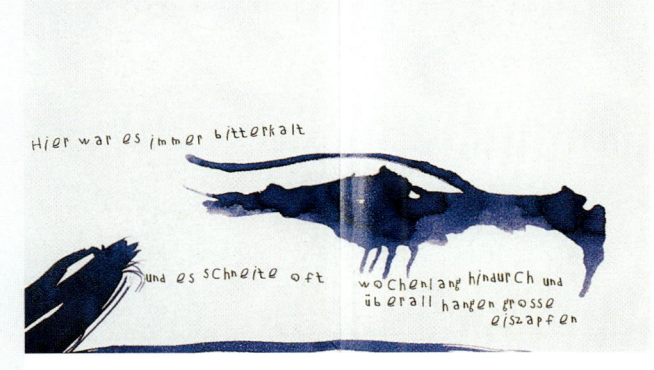

... he lived all alone in the far, cold north ...

... it was always bitter cold there ...
... and it would often snow for weeks without end and huge icicles hung from everywhere ...

... the small giant always had a lot of time and observed his surroundings carefully. He could see very well and accurately with his big, big eyes ...

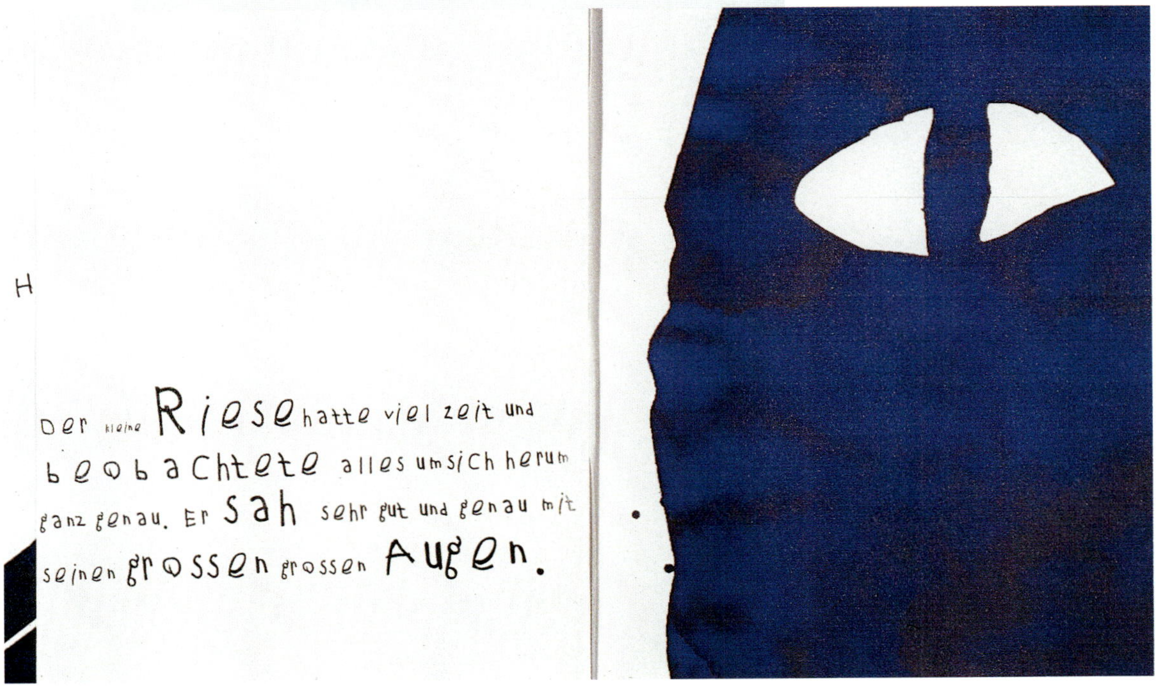

Heart Sutra: The Process | Heart Sutra: Der Prozess ᵀⁱᵗˡᵉ ✳ **Exhibition** | Ausstellung ᴹᵉᵈⁱᵘᵐ
2 ˢᵗᵘᵈʸ ʸᵉᵃʳ   Yale School of Art ᶜᵒˡˡᵉᵍᵉ   USA ᶜᵒᵘⁿᵗʳʸ
Paul Elliman, Matthew Carter, Jonathan Hoefler ᴾʳᵒᶠᵉˢˢᵒʳˢ

Li Wei ˢᵗᵘᵈᵉⁿᵗ **69**

✳ »This book documents my working process of a semester-long project: to represent my daily meditative experience with ›Heart Sutra‹ (a Buddhist scripture) and eventually design an exhibition for such an experience.«

»Dieses Buch dokumentiert meinen Arbeitsprozess für ein Projekt über den Zeitraum eines Semesters: meine täglichen Erfahrungen mit Meditation anhand der buddhistischen Schrift ›Heart Sutra‹. Anschließend habe ich eine Ausstellung über diese Erfahrungen gemacht.«

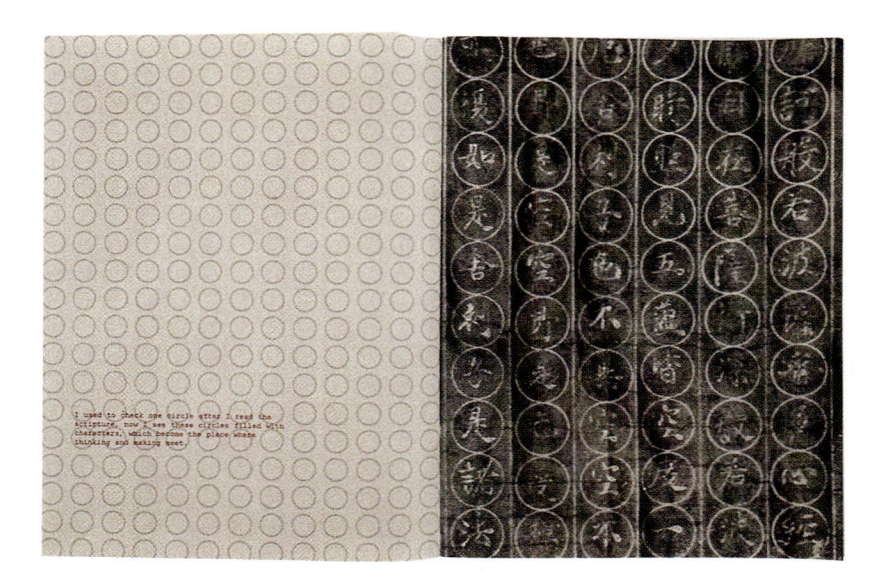

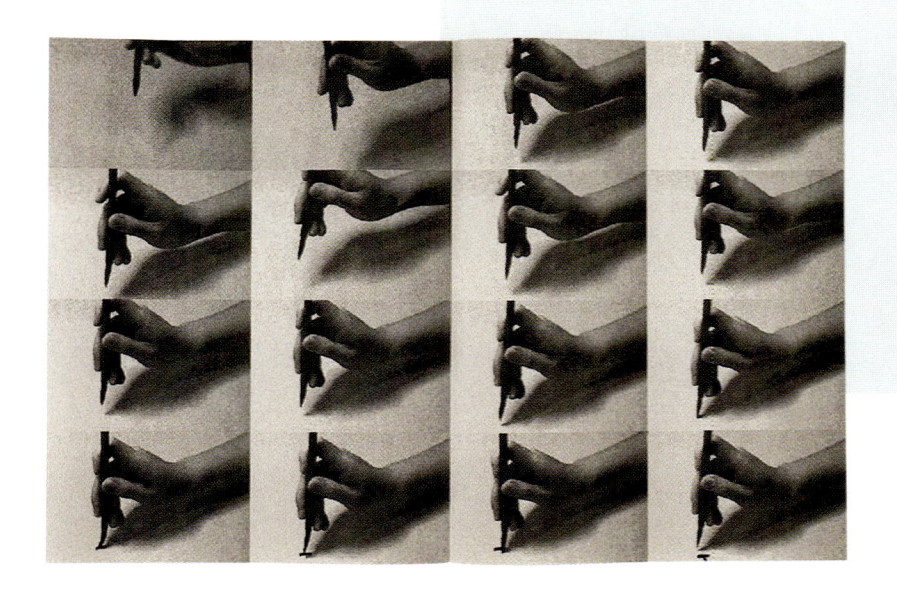

proposal 1
projection on the screen:
text of *Heart Sutra*

Isn't the stillness a repetition
of itself in time?

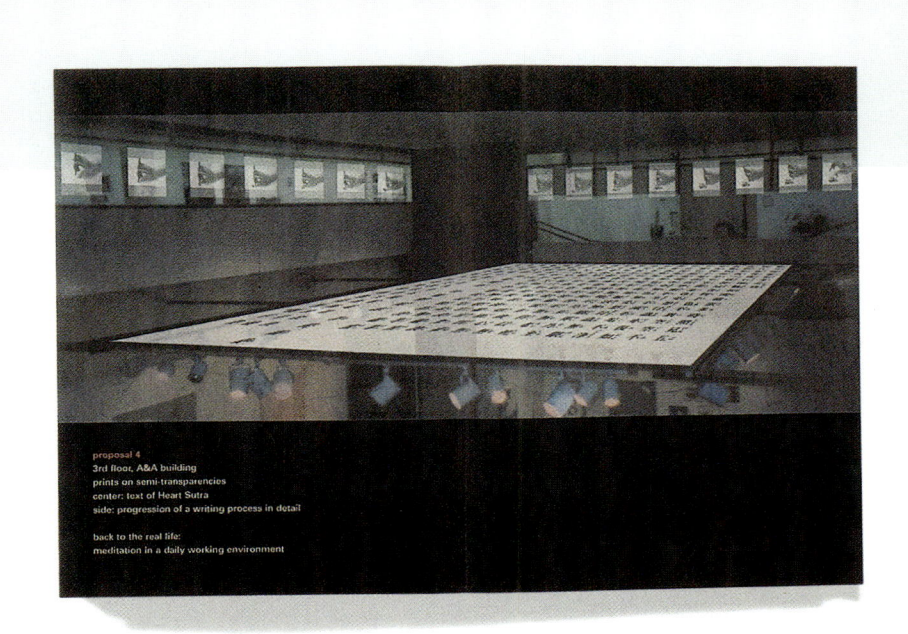

proposal 4
3rd floor, A&A building
prints on semi-transparencies
center: text of Heart Sutra
side: progression of a writing process in detail

back to the real life:
meditation in a daily working environment

Doreen Kiepsel Student

70

A Card Collection | Eine Kartensammlung Title   5 Study Year
Muthesius Hochschule Kiel College   Germany Country

→ In this collection of cards, cut-out words from magazines are combined with drawings to produce an opposition. The pictures react to the words and the words to the pictures. The cards can be put together to compose little stories, always with a different meaning.   In dieser Kartensammlung werden aus Zeitschriften ausgeschnittene Wörter mit Zeichnungen kombiniert und bekommen ein anderes Gegenüber. Die Bilder reagieren auf die Worte und umgekehrt. Als Reihe können die einzelnen Karten zu kleinen Geschichten zusammengestellt werden, die sich immer anders darstellen.

Bidets and Life Title Fanzine | Fanmagazin Medium
4 Study Year American University of Beirut College Lebanon Country
Leila Musfy Professor

71
Fadi Baki Student

»A book for all those who wanted to know more about toilet paper, bidets and other things, but never dared to ask … and for Omar, without whom I would have never realized that some people don't use the bidet.« | »Ein Buch für alle, die schon immer mehr über Toilettenpapier, Bidets und andere Dinge erfahren wollten, aber nie zu fragen wagten – und für Omar, ohne den ich nie bemerkt hätte, dass manche Menschen das Bidet gar nicht benutzen.«

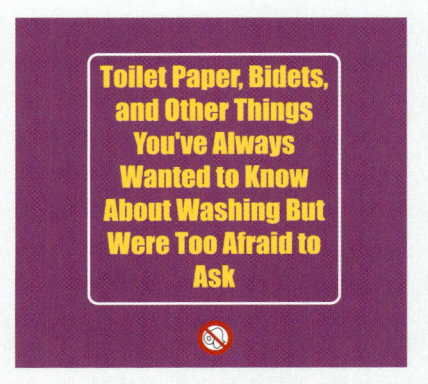

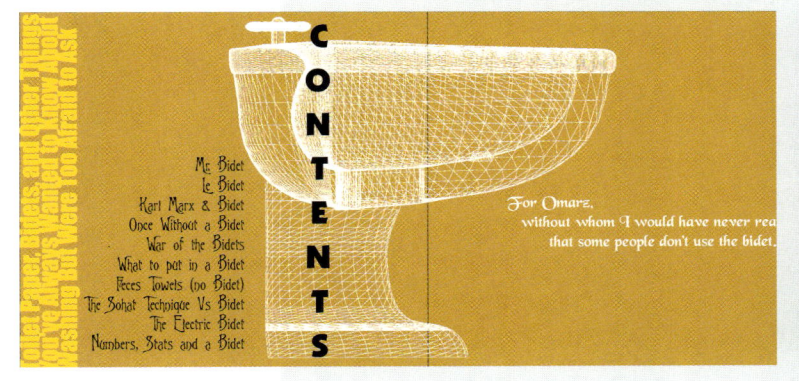

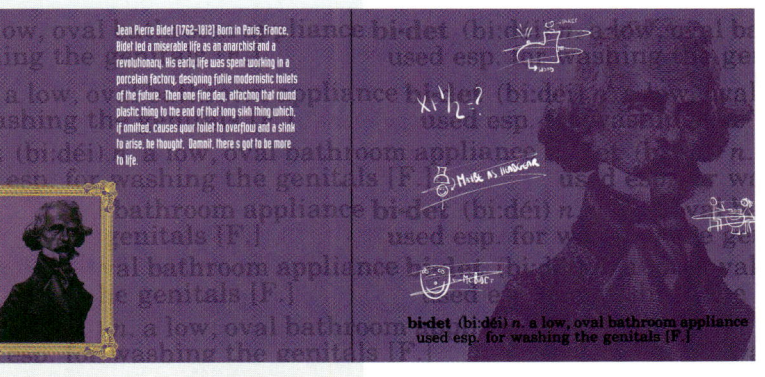

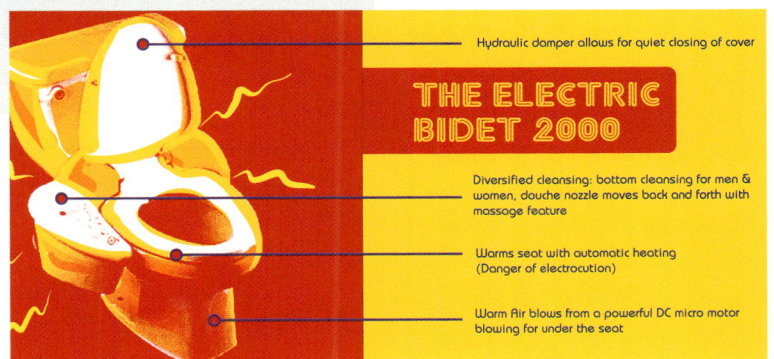

Kontemplasi **Title** → Design for a photographic exhibition | Ausstattung für eine Fotoausstellung **Project** ⤴ 4 **Study Year** ➢ Jakarta Institute of Arts **College** ✤ Indonesia **Country** ⤴ Siti Turmini **Professor**

Lembu Wiworo Jati **Student** **72**

✤ The theme of the exhibition is »Contemplation.« It features black and white photographs of seven students from the Jakarta Institute of Arts.
➢ Das Thema der Ausstellung ist »Kontemplation«. Die Ausstellung zeigt Schwarzweißfotografien von sieben Student/inn/en des Jakarta Insitute of Arts.

73
Stefanie Matter Student

On the Edge of Language | An den Rändern der Sprache Title → Book, Poster and Illustrations about Ernst Jandl | Buch, Plakat und Illustrationen über Ernst Jandl Project ✂ 5 Study Year ❷ FH Anhalt College ❾ Germany Country ✈ Erhard Grüttner Professor

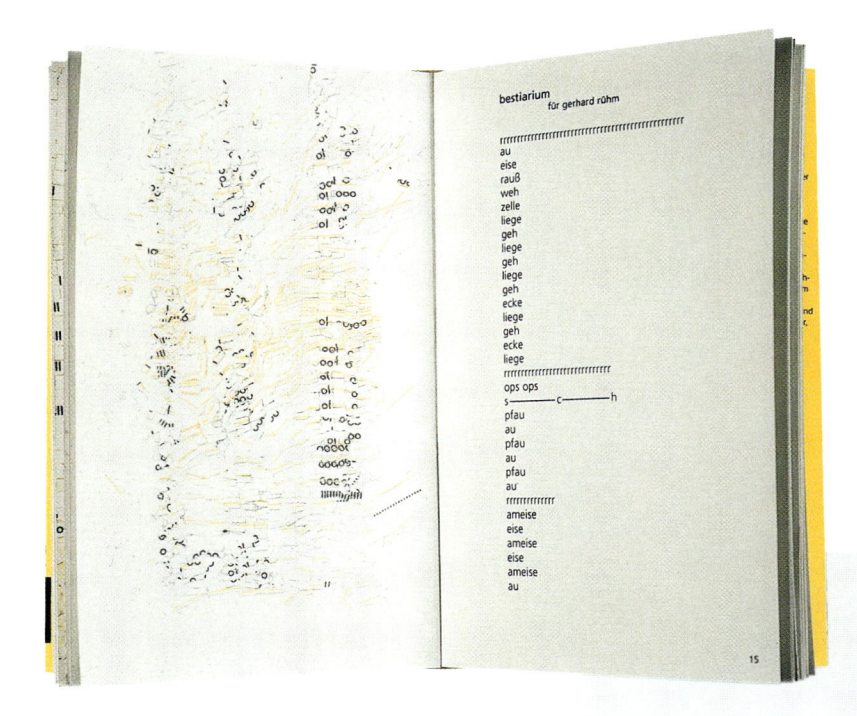

→ These illustrations were made for the collection of poems »Aloud and Quiet« by Ernst Jandl. Along with this, a poster had to be designed for a fictitious reading. ◆ Die Illustrationen entstanden zu dem Gedichtband »Laut und Leise« von Ernst Jandl. In diesem Zusammenhang wurde auch ein Plakat für eine fiktive Lesung entworfen.

Isabell Große Holtforth Student

① ✼ Rituals for falling asleep are printed on one side of the pillow, and for waking up on the other. The instructions are to be used while laying in bed.
✼ Der Kopfkissenbezug ist auf der einen Seite mit Einschlafritualen bedruckt und auf der anderen Seite mit Aufwachritualen. Diese Lernhilfe soll direkt im Bett benutzt werden.

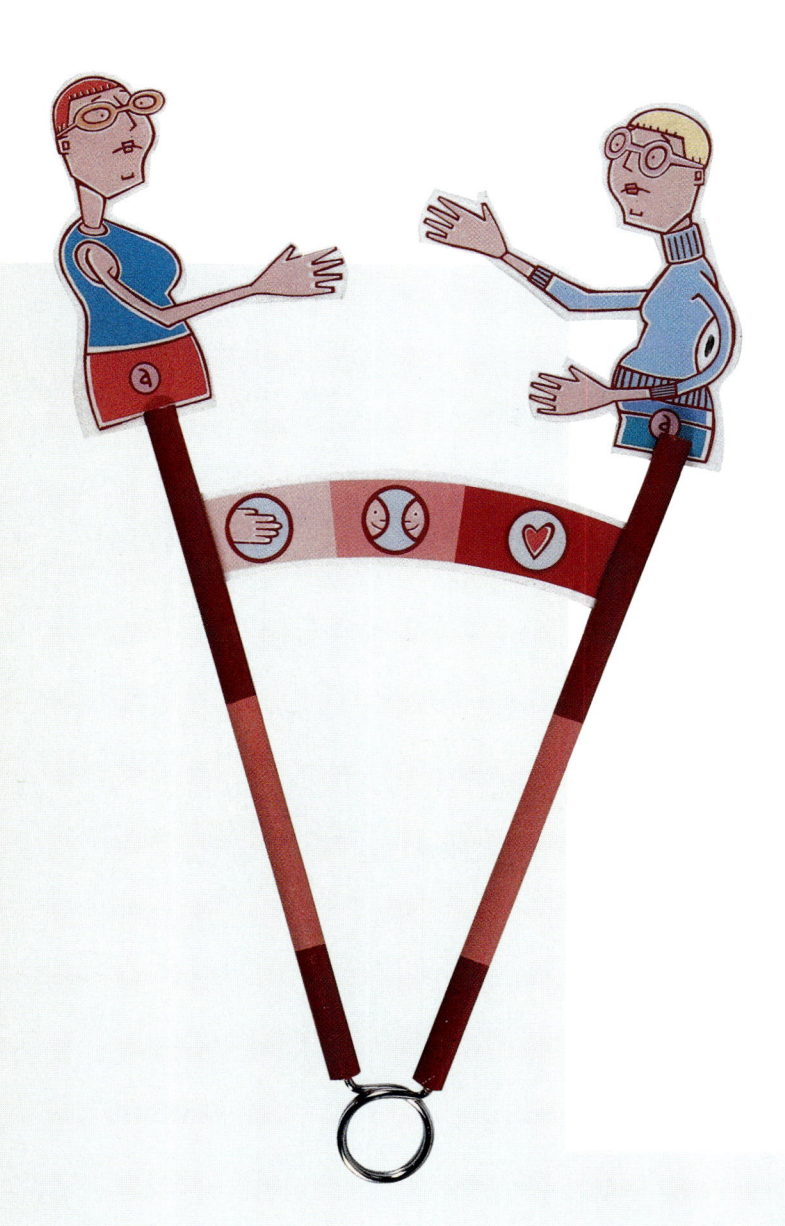

② ✦ By choosing a situation between the figures on the scale, every greeting and parting ritual may be learned. The figures may be replaced at will.
✦ Anhand der Skala zwischen den Stäben kann die jeweilige Begrüßungs- und Abschiedssituation einstudiert werden. Die Figurenpaare können – je nach Anlass – ausgetauscht werden.

③ → 12 different tablecloths make it easier for the user to learn the etiquette for various eating-situations.
→ 12 verschiedene Tischsets helfen dem Benutzer, die richtigen Verhaltensweisen für unterschiedliche Essenssituationen zu erlernen.

The Everyday without Effort – a Modern Domestic Ritual Primer
Alltag ohne Mühe – ein moderner Ritualheimtrainer *Title* **5** *Study Year*
HfK Bremen *College* **Germany** *Country* **Wolfgang Jarchow** *Professor*

❹ ▸ By using these two manuals one can practice »dressing rituals« with a young woman or man. The »Modern Domestic Ritual Primer« also contains ritual textile labels, which can be sewn into the clothing to make it easier to use in everyday life.
▸ Mithilfe zweier Handbücher können wahlweise an einer jungen Dame oder an einem jungen Herrn Bekleidungsrituale eingeübt werden. Außerdem enthält der moderne Ritualheimtrainer Textilkennzeichen, die in die persönliche Kleidung eingenäht werden können und so die tägliche Benutzung von Kleidung erleichtern.

➤ Cover / Titel

★ »›The Everyday without Effort‹ is a domestic ritual primer for beginners and promises quick results – without effort. When you are confident in the rituals, you will experience a sense of place and protection, you will have a sense of belonging and, above all, your quality of life will improve. Your life will have structure and you'll be able to keep a straight line. Knowing the rituals gives you security within the cosmic whole. The primer contains exercises for the six essential moments in everyday life: falling asleep/waking up (image ① ✳), doing the wash, getting dressed (image ❹ ▸), eating (image ③ ➝), greeting and parting (image ② ✢), giving comfort and experiencing pleasure.« ❦ »Der ›Alltag ohne Mühe‹ ist ein moderner Ritualheimtrainer für Anfänger und bietet schnelle Erfolge – ohne Mühe. Wenn Sie die Alltagsrituale beherrschen, erlangen Sie persönliche Orientierung, Schutz, Zugehörigkeit und vor allen Dingen steigern Sie Ihre Lebensqualität. Sie geben Ihrem Tagesablauf Struktur und wirken Haltlosigkeit sinnvoll entgegen. Das beherrschen der Alltagsrituale gibt Ihnen Geborgenheit im kosmischen Ganzen. Der Ritualheimtrainer enthält Lernmittel für die sechs wesentlichen Bereiche des Alltags: Einschlafen/Aufwachen (Abbildung ① ✳), Waschen, Bekleiden (Abbildung ❹ ▸), Essen (Abbildung ③ ➝), Begrüßen/Verabschieden (Abbildung ② ✢) sowie sich trösten und sich freuen.«

Self-Help – Communication | Selbsthilfe – Kommunikation Title
✱ **Book** Medium ✱ **8** Study Year ✱ **FH Hamburg** College † **Germany** Country
✱ **Prof. Kroye, Welfhard Kraiker** Professors

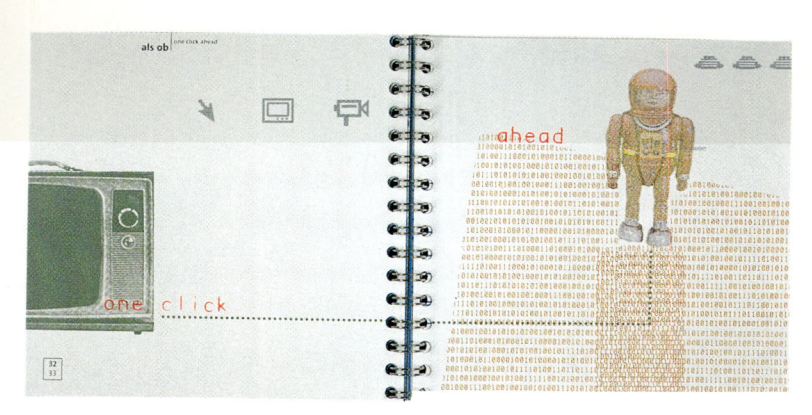

Jan Kruse Student **75**

⟩ This »self-help« manual familiarizes you with communication in its most beautiful form: miscommunication. ⑨ Das Hilf-Dir-Selbst-Handbuch beschäftigt sich mit Kommunikation in ihrer schönsten Form: Der Kommunikationsstörung.

» Places with a highly communicative character are: public toilets, laundrettes and car parks. The rule is as follows: the more unpleasant and dark a place is, the greater your chance is to meet someone you will really like. «

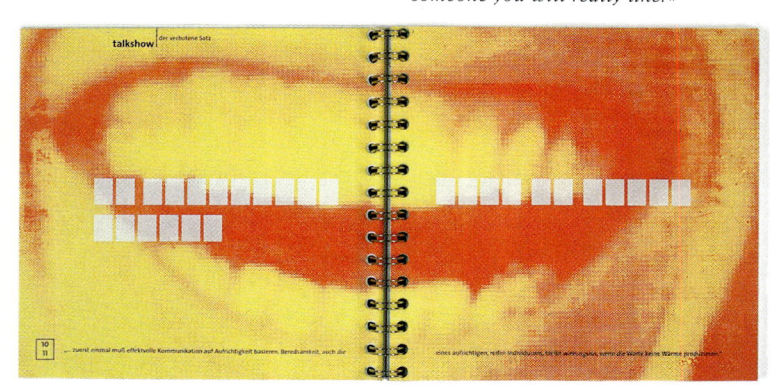

»Plätze mit hohem kommunikativem Charakter sind z.B. öffentliche Toiletten, Waschsalons und Parkhäuser. Es gilt die Faustregel: Je dunkler und unwirtlicher, desto größer die Aussicht auf Erfolg jemanden kennenzulernen der einem wirklich am Herzen liegen wird.«

⌄ Please, don't move. The smallest body movement speaks volumes and brings your true face into the light.
☱ Bitte nicht bewegen. Jede kleinste Bewegung ihres Körpers spricht Bände und würde ihr wahres Gesicht an den Tag bringen.

Claudia Atencia Student

76

Cities | Städte Title ✦ Book Medium ✦ 1 Study Year
School of Visual Arts, New York College USA Country
Warren Lehrer Professor

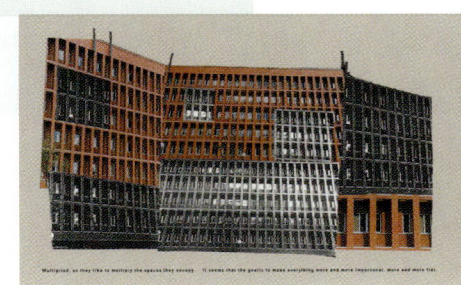

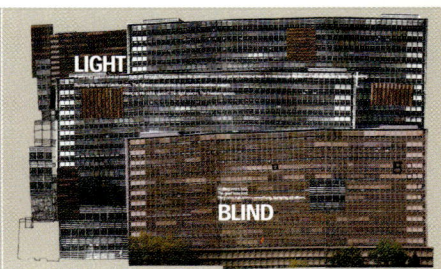

➤➤ The book »Cities« is divided into two chapters. The first, »The City as Author,« contains black and white imagery (mostly photographic) of what can be interpreted as »City Drawings.« The second, »City as a Subject,« is a colourful chapter in which the city is shown in watercolours and busy photo-montages. All pages are printed on normal paper, but one is made from sandpaper to represent asphalt. Last of all, the cover is soft plastic to resemble the colour and texture of city streets.

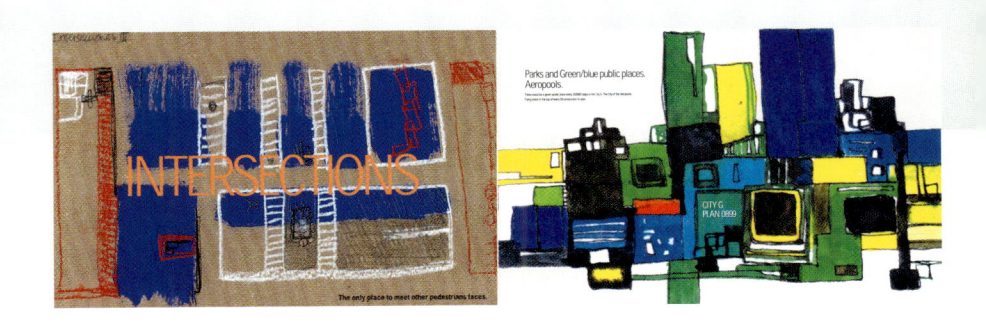

➤➤ Das Buch »Cities« ist in zwei Kapitel unterteilt. Das Erste »The City as Author« enthält Schwarzweißabbildungen (meist Fotos), die man als »Städtezeichnungen« bezeichnen könnte. Das zweite Kapitel »City as a Subject« ist dagegen sehr farbenfroh und zeigt die Stadt in Wasserfarben und geschäftigen Montagen. Alle Seiten sind auf Papier gedruckt, bis auf eine, die auf Sandpapier gedruckt wurde, um den Asphalt der Straße nachzuempfinden. Auch das Cover aus weichem Plastik erinnert in seiner Farbe und Textur an Asphalt.

Question – Answer | Frage – Antwort Title • Poster Medium * American University of Beirut College 🍂 Lebanon Country ☐ Leila Musfy Professor

Tarek Atrissi Student **77**

♥ Leila Musfy Contributing Editor

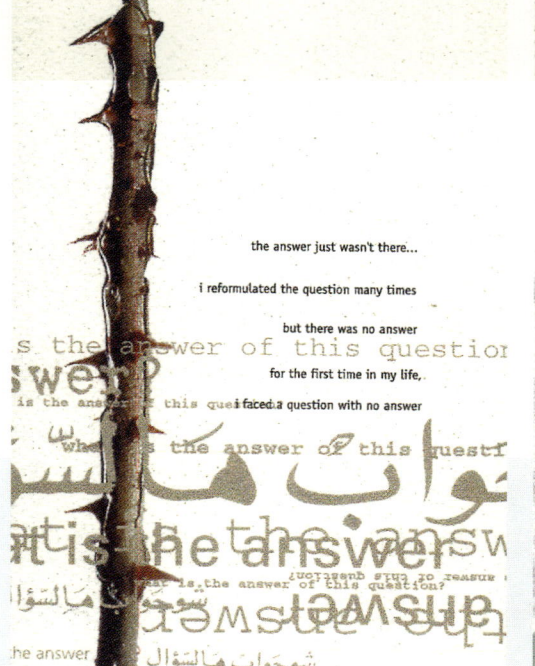

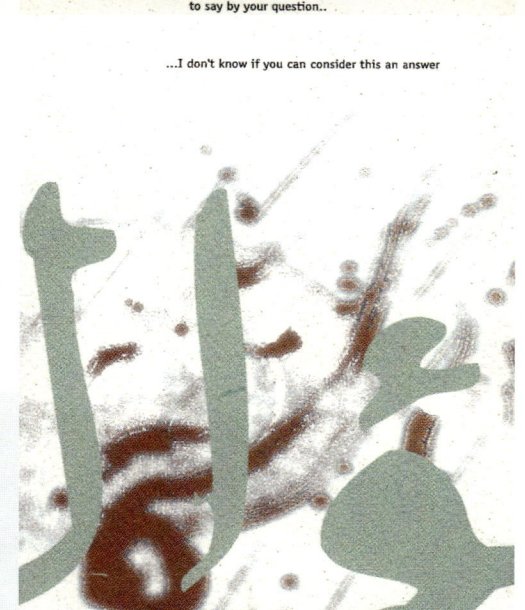

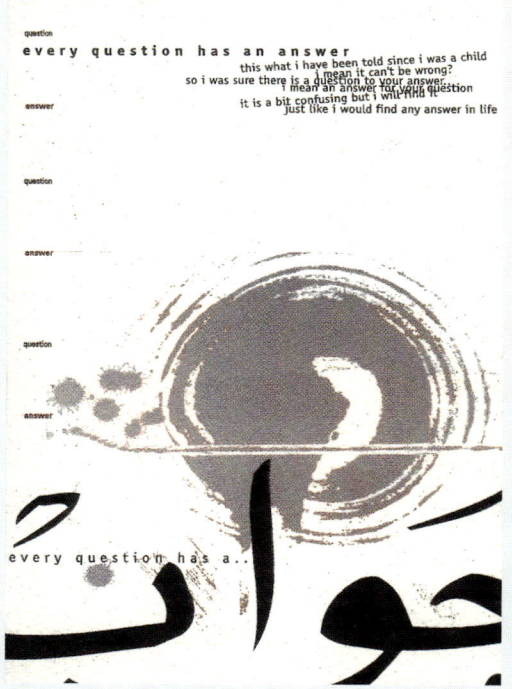

↥ »Question – Answer« uses two opposite terms and expresses them through a typographic experiment. It addresses the unanswered questions in life.
↥ »Frage – Antwort« benutzt zwei gegenpolige Begriffe und drückt sie durch ein typografisches Experiment aus. Es richtet sich an alle unbeantworteten Fragen im Leben.

Kutlay Sindirgi Student **78**

♥ Sadik Karamustafa Contributing Editor

Açik Title ✳ Campaign for a radio station | Kampagne für einen Radiosender Project ♥ 3 Study Year ✳ Mimar Sinan Üniversitesi, Istanbul College 🏛 Turkey Country ⚱ Esen Karol Professor

»Açik« means »Open«. This project is a promotional series for »Açik Radyo,« a progressive radio station in Turkey. The philosophy of the station is to be open to all the colours and sounds of the universe. 👽 »Açik« bedeutet »offen«. Die Arbeit ist eine Anzeigenserie für »Açik Radyo«, einen progressiven Radiosender in der Türkei. Die Philosophie des Senders ist es, offen für alle Farben und Klänge des Universums zu sein.

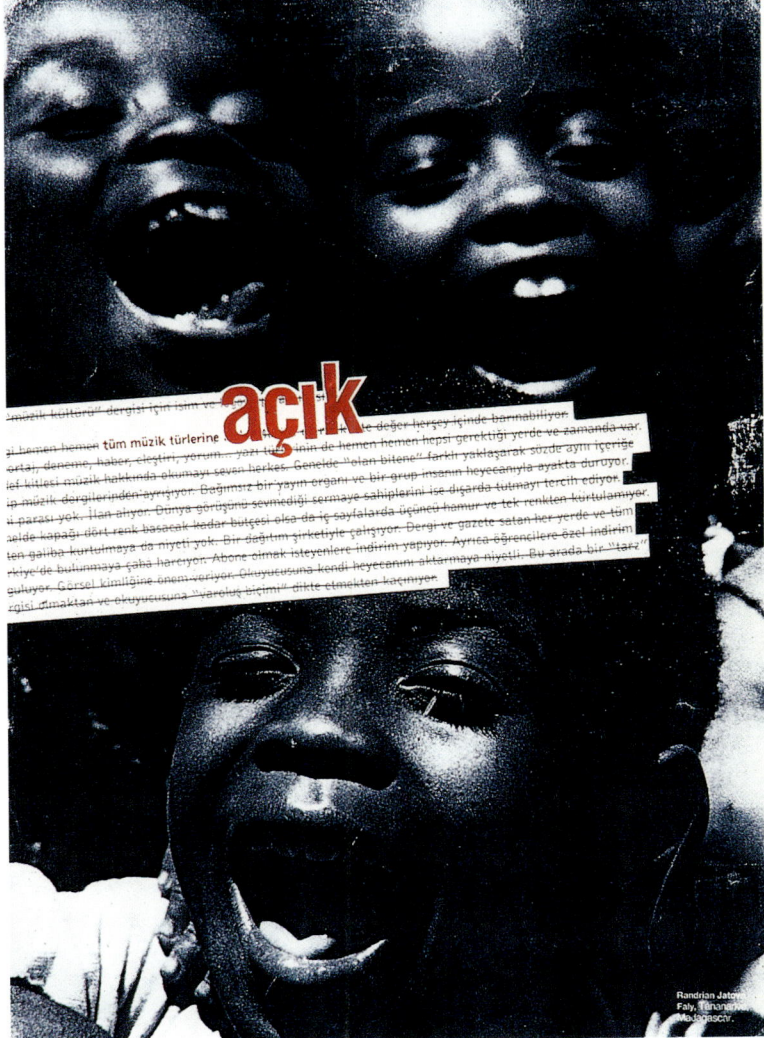

Nadine Chahine Student

Arabic Type Design and the Arabesque Title ⇒ 4 Study Year
American University of Beirut College ⇒ Lebanon Country → Leila Musfy Professor

→ This project is based on the 6 letters in the Arabic word »abjadiah,« meaning »alphabet.« Arabesque compositions were formed using these letters that were then applied to a set of coasters and a tray. ▫ Dieses Projekt basiert auf den 6 Buchstaben des arabischen Wortes für Alphabet: »abjadiah«. Aus den Buchstaben wurden arabeske Kompositionen geformt, mit denen anschließend ein Set Untersetzer und ein Tablett gestaltet wurden.

Mozart Title ‖ CD Cover Medium ✢ 4 Study Year ✦ Shanghai Light Industry College College ▲ China Country 🚌 Hormann, Peter Krüll Professors

80

Liu Bin, Fang Yi Students

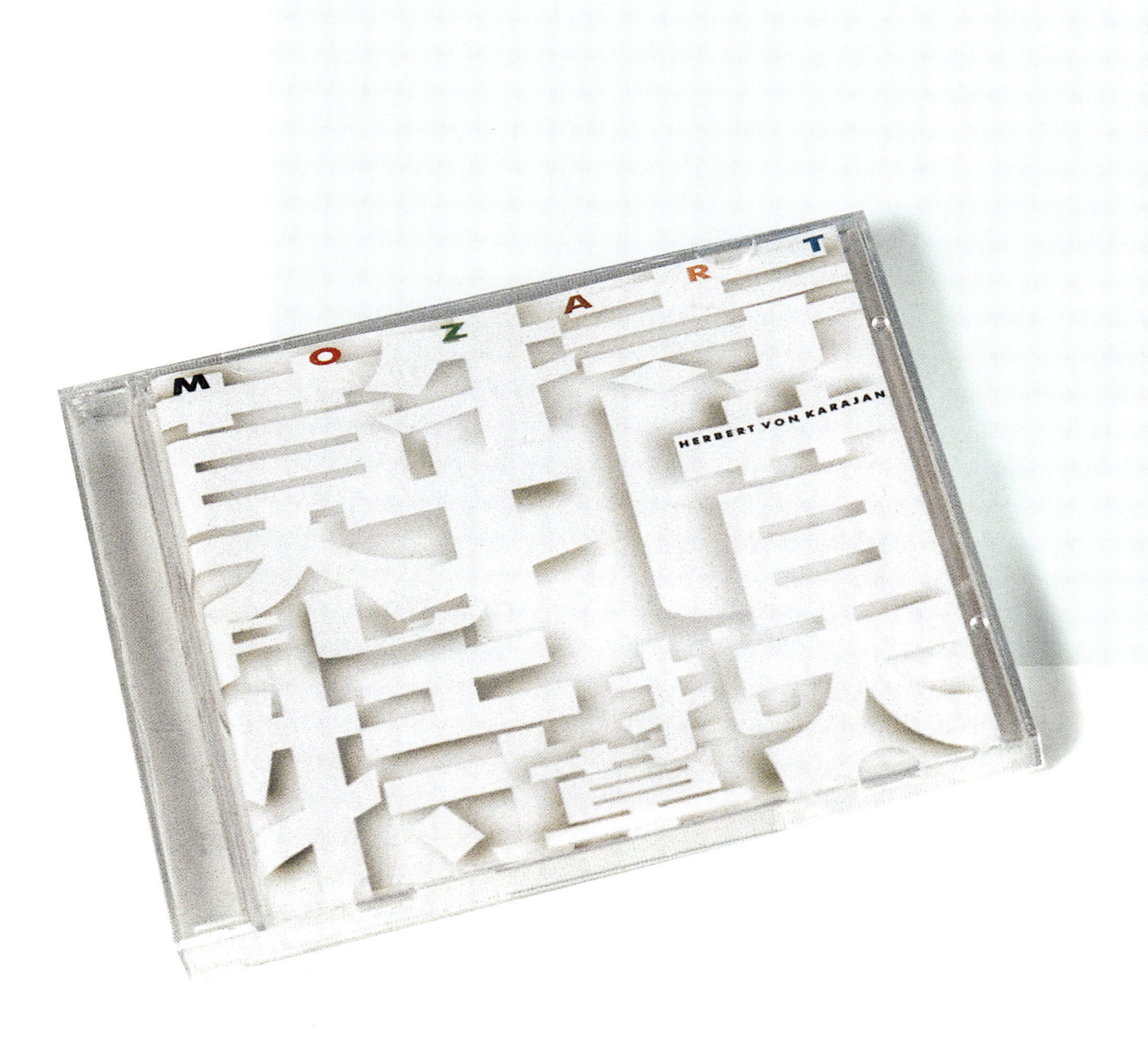

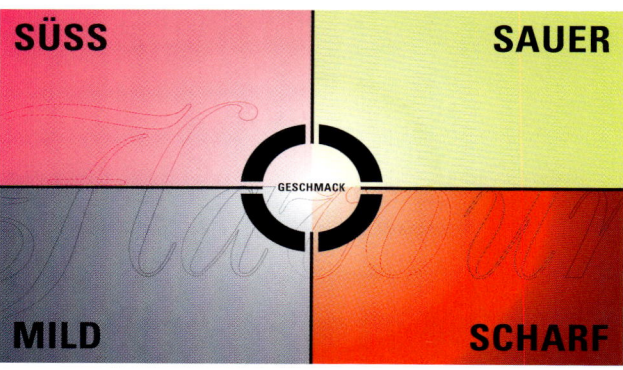

Cooking Without Recipes | Kochen ohne Rezepte Title ✓ Cookbook | Kochbuch Medium ✳
5 Study Year 💬 HfK Bremen College † Germany Country 🗾 Eckhard Jung Professor

✳ The »Taste-Axis« charts the food's taste in four quadrants (sweet, sour, mild and hot).
▲ Das Geschmacksachsenkreuz zeigt in vier Quadranten (süss, sauer, mild und scharf) an, welche geschmackliche Tendenz eine Speise hat.

⑥ All good and well-designed cookbooks describe how to make tarts and parfaits. But how to vary and combine their individual tastes is included in this one. »Cooking Without Recipes« is a book to inspire advanced cooks and encourages them to cook creatively (supposing their already thorough knowledge of cooking). Therefore, a large range of food and taste combinations are presented based on basic methods, e.g. frying, streaming, scalding, etc. The ten chapters deal with various subjects such as meat, fish, vegetables, etc., and contain several photos and a page of text.

Ellen Jacoby Student
81

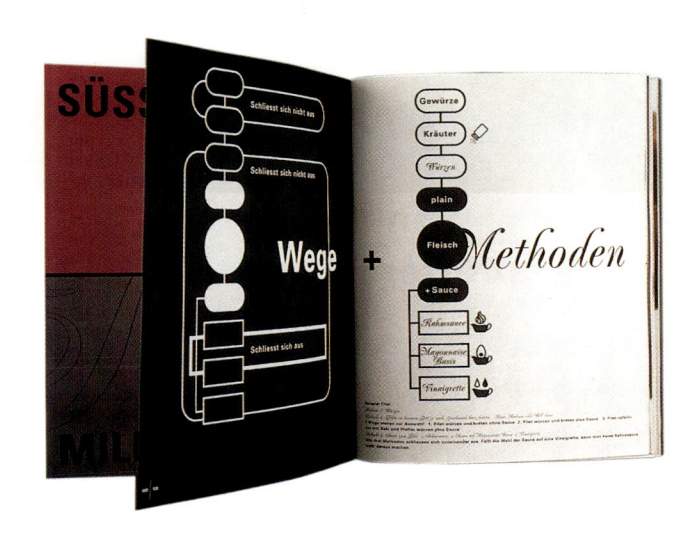

✱ The text page shows alternative combinations of food tastes.
❏ Die Textseiten zeigen alternative Geschmackskombinationen einer Speise.

✱ Wie man Tartes und Parfaits macht, steht in all den guten und schönen Kochbüchern. Wie man diese Methoden geschmacklich variiert und kombiniert, steht in diesem. ✈ Kochen ohne Rezepte ist ein Buch, das den fortgeschrittenen Koch (Kenntniss der Grundmethoden und Prozesse vorausgesetzt) inspirieren und ihn zum kreativen Kochen anregen soll. Hierzu werden mögliche Variationen von Speisen und unterschiedlichste Geschmackskombinationen dargestellt, die auf den bekannten Grundmethoden wie z.B. Braten, Dünsten, Blanchieren, etc. basieren. ✱ Die 10 Kapitel behandeln unterschiedliche Bereiche wie z.B. Fleisch, Fisch, Gemüse usw. und bestehen jeweils aus mehreren Bildseiten und einer Textseite.

⊛ The photos give a visual impression of a taste combination and tell where its description can be found.
➤ Die Bildseiten geben einen visuellen Eindruck einer bestimmten Geschmackskombination und zusätzlich werden Angaben gemacht, wo die schriftliche Beschreibung der Geschmackskombination auf der Textseite zu finden ist.

Slam Poetry *Title* • Newspaper | Zeitung *Medium* • Höhere Schule für Gestaltung, Basel *College* • Switzerland *Country* • Leander Eisenmann *Professor*

Ludovic Balland *Student* **82**

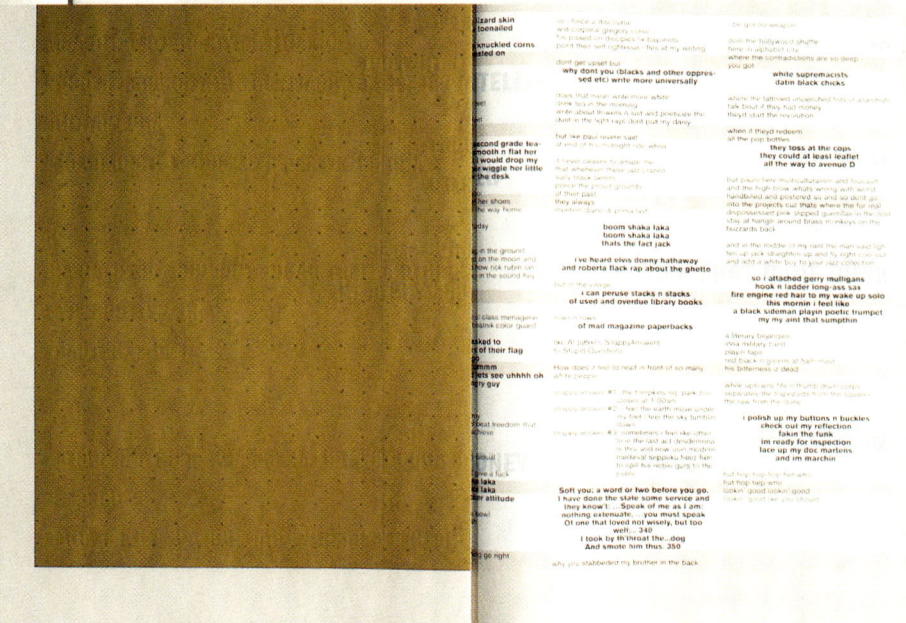

»Slam Poetry is contemporary poetry with strong connections to '60s beat poetry taking place live in open spaces, in bars or cafés: direct, immediate and engaging. The idea is to make overlapping words and sounds readable, translating them onto paper without taking away their energy. By overprinting the previous edition, the pages become increasingly loud and heavy. Sentences and words mix, fall back and fill in the spaces.« »Slam Poetry ist zeitgenössische Lyrik mit engem Bezug zur Beat-Poesie der 60er Jahre, die sich live abspielt, meist in öffentlichen Räumen wie Bars oder Cafés: direkt, unmittelbar, engagiert. Die Idee meiner Arbeit ist es, diese Überlagerung von Tönen und Wörtern sicht- und lesbar zu machen, sie ins starre Printmedium zu übertragen, ohne ihnen ihre Lebendigkeit zu nehmen. Durch einen fortlaufenden Überdruck der alten Ausgabe werden die Seiten immer dichter und immer lauter. Sätze und Wörter vermischen sich, gehen nach hinten und füllen den Raum.«

Identity for the HfG Karlsruhe | Erscheinungsbild für die HfG Karlsruhe Title
4 Study Year Hochschule für Gestaltung Karlsruhe College Germany Country
Gunter Rambow Professor

83

Jan Haux, Adrian Krell, Matthias Megyeri Students

This identity system has three levels (or areas) that overlap in such a way that, by moving them over and alongside each other, various formal compositions are produced. They make it possible to react to a constantly changing range of tasks in different types of media. The overlapping and interfolding fields represent the interdisciplinary way of working at the art college. Die Idee des Erscheinungsbildes sind drei sich überlagernde Flächen oder Ebenen, die in ständiger Bewegung zueinander unablässig neue formale Konstellationen ergeben. Sie ermöglichen es, in verschiedenen Medien auf immer neue Anforderungen zu reagieren. Die Überlagerung und Durchdringung beschreibt das interdisziplinäre Arbeiten an der HfG.

Sarah Schroeder, Ilona Grunau, Maike Hoffmann **Students** **84**

insideout **Title** Catalogue **Medium** 2 **Study Year**
FH Düsseldorf **College** Germany **Country** Roland Henß **Professor**

Each year an exhibition entitled »new« takes place at the College of Düsseldorf. There, design coursework is presented and made accessible to a broader audience. The »insideout« catalogue arose from this event.

Einmal im Jahr findet an der FH Düsseldorf die Ausstellung »neu« statt. Dort werden die im Fachbereich Design entstandenen Arbeiten präsentiert und einem breiten Publikum zugänglich gemacht. Zu diesem Anlass ist erstmalig der Ausstellungskatalog »insideout« entstanden.

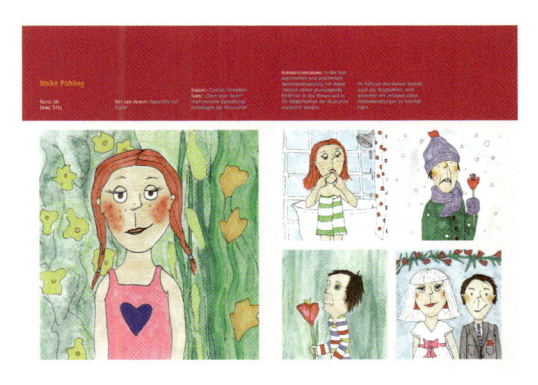

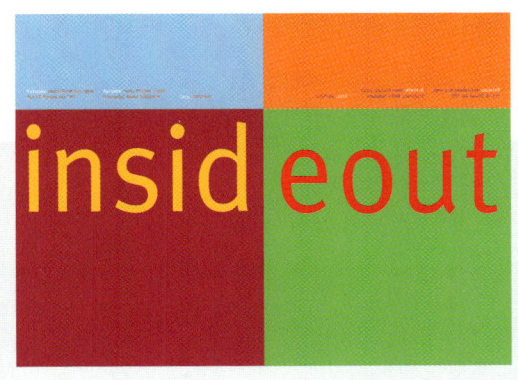

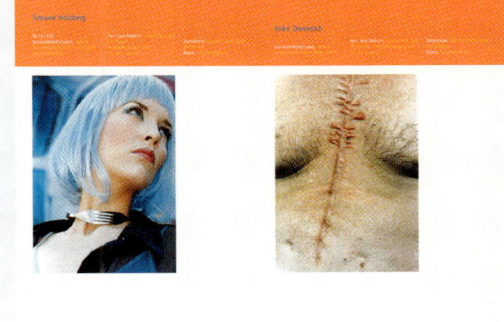

About Habits | Über Gewohnheiten Title ◆ **Lecture** | Vortrag Medium ✱
5 Study Year ⊞ **HfK Bremen** College ✲ **Germany** Country ▭ **Eckhard Jung** Professor

Friederike Lambers Student

85

☛ »About Habits« is a lecture about everyday life; its actions, rituals, conventions, customs and boundaries. Sixty-eight image and text panels complement the lecture, hung up one after another over the course of the event, building an installation of text and image. ✧ »Über Gewohnheiten« ist ein Vortrag über den Alltag, täglich ausgeführte Handlungen, Rituale, Konventionen, Sitten und Grenzüberschreitungen. Zur besseren Verständlichkeit wird der Vortrag durch 68 Bild- und Texttafeln ergänzt, die während der Veranstaltung nach und nach aufgehängt und zu einer Bild-Text-Installation ergänzt werden.

① Monday – a normal day: Everyone needs habits to bring stability to their everyday lives. Three people document their morning rituals with images.
❶ Montag – ein ganz normaler Tag: Jeder Mensch braucht Gewohnheiten, um Stabilität in seinen Alltag zu bringen. Drei Menschen beschreiben in Bildern ihre morgentlichen Rituale. ② Hello – Greetings are ritualised differently in different cultures. Here Donald Duck meets Scrooge; Honecker meets Breschnev.
❷ Guten Tag – Begrüßungen werden in unterschiedlichen Kulturen auf verschiedene Weise ritualisiert. Hier: Donald trifft Dagobert, Honecker trifft Breschnew.

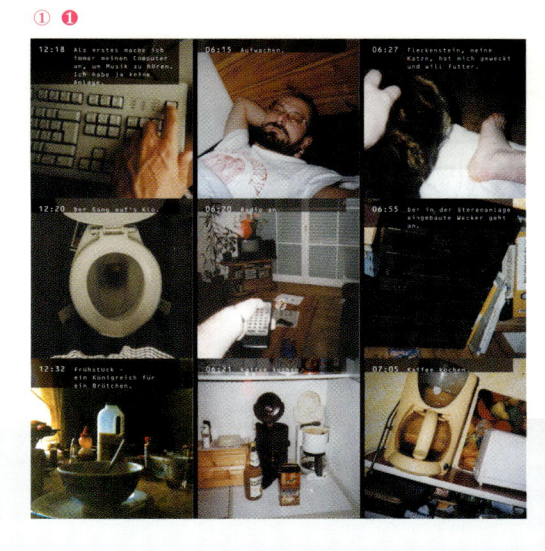

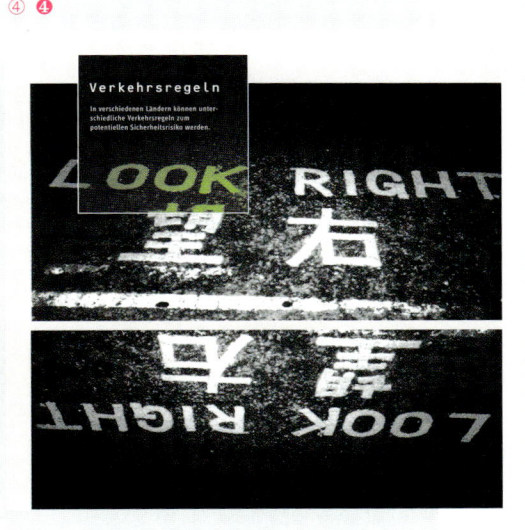

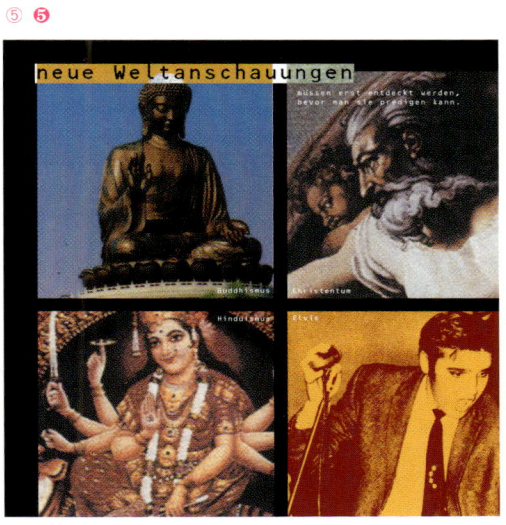

③ A special day – Society has created many rituals, such as the family feast. These events symbolize the transition from one part of life to another. Here, the first day of school. Ein besonderer Tag – es gibt zahlreiche Rituale, die von der Gesellschaft erschaffen worden sind, z.B. Familienfeiern. Diese Feste symbolisieren den Übergang zwischen zwei Lebensabschnitten. Hier: Erster Schultag. ④ Discovering habits – habits are automatic. That is why one is not aware of them. One only notices them when something has changed or one is brought off-course: different traffic laws could become potential safety risks. ❹ Gewohnheiten entdecken – Gewohnheiten sind automatisiert. Deshalb werden sie nicht mehr bewusst wahrgenommen. Meist werden sie erst entdeckt, wenn sich etwas verändert hat oder man in seinem Tagesablauf gestört wird: unterschiedliche Verkehrsregeln können zum potentiellen Sicherheitsrisiko werden. ⑤ Only he who knows his boundaries, knows what lies beyond them: in many spheres people have questioned the norm, investigated new methods and discovered new things. Innovation and creativity are a result of overcoming habits. Here, e.g.: religion. ❺ Nur wer seine Grenzen kennt, kennt auch das Land dahinter: in unterschiedlichen Bereichen haben Menschen das Normale hinterfragt, andere Wege ausprobiert und Neues entdeckt. Innovation und Kreativität entstehen aus der Überwindung der Gewohnheit. Hier als Beispiel: Religionen.

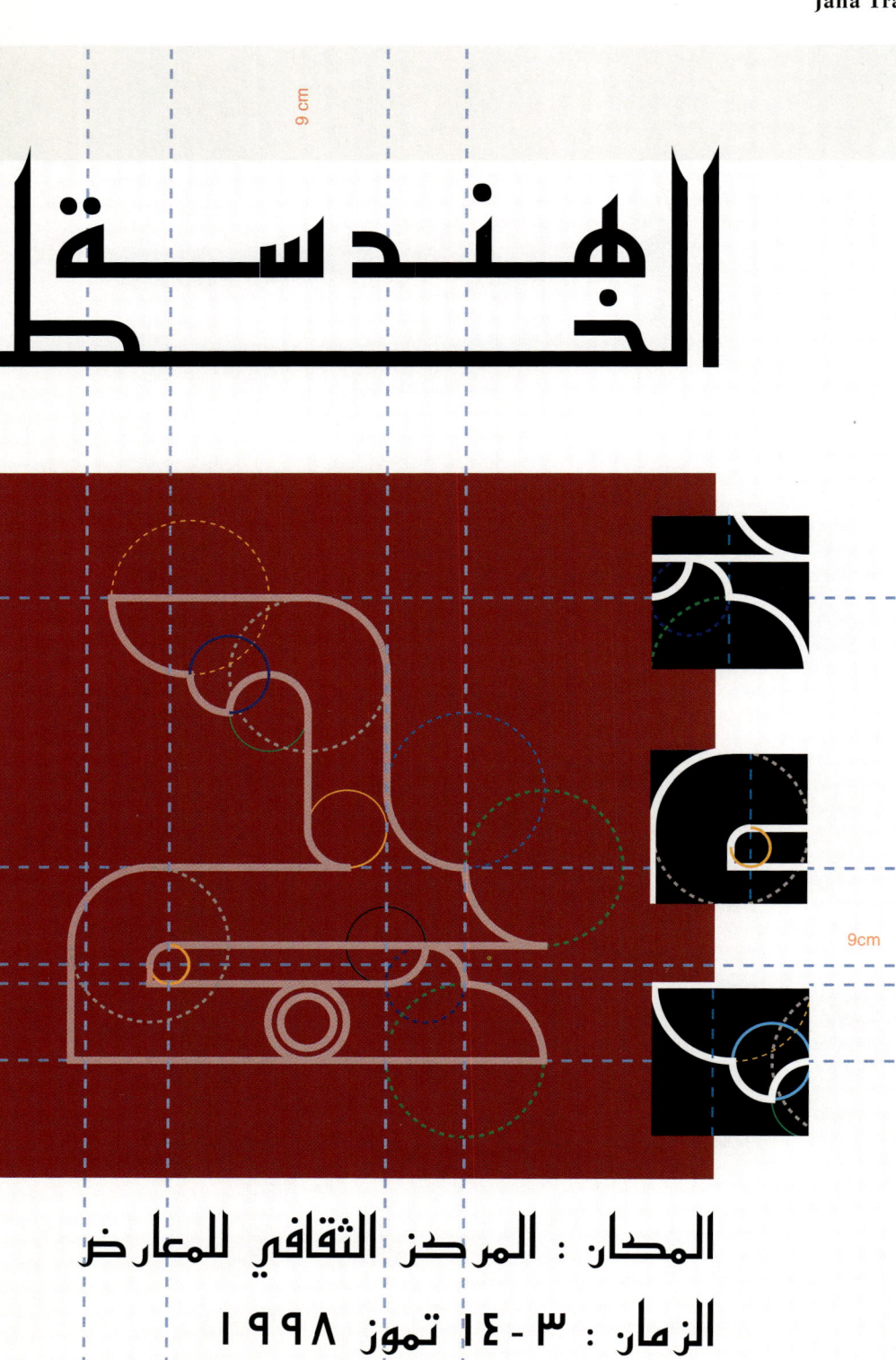

Typographic Exhibition | Typografische Ausstellung Title * Poster Medium
4 Study Year * American University of Beirut College * Lebanon Country * Leila Musfy Professor

Jana Traboulsi Student

86

الهندسة الخط

المكان : المركز الثقافي للمعارض
الزمان : ٣-١٤ تموز ١٩٩٨

Candice S. Davidian Student 87

National Mail Title ▲ Logotype for Lebanese Post | Zeichen für die Libanesische Post Project
✳ 4 Study Year ✳ Notre Dame University College ✳ Lebanon Country | John Kortbawi Professor

For this logo that takes on the form of a stamp, the colour red was chosen to attract attention and to suggest speed and energy. The Arabic type was developed from the Latin typeface »Bodoni« in order to come to a middleground where East meets West. ✚ Für das Zeichen, das die Form einer Briefmarke hat, wurde die Farbe Rot gewählt, um Aufmerksamkeit zu erregen und die Assoziation mit Geschwindigkeit und Energie hervorzurufen. Der arabische Schriftzug wurde aus der lateinischen Schrift »Bodoni« entwickelt, um dort Konsistenz herzustellen, wo Ost auf West trifft.

The Future of Solidarity | Die Zukunft der Solidarität Title * Poster Medium *
4 Study Year * FH Dortmund College † Germany Country * Fons Matthias Hickmann Professor

Christiane Möller Student **88**

— On the 50th anniversary of the German Trade Unions Federation, a poster contest was held for German art schools with the theme »The Future of Solidarity.« The idea behind the poster design was to let employees make their own statement about solidarity. For that reason the posters were pinned on blackboards with a request that they be filled out in factories and companies. ↠ Anlässlich seines 50-jährigen Bestehens hat der Deutsche Gewerkschaftsbund einen Plakatwettbewerb mit dem Thema »Die Zukunft der Solidarität« an deutschen Design-Hochschulen ausgeschrieben. Die Idee für die Plakatgestaltung ist es, Arbeitnehmern die Möglichkeit zu geben, selber Aussagen zur Solidarität zu treffen. Zu diesem Zweck wurden die Plakate an den schwarzen Brettern von Fabriken und Unternehmen aufgehängt mit der Aufforderung, sie zu ergänzen.

The Future of Solidarity is ... in danger ... and ... so endangers our future ... but also ... challenges us!

♥ Leila Musfy Contributing Editor

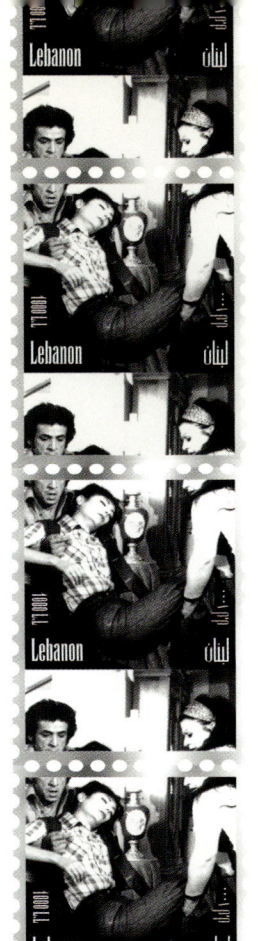

Ali Cherry Student

Black-and-white TV | Schwarzweißfernsehen Title ▲ Stamps | Briefmarken Medium ✱
American University of Beirut College † Lebanon Country ✦ Leila Musfy Professor

▲ This series of postage stamps is an homage to the black-and-white TV series that have been showing in Lebanese TV for the past 30 years. The project was made in connection with the theme »Beirut – Cultural Capital of the Arab World, 1999.« ▢ Diese Briefmarkenserie ist eine Hommage an Schwarzweißfernsehserien, die seit mehr als 30 Jahren im libanesischen Fernsehen gesendet werden. Das Projekt wurde im Zusammenhang mit dem Thema »Beirut – Kulturhauptstadt der Arabischen Welt, 1999« entwickelt.

Anne Breucha Student 90

Rooms of Power | Machträume Title ❋ Book Medium ❋
Merz Akademie Stuttgart College ✝ Germany Country ❋
Gabriele Götz, Diedrich Diedrichsen Professors

»Rooms of Power« is a book about the theories of Gilles Deleuze and Félix Guattari, published in their books »Anti-Oedipus« and »A Thousand Plateaus« in 1972 and 1980. The central figure in these texts is the idea of the Nomad, which is presently experiencing a renaissance in the context of globalization and virtual reality. The book »Rooms of Power« reflects this period of globalization, and shows how limited our movements are and how much we limit ourselves. Die Arbeit »Machträume« beschäftigt sich mit den Theorien von Gilles Deleuze und Félix Guattari, die in den ihren Büchern »Anti-Ödipus« und »Tausend Plateaus« 1972 bzw. 1980 veröffentlicht wurden. In diesen Texten spielt der Begriff des Nomaden eine zentrale Rolle, der heute im Zusammenhang mit der Globalisierung und virtuellen Realitäten eine Renaissance erlebt. In dem Buch »Machträume« soll das Zeitalter der Globalisierung reflektiert werden. Es soll bewusst gemacht werden, wie eingeschränkt und einschränkend wir uns bewegen.

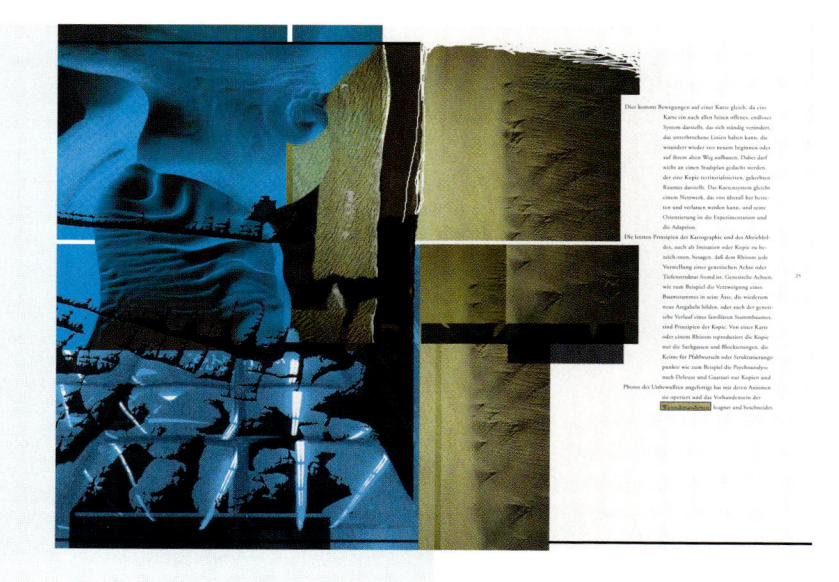

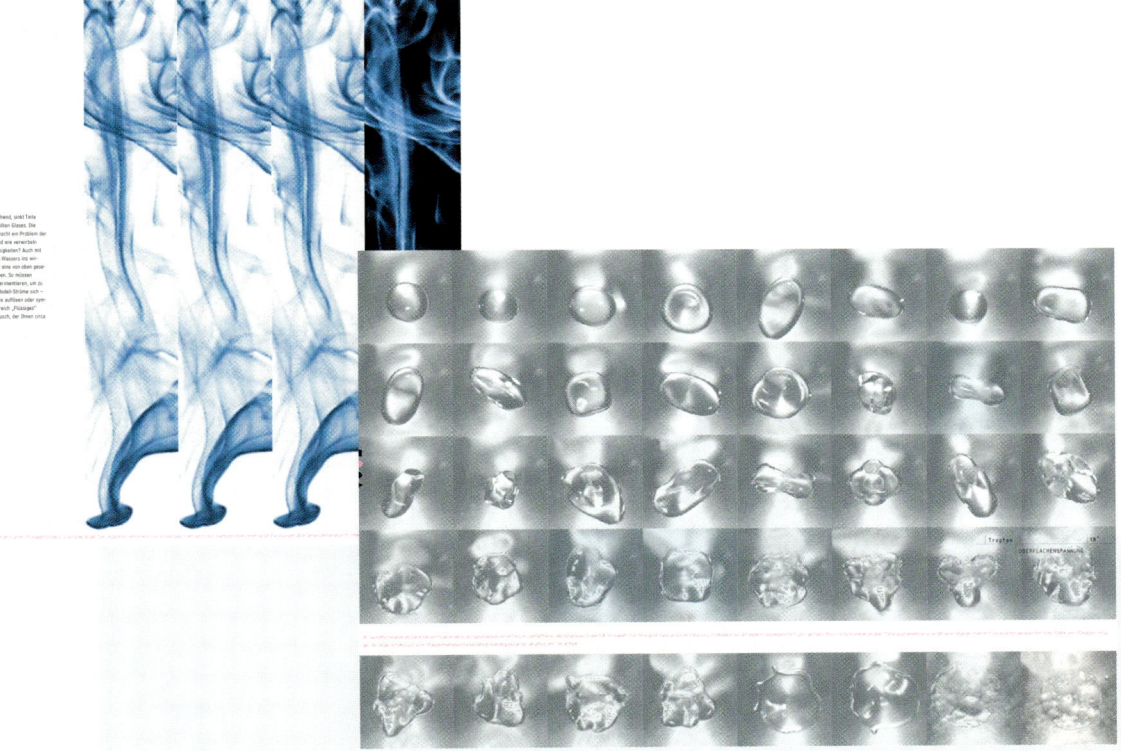

Light-blue – Water Fascination | Lichtblau – Faszination Wasser Title
Book Medium   5 Study Year   FH Würzburg College   Germany Country
Uli Braun Professor

Doreen Ambrosius Student   **91**

The book about water is divided into four parts: »elementary,« »solid,« »fluid« and »gaseous.« It begins at -273°C and ends at +374°C, water's critical point. The Celsius scale is set on the right margin, acting as pagination. The themes are as follows: the basics of molecules (-97°C), artificial snowcrystals (-22°C/-6°C) and steam (+100°C). The endpaper and chapter quotations were taken from the »Water Hymn« in James Joyce's »Ulysses.«

Das Buch zum Thema Wasser ist in vier Teile gegliedert: »elementar«, »fest«, »flüssig« und »gasförmig«. Es beginnt bei -273°C und endet bei +374°C, dem kritischen Punkt. Als Paginierung dient eine Celsiusskala, die sich am rechten Seitenrand befindet. Die Themen reichen dabei von molekularen Grundlagen (-97°C) über künstliche Schneekristalle (-22°C/-6°C) bis hin zu Wasserdampf (+100°C). Schmutztitel und Unterkapitelzitate sind der Wasserhymne von »Ulysses« von James Joyce entnommen.

Land Surveyor's Office | Büro für Landvermessung Title ✳ Identity | Erscheinungsbild Project
✳ 3 Study Year ▲ FH Darmstadt College ✧ Germany Country ◆ Kai Krippner Professor

Viola Läufer Student **92**

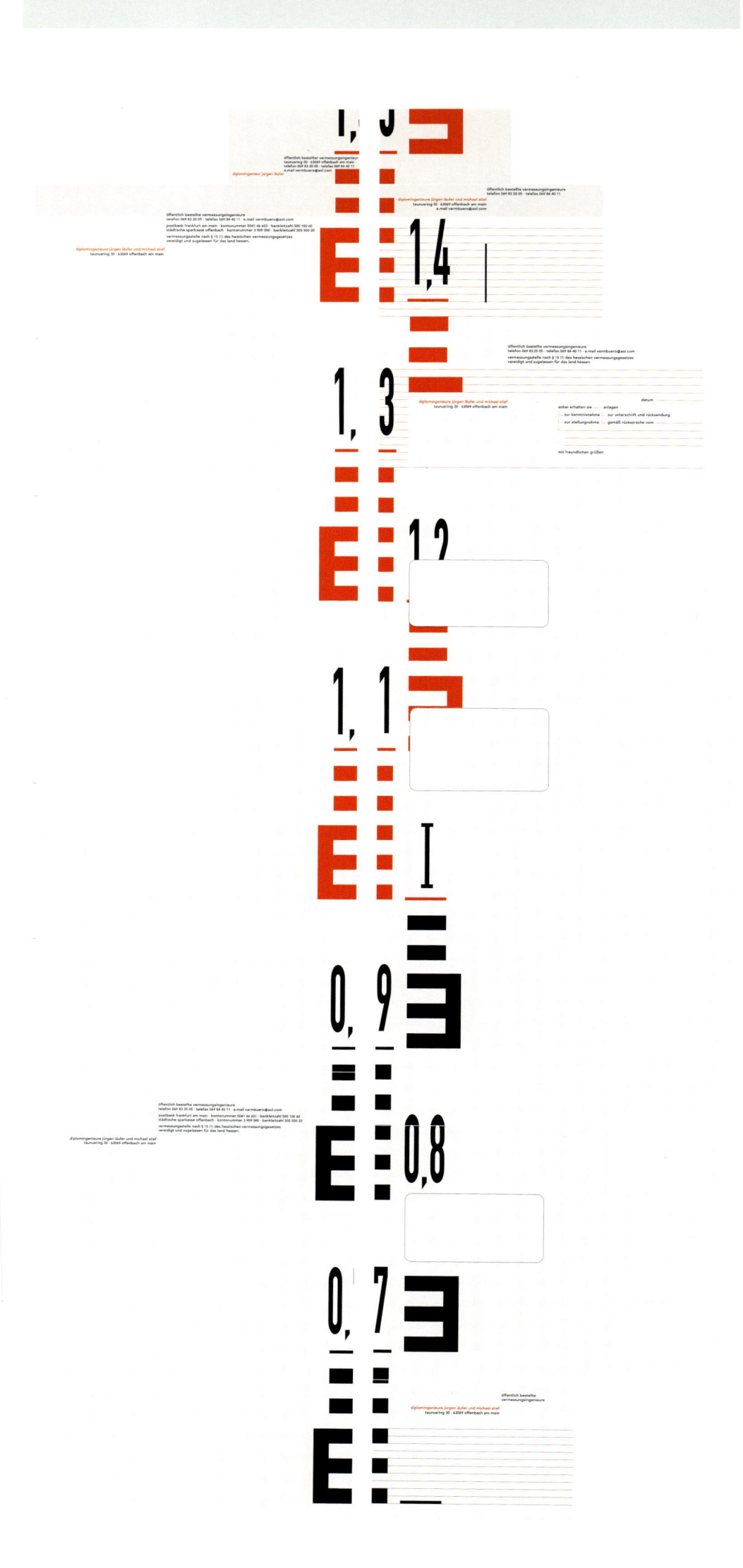

Shau Chung Shin Student

93

Identity system for a Chinese homeopathic doctor | Erscheinungsbild für eine Chinesische Heilpraktikerin Project ❖ 3 Study Year ➪ **FH Darmstadt** College ❖ **Germany** Country ▲ **Kai Krippner** Professor

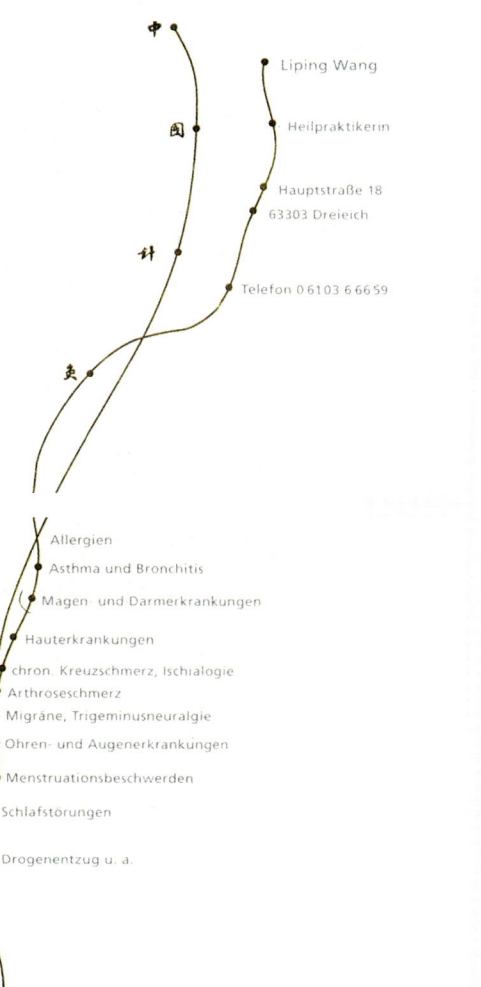

Business Card ...
Visitenkarte ...

中
国
针
灸

Liping Wang
Heilpraktikerin
Hauptstraße 18
63303 Dreieich
Telefon 0 6103 6 66 59

Allergien
Asthma und Bronchitis
Magen- und Darmerkrankungen
Hauterkrankungen
chron. Kreuzschmerz, Ischialgie
Arthroseschmerz
Migräne, Trigeminusneuralgie
Ohren- und Augenerkrankungen
Menstruationsbeschwerden
Schlafstörungen
Drogenentzug u. a.

Bescheinigung

Der/die umseitig genannte Patient/in leidet an

Die bisherige medikamentöse Behandlung führte zu keiner
wesentlichen Beschwerdelinderung.

Eine Akupunkturbehandlung (Nadelakupunktur)
mit voraussichtlich   Sitzungen ist vorgesehen.

Die Kosten pro Sitzung betragen
Der Zeitaufwand pro Sitzung beträgt 60. bis 90 Minuten.
Die Akupunktur wird von mir selbst durchgeführt.

Dreieich,

Liping Wang
Heilpraktikerin

Darm Meridian

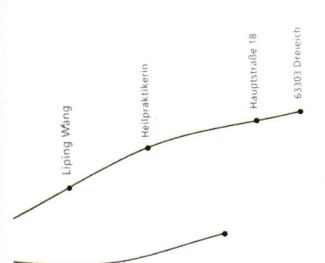

Form ...
Formular ...

Liping Wang
Heilpraktikerin
Hauptstraße 18
63303 Dreieich

Kreisgesundheitsamt Kreis Offenbach
Postfach 11163
63011 Offenbach am Main

Envelope ...
Briefumschlag ...

Ozan Erdogan Student

94

Bastard Title ❖ Typeface and Type Book | Schrift und Schriftmusterbuch Medium ◆
4 Study Year ✷ Mimar Sinan Üniversitesi, Istanbul College ▲ Turkey Country ❄
Esen Karol Professor

✷ This project contains the design process of the font »Bastard« and also a book presenting the font in practical use. ❊ Das Projekt umfasst die Gestaltung der Schrift »Bastard« sowie ein Schriftmusterbuch, in dem die Schrift in illustrativen Anwendungen vorgestellt wird.

Arabic and Latin Text | Arabische und Lateinische Texte Title
2 Study Year • Notre Dame University, Beirut College • Lebanon Country
• John Kortbawi, Yara Khoury Professors

Christine Akmakji Student

∗ These pages are part of a foundation project for typography class: the purpose is to examine the possible combinations of Arabic and Latin text. ∗ Die Seiten sind Teil einer Grundlagenarbeit im Fach Typografie: es sollen Möglichkeiten der Kombination von arabischem und lateinischem Text erforscht werden.

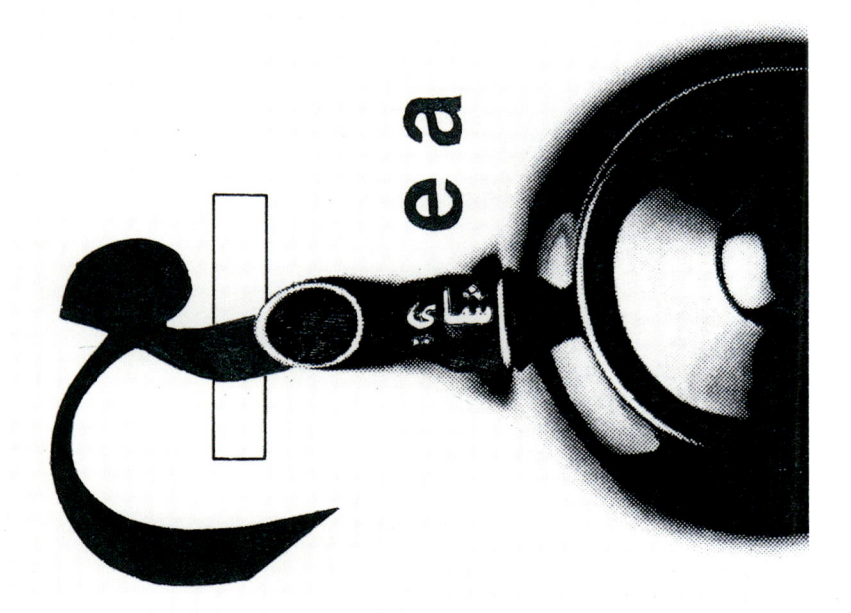

Lena Schalén Student

96

Cavity Prevention | Spatienprophylaxe Title ✢ **Posters** Medium ✢
4 Study Year ❣ **GH Kassel** College ✎ **Germany** Country ☆
Christof Gassner Professor

❋ »Cavity Prevention« is about »spacing,« the topic of the »Forum Typographie« at the Leipzig College of Graphic and Book Arts. The convention participants were invited to tear off a portion of the poster, each containing a piece of dental floss and a toothpick for preventing spatium (cavities). By the tearing off of the portions, the six posters were then »spaced.«

❋ »Spatienprophylaxe« ist der Titel einer Arbeit zum Thema »Spatium« des »Forum Typographie« an der Hochschule für Grafik und Buchkunst Leipzig. Die Teilnehmer des Kongresses waren dazu eingeladen, sich Zahnstocher und Zahnseide zur Vorbeugung von Spatium (Karies) abzutrennen. Durch die Entfernung der Spatienprophylaxen wurden die 6 A1 Plakate »spationiert«.

Cornelia Hofmann Student

97

Grown Type Title ▲ Typeface Design | Schriftgestaltung Project ✛ 4 Study Year
FH Nürnberg College ✱ Germany Country ✱ Peter Krüll Professor

In most cases, letterforms are made from geometric shapes. But what would happen if nature were to design a font? Could someone develop a font that grows during its lifespan and then dies at a certain point? With mould growth, it is possible to initiate a letterform and then let nature's design process take over. The only point of intervention was the selection of the most beautiful moments of growth and photographing them. The fonts »Mould Bold« and »Mould Inside« were created from this material.

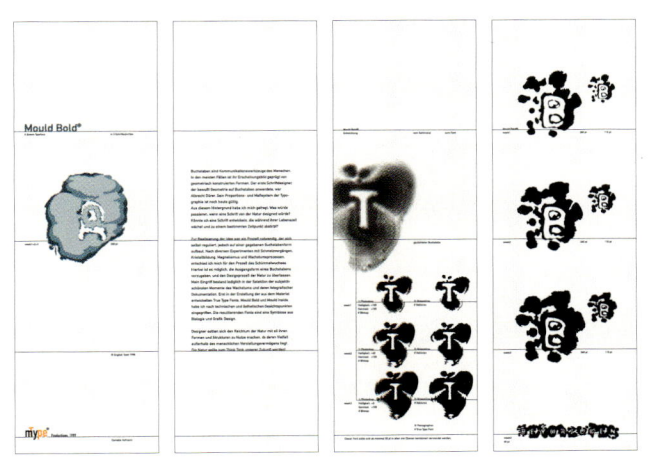

Buchstaben sind in den meisten Fällen geprägt von konstruierten, geometrischen Formen. Aber was wäre, wenn eine Schrift von der Natur gestaltet würde? Könnte man eine Schrift entwickeln, die während ihrer Lebenszeit wächst und zu einem bestimmten Zeitpunkt stirbt? Bei dem Prozess des Schimmelwuchses ist es möglich, die Ausgangsform des Buchstabens vorzugeben und den Designprozess der Natur zu überlassen. Der Eingriff bestand lediglich in der Auswahl der schönsten Momente des Wachstums und deren fotografischer Dokumentation. Aus diesem Material sind die TrueType Schriften »Mould Bold« und »Mould Inside« entstanden.

Bird Perch | Vogelstange Title ✧ Packaging | Verpackung Medium ✲ 2 Study Year
Shih Chien University, Taipei College ▪ Taiwan Country ● Pi-I Chixng Professor

98 Zhi-Zhong Lue Student

Stefan Walz Student

99

World Book | Weltbuch Title ❄ 3 Study Year ❄ Merz Akademie Stuttgart College ▲ Germany Country ▲ Joost Bottema Professor

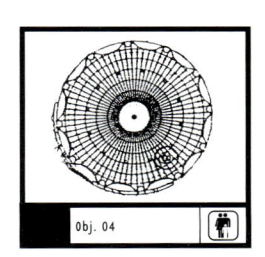

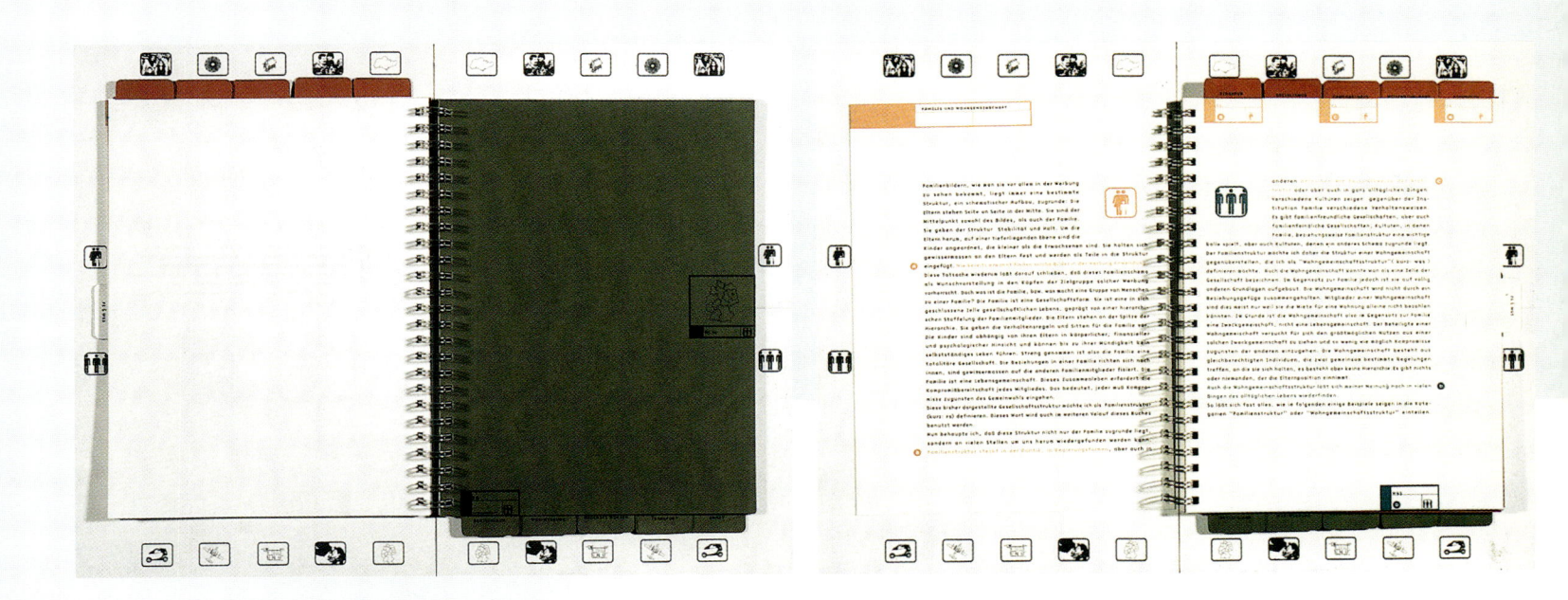

↪ This book is about forms of contact, trends, and structures in our society. It presents two basic forms of living together, the family and flat-sharing communities. The structure is hypertextual. The first two pages introduce the chapters using symbols. These symbols then lead one on different paths on which one can gather information. But of course, you can also read the book from front to back. ↪ Das Buch handelt von Formen des Umgangs, von Strömungen und Strukturen unserer Gesellschaft. Als die zwei Grundformen des Zusammenlebens werden die Familie und die Wohngemeinschaft vorgestellt und anschaulich gemacht. Das Buch selbst hat einen hypertextähnlichen Aufbau. Ausgehend von den ersten zwei Seiten, auf denen die Kategorien anhand von Bildsymbolen vorgestellt werden, kann man unterschiedlichen Informationssträngen und Wahlmöglichkeiten folgen, die mit Beispielen die Kategorien veranschaulichen. Man kann das Buch aber selbstverständlich auch von vorne bis hinten durchlesen.

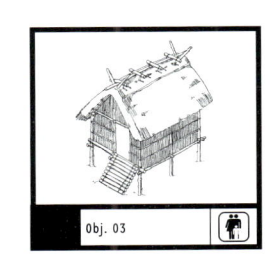

Wattanapol Ruenroeng Student **100**

♥ Debra Drodvillo Contributing Editor

Bugs Title ‖ Book Medium ‖ 2 Study Year ❣ University of the Arts, Philadelphia College
♣ USA Country ✺ Jan Almquist Professor

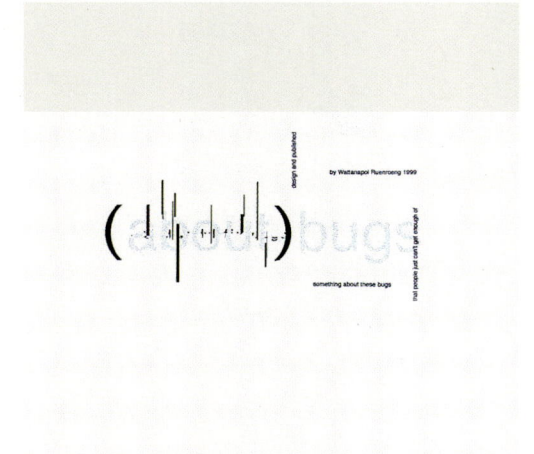

✺ In this book three individuals (chapters) are tied around the theme »Bugs.« The first individual is fixated on the Volkswagen Beetle (favourite object), the second individual is a computer programming major who fixes »bugs« (vocation), and the third is a small, timid individual who never kills »bugs« (personality). ✵ Dieses Buch ist in drei Kapitel aufgeteilt. Jedes Kapitel beschäftigt sich mit je einem Individuum, das mit dem zentralen Thema »Bugs« in Zusammenhang steht. Das Lieblingsobjekt der ersten Person ist ein VW Käfer. Das zweite Kapitel handelt von einem Computerprogrammierer, der auf das Suchen von Fehlern (bugs) in Programmen spezialisiert ist (Berufung) und das Dritte von einem kleinen, ängstlichen Mann, der keinem Käfer etwas zuleide tun könnte (Persönlichkeit).

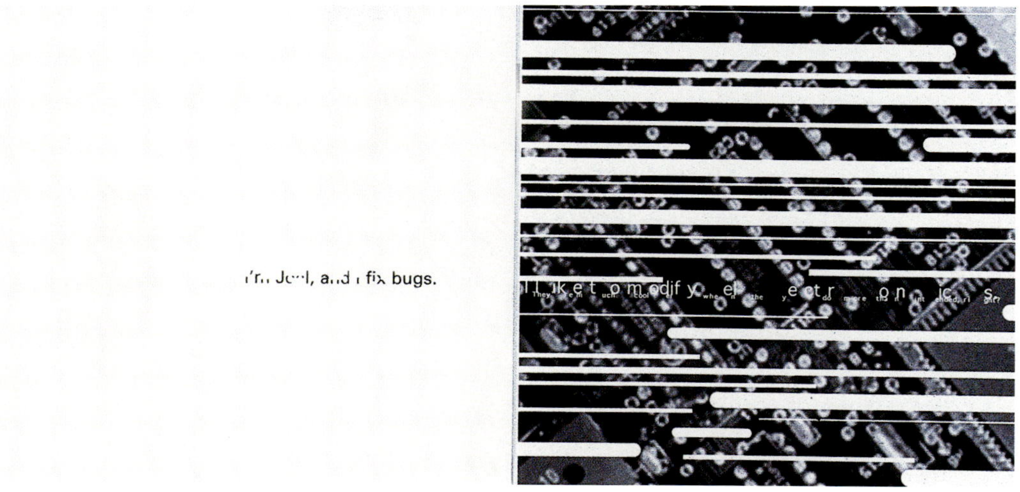

Missing Heart and Missing Bones | Fehlendes Herz und fehlender Knochen Title
Calligraphy | Kalligraphie Project   Hong Kong Baptist University College
China Country   Wendy Wong Professor

Lap-yan Wong Student

These posters are an appeal for donating organs and bone marrow. The pages look like the typical exercise books one uses to learn calligraphy. The Chinese characters have two parts. One part is only an outline to be redrawn and filled in by the pupils. In the poster for blood donation, the outline of the character »Heart« is contained within the strokes that form the character »Forgetting.« The headline reads: »Every day, 20 dangerously-ill people are waiting for a heart transplant.« ▲ In the poster for bone marrow donation, the »Bone« element of the character »Bone Marrow« is left as an outline whose components are the characters »Bones« and »Bury.« »Every day, 80 people are waiting for a donation of bone marrow while they prepare to be buried.«

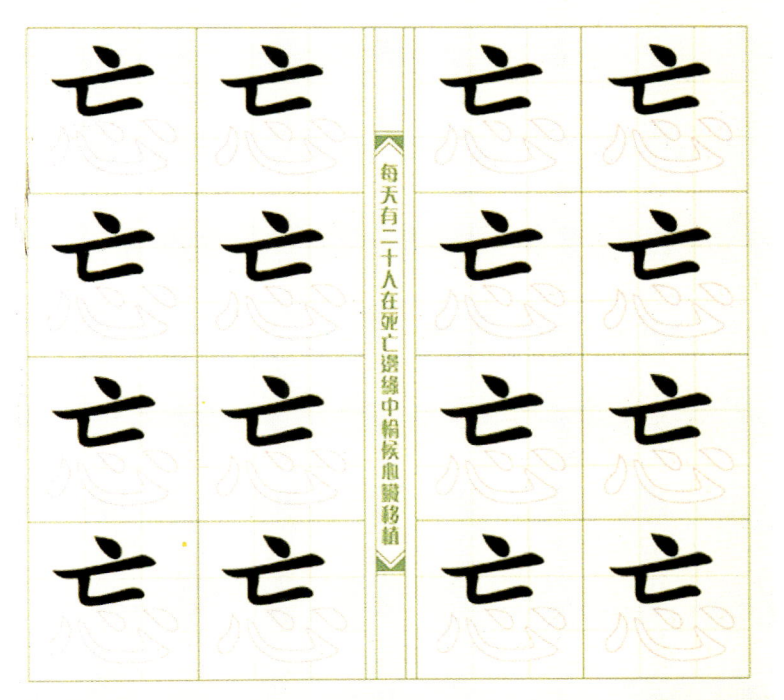

Die Plakate rufen dazu auf, Organe bzw. Knochenmark zu spenden. Sie sehen aus, wie die Seiten eines typisch chinesischen Übungsbuches. Die Zeichen auf dem Plakat bestehen aus zwei unterschiedlichen Teilen. Ein Teil ist nur eine Outline und soll von den Schülern nachgezeichnet und ausgefüllt werden. In dem Plakat für das Blutspenden ist der Wortteil »Herz« aus dem Wort »Vergessen« als Outline abgebildet. Die Überschrift lautet: »Jeden Tag warten 20 todkranke Menschen auf eine Herztransplantation«. In dem Plakat für die Knochenmarkspende ist die Komponente »Knochen« aus dem Wort »Knochenmark« unausgefüllt, welches seinerseits aus den Worten »Knochen« und »begraben« besteht: »Jeden Tag warten 80 Menschen auf eine Knochenmarkspende, während sie sich auf ihre Beerdigung vorbereiten.«

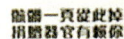

Changed Priorities Ahead | Geänderte Vorfahrt Title ✳ Booklet | Broschüre Medium
✢ 4 Study Year ❣ London College of Printing College ✿ Great Britain Country ✯
Teal Triggs, Joe Ewart Professors

Willem Heskes, Dionysios Livanis, Nadim Matta,
Dima Schneider, Niall Sweeney, Alan Zaruba Students

102

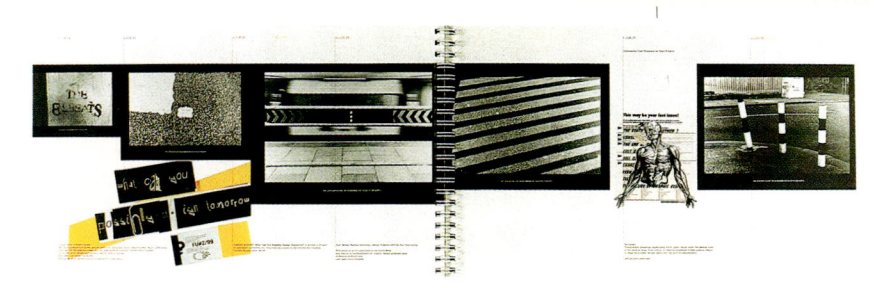

✣ »Changed Priorities Ahead« is a calendar documenting the studies of 6 students enrolled in the MA Typo/graphic Studies programme at the London College of Printing. Its structure is intended to reveal the framework the course is based on. More importantly, the calendar highlights the value of the student experience. Each day of 1999 is listed – with entries spanning from the first project completed by students up to the final stages of their Major Project thesis. »Changed Prorities Ahead« operates as a Degree Show Catalogue for these students as well as a general promotional piece for the MA programme. ✝ »Changed Priorities Ahead« ist der Name eines Kalenders, der die Studienzeit von 6 Studenten dokumentiert, die am Londoner College of Printing Typografie und Grafik studiert haben (MA). Die Struktur des Kalenders soll aufzeigen, auf welchem Prinzip und somit welchem Gerüst der Studiengang aufbaut. Wichtiger ist es aber, dass die Studenten ihre Erfahrungen in dem Kalender aufgezeichnet haben. Jeder Tag aus dem Jahr 1999 ist aufgeführt. Die Einträge umfassen die ersten Arbeiten der Studenten bis hin zu den Endeintragungen über ihre Abschlussarbeiten. »Changed Priorities Ahead« funktioniert als Katalog für die Abschlussarbeiten der Studenten und als Werbung für das MA Programm.

Isabell Große Holtforth Student

Muses | Musen Title || Dividers | Trennseiten Project ▲ 5 Study Year
HfK Bremen College ■ Germany Country ☆ Bernd Bexte Professor

❋ These seperate pages enclose the lecture timetable for the School of Fine Arts in Bremen and illustrate the muses of Greek mythology. ▶ Die einzelnen Seiten sind Zwischentitel für das Vorlesungsverzeichnis der Hochschule für Künste Bremen und zeigen die verschiedenen Musen aus der griechischen Mythologie.

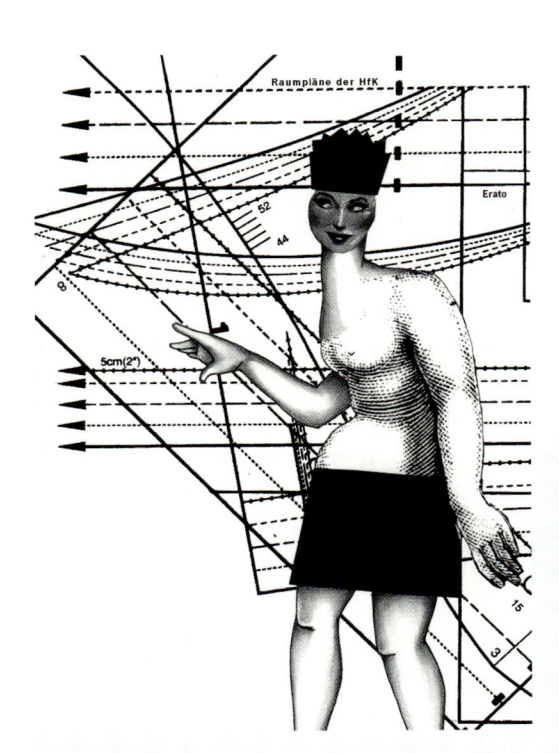

Cloud Chart | Wolkentabelle Title • Photography Medium
2 Study Year * Yale School of Art College • USA Country

Li Wei Student

104

»Weather sets the mood of each day, and the changing clouds can never be separated from the whole picture of our daily lives. ›Cloud Chart‹ is a series of photographs I took daily from the roof of my studio over a period of one month. It is my observation of repetition and difference from one specific location at different times. At a particular time of a day, continuously, I took four snapshots from the sky to the street. The shots captured a different cloud formation and its coexisting street-level surroundings each day. The visual experience of the same street is never the same. I established a visual structure in my Cloud Chart that reinforces comparison and contrast in order to deliver the message of difference within repetition.« »Das Wetter legt die Stimmung eines ganzen Tages fest, und die sich stets wechselnden Wolken sind untrennbar mit den Bildern unseres täglichen Lebens verbunden. ›Wolkentabelle‹ ist eine Serie von Fotografien, die ich über einen Zeitraum von einem Monat von dem Dach meines Studios aus gemacht habe. Sie ist meine Beobachtung von Veränderung und Gleichheit eines bestimmen Ortes zu unterschiedlichen Zeitpunkten. Zu einem bestimmten Zeitpunkt eines jeden Tages in dieser Zeitspanne, machte ich vier Schnappschüsse vom Himmel bis hinunter zur Straße. So fing ich verschiedene Wolkenformationen und die dazugehörigen Stimmungen auf der Straße ein. Die visuelle Erfahrung einer Straße ist nie die Gleiche. In meiner Wolkentabelle habe ich eine visuelle Struktur benutzt, die Vergleiche ermöglicht und Unterschiede aufzeigt, um zu verdeutlichen, dass Unterschiede in der Wiederholung bestehen.«

Sarah Winter Student **105**

The blood. The red. The flow. | Das Blut. Das Rot. Das fließt. Title
Book Medium **4** Study Year **GH Kassel** College **Germany** Country
Christof Gassner Professor

This book deals with the colour red and its association with blood.
Das Buch beschäftigt sich mit der Farbe Rot und den Assoziationen im Zusammenhang mit Blut.

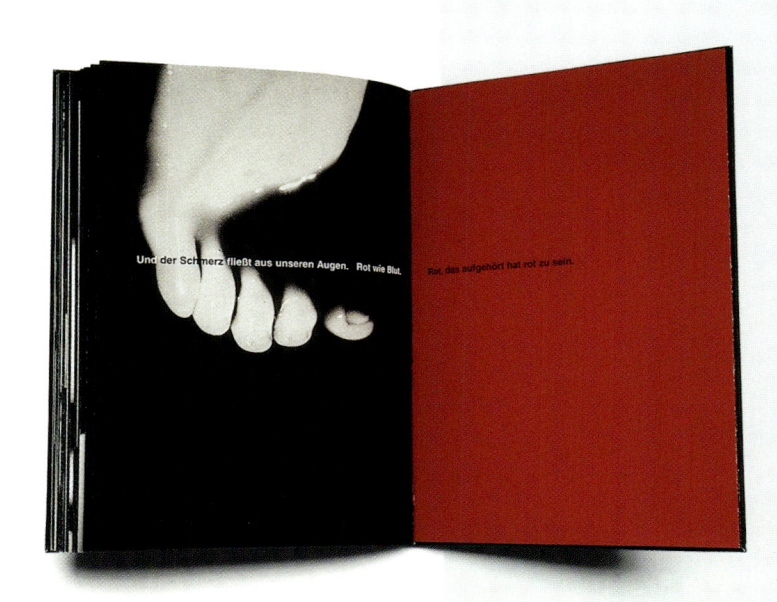

German World Hunger Relief | Welthungerhilfe Title ‹ Poster Medium
4 Study Year ✳ FH Düsseldorf College ❖ Germany Country ✩
Wilfried Korfmacher Professor

⭐ 106

Jan Tittelbach, Jörg Morsbach Students

Bier und Bewegung gut gegen Weihnachts-Völlerei

WELTHUNGERHILFE: Spendenkonto 1115 Sparkasse Bonn BLZ 380 500 00

+
Beer and exercise good for Christmas gluttony

❂ »›German World Hunger Relief‹ is one of the biggest independent foreign aid organizations in Germany. Its humanitarian work in Africa, Asia and Latin America is financed by donation, national subsidy, the EU and the UN. The aim of the campaign is to make the brand of ›German World Hunger Relief‹ stand out against its competitors and above all to motivate non-donors. We decided that the images should speak directly and make one choose sides because they won't be printed often and they need to be effective. The concept is simple: We show pictures of desperate people, whose only concern is survival, to contrast headlines extracted from tabloids, which only address the wishes and worries of our material society. This kind of advertisement is hard and unpleasant and should instigate a dialogue. We at least hope it does.«

✤ »Die Welthungerhilfe ist eine der größten nichtstaatlichen Entwicklungshilfe-organisationen in Deutschland. Ihre humanitäre Arbeit in Afrika, Asien und Lateinamerika finanziert sie mit Spenden aus der Bevölkerung und Zuschüssen der Bundesregierung, der EU und der Vereinten Nationen. Ziel der Kampagne ist es, die Marke Welthungerhilfe von der Konkurrenz abzuheben und vor allen Dingen die Nicht-Spender zu aktivieren. Wir haben uns für eine polarisierende und plakative Ansprache entschieden, da die Kampagne ihre Wirkung auch bei geringer Schaltfrequenz und entsprechend geringem Werbedruck entfalten muss. Das Prinzip ist denkbar einfach: Wir stellen Bilder geschundener Menschen, deren einzige Sorge das Überleben ist, Ausrissen aus Boulevardblättern gegenüber, die die banalen Sorgen oder Wünsche unserer Überflussgesellschaft dokumentieren. Diese Art der Ansprache ist hart, unangenehm und dürfte für Diskussionen sorgen. Darauf spekulieren wir.«

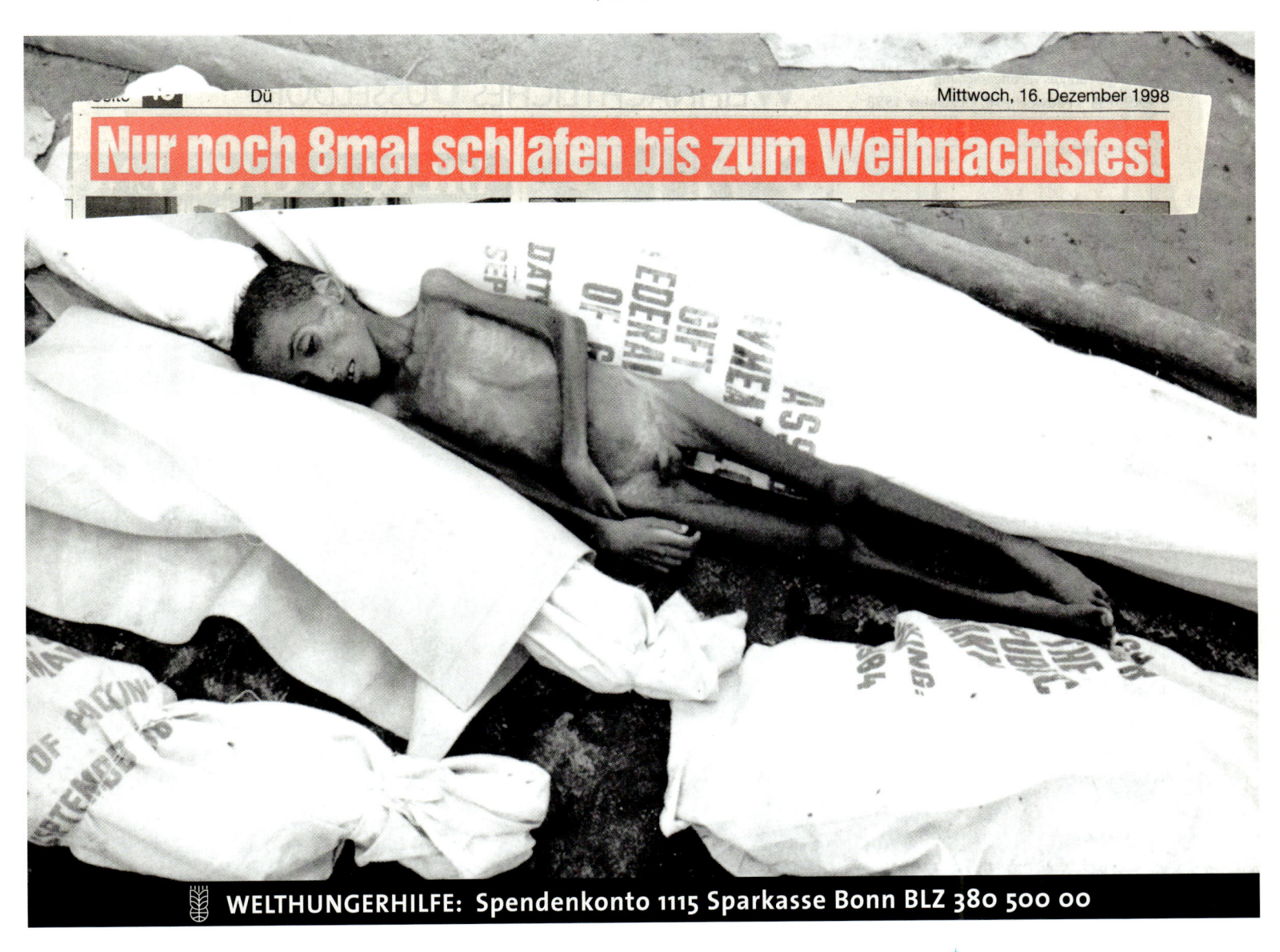

+
*Close your eyes only eight more times,
then it will be Christmas Day.*

Bethany Koby Student

✸ **107**

Trace | Spur Title ✢ Installation Medium ✢ 4 Study Year
Rhode Island School of Design College ✎ USA Country ☆
C. Maxx Stevens Professor

✳ This installation deals with memory – past and present – as well as history. The projections of Victorian furniture on the walls of an old building show what is present; what was, in the past; and what could be, in future. The installation consists of 10 rooms to walk through and experience. ✡ Diese Installation handelt von der Idee der Erinnerung, der Vergangenheit, der Gegenwart und der Geschichte. Die Projektionen von viktorianischen Möbeln auf die Mauern eines alten Gebäudes zeigen, was Gegenwart ist, was Vergangenheit war und was Zukunft sein könnte. Die Installation umfasst 10 Räume, durch die man gehen und in denen man etwas erleben kann.

The Explanation of Flight | Die Darstellung des Fliegens Title
Projection | Projektionen Medium 5 Study Year
Hochschule für Grafik und Buchkunst Leipzig College Germany Country
Ruedi Baur Professor

Berit Kaiser Student

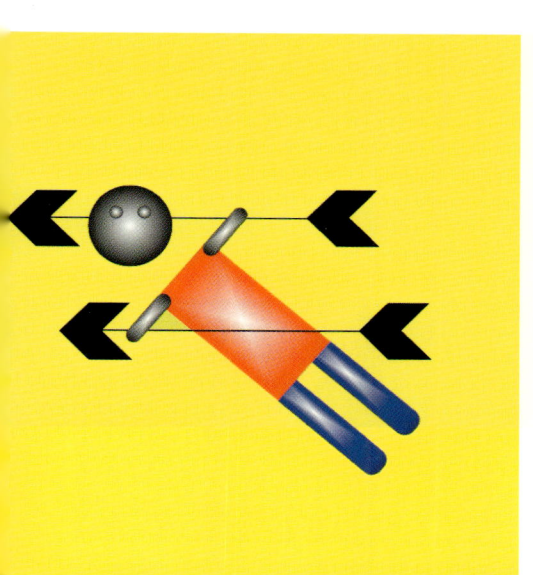

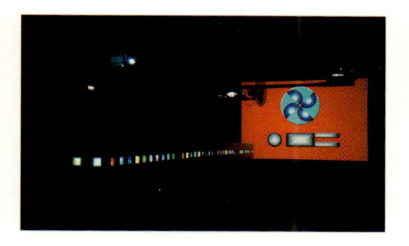

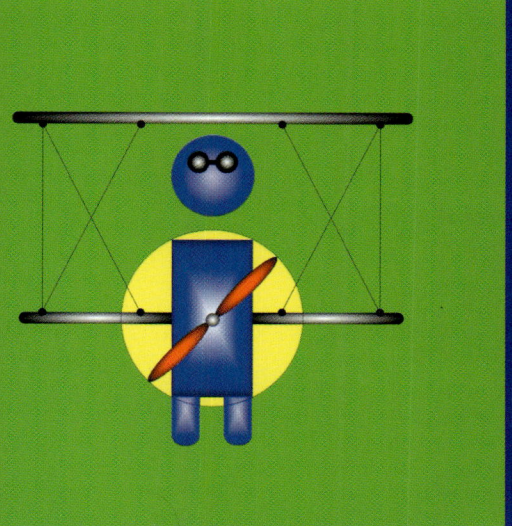

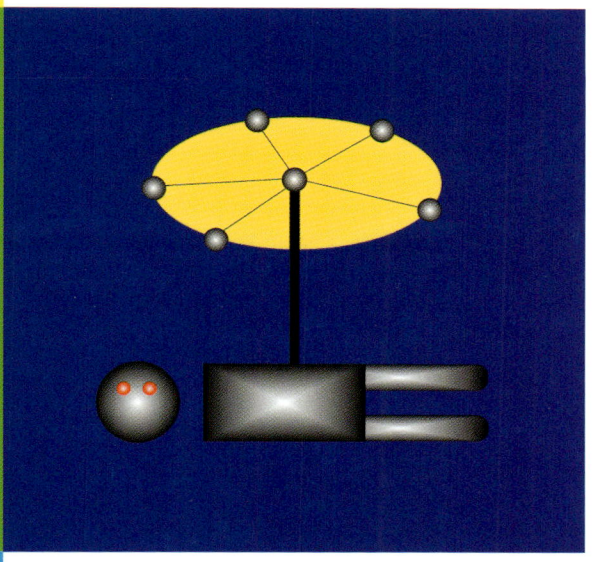

108

❖ »Airplanes are part of everyday life. They are the No. 1 form of transportation: in distance, speed and comfort. But still their development has not yet reached what people had dreamed of centuries ago: for humans to fly independently. Throughout history there have been many familiar images of flight: messengers with golden wings, the first hot air balloons and early bird-like flying apparati. My diploma thesis consist of approx. 300 pictograms showing human flight in different ways. The pictures show humans flying with various insignia of flight: propellers, dragons, umbrellas, magic wands, feathers, sails, wings, balloons ... Because it is impossible to experience flying on the paper this work was then rendered in three dimensions. A machine built for presentation allows one to experience both the form and function of flight.« ▲ »Flugzeuge gehören zum Alltag. Sie sind Transportmittel Nr. 1 was Geschwindigkeit, Entfernung und Komfort betrifft. Dennoch ist mit der Entwicklung des Flugzeuges nicht das erreicht, was sich die Menschen vor Jahrhunderten erträumt hatten: den freien Menschenflug. Aus der Geschichte sind eine Vielzahl von Flugmotiven bekannt. Von Götterboten mit goldenen Flugsandalen, über erste Gas- und Heißluftballons bis zu vogelähnlichen frühen Flugapparaten. Meine Diplomarbeit besteht aus etwa 300 Zeichen, die den freien Menschenflug auf verschiedene Weise illustrieren. In den Zeichen fliegt der Mensch selbst mit verschiedenen Attributen des Fluges: Propeller, Drachen, Regenschirm, Zauberstab, Federn, Segel, Schwingen, Ballons ... Da sich das Fliegen nicht auf dem Papier, sondern nur im Raum erleben lässt, wurde die Arbeit erweitert. Ein Präsentationsmaschine veranschaulicht durch seine Form und Funktion das Fliegen auf materieller Ebene.«

Royal Astronomy | Königliche Astronomie Title ✦ CD Packaging and promotional material | CD Verpackung und Werbematerial Project ✦ 1 Study Year ♥ School of Visual Arts, New York College ✎ USA Country ☆ Stefan Sagmeister Professor

♥ Steven Heller Contributing Editor

Peter Kienzle Student **109**

✳ »Invisibility« is the design concept behind the repackaging and promotion of the CD »Royal Astronomy« by µ-ziq. The front cover of the jewel case is silkscreened, blurring the vision. But even after taking the booklet out, the image is out of focus and the subject's back is turned on you. You never get to see his face. In logical conclusion, the »Action Set« contains Royal-Gear-Fashion. ✦ Das Konzept bei der Gestaltung und Werbung der CD »Royal Astronomy« von »µ-ziq« ist Unsichtbarkeit. Das Cover ist halbtransparent und macht das dahinter liegende Bild unscharf. Nimmt man das Bild aus der Hülle heraus, stellt man fest, dass es immer noch unscharf ist. Der darauf abgebildete Mann dreht dem Betrachter den Rücken zu. Man bekommt das Gesicht nie zu sehen. Darüberhinaus beinhaltet das zur CD gehörende »Action Set« die passende Royal-Gear-Mode.

Bethany Koby Student **110**

Atonal Title — Experimental music identity packaging | Erscheinungsbild für einen Musikverlag für expermientelle Musik Project — 2 Study Year — Rhode Island School of Design College — USA Country — Matthew Monk Professor

This packaging plays off the methodologies of the experimental music genre and its intention to push, both visually and audibly, the boundaries of music. By using everyday found objects like plastic baggies, Band-Aids, Advil, etc. the package echoes the avant-garde and progressive feeling of this type of music. The 3-D display is less a display case for use, and more an aesthetic arrangement for promotional items. The bags are arranged on the wall such that one can read the word »Atonal.« Die Verpackung spielt mit der Methodik der experimentellen Musik und ihrer Intention, die Grenzen der Musik audio-visuell zu verschieben. Indem alltägliche Materialien verwendet wurden, wie z.B. Plastiktüten, Pflaster und Tabletten, spiegelt die Verpackung das progressive, avantgardistische Gefühl der Musik wider. Das 3D-Display ist weniger ein Gebrauchsgegenstand als vielmehr ein ästhetisches Arrangement für die Artikel. Die Tüten sind so an der Wand angeordnet, das der Betrachter das Wort »atonal« lesen kann.

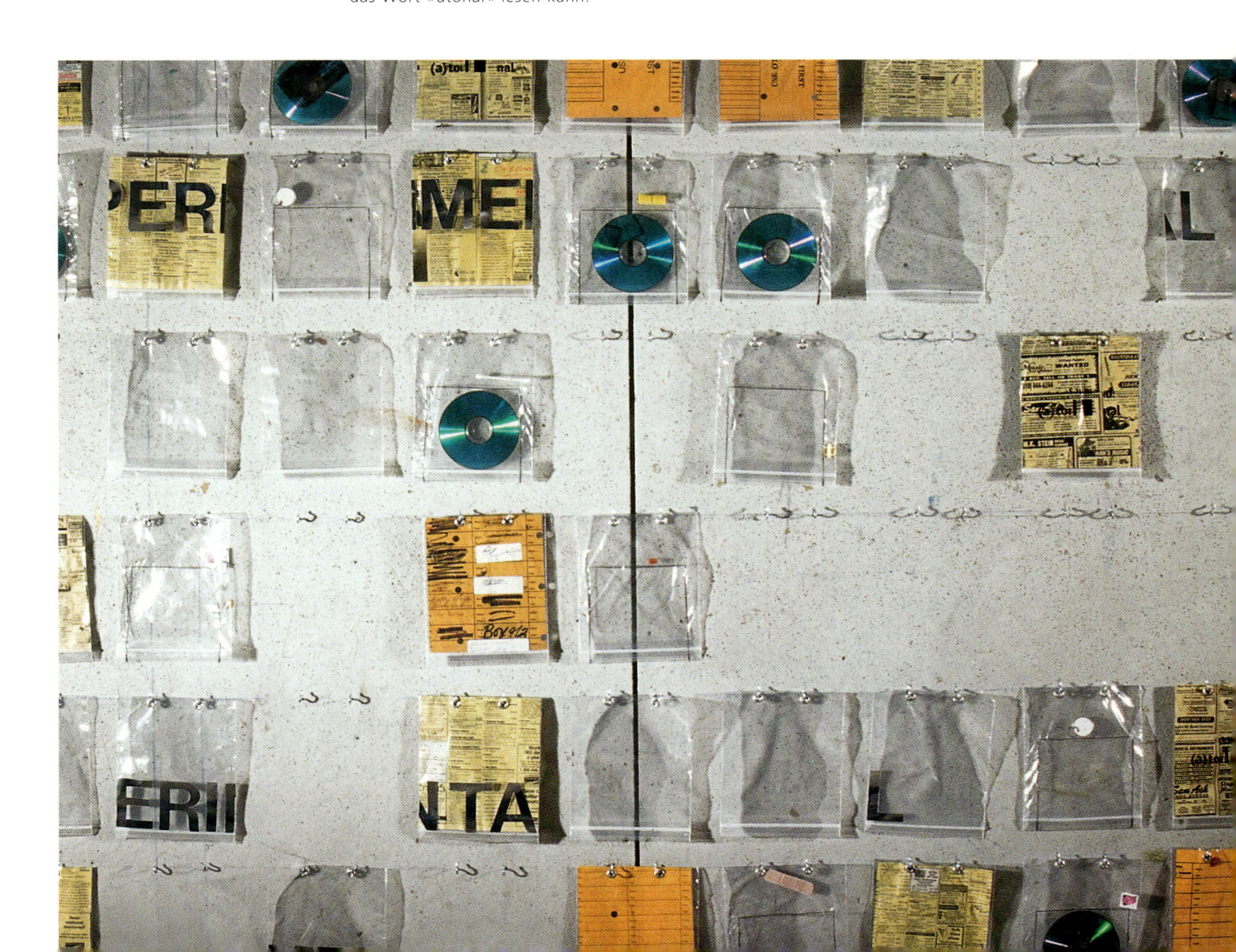

Eva Heibl Student 111

Milk | Milch Title ✣ Packaging | Verpackung Project ✣ 3 Study Year ❢ Universität für angewandte Kunst Wien College ✎ Austria Country ✭ Walter Lürzer Professor

⌒ »I've designed the package according to the way milk is: raw« ⌒
»Ich habe die Packung so gestaltet, wie die Milch ist: roh.«

Small Plot of Land | Kleines Stück Land Title ✢ Illustration Project ✢
3 Study Year ❢ Hungarian Academy of Crafts and Design College
Hungary Country ☆ Molnár Gyula Professor

László Nagy Student **112**

⌒ For the exhibition »Make Me a School,« celebrities in art, design, science and architecture were invited to present ideas for changing the academy. The sent-in materials were also to be an inspiration for a future art school. The design of the exhibition in which the solutions were shown was a cooperation with students from the College of Art, Halle – Burg Giebichenstein.

❖ *The drawers in the steps are to make the stairway into a space for communication and inspiration.*
❖ *Die Schubladen in den Treppen sollen das Treppenhaus zu einem Kommunikations- und Inspirationsraum machen.*

❖ *The pathway to the exibition leads you through a tunnel in which all the students who have ever studied at the College for Graphic and Book Arts are recorded.*
❖ *Der Weg zur Ausstellung führt durch einen Tunnel, in dem alle Studenten vermerkt sind, die jemals an der Hochschule für Grafik und Buchkunst studiert haben.*

❖ *Pavilion for cultural disaster:*
The pavilion is to be big enough for one person to sit and stand within. It is made from a dense structure that allows the user to observe others without themselves being seen.
❖ *Pavillon für kulturelles Desaster:*
Der Pavillon sollte so groß sein, dass darin ein Person sitzen und stehen kann. Er besteht aus einer dichten Struktur, die es dem Benutzer erlaubt, andere zu beobachten ohne selbst gesehen zu werden.

Make Me a School | Mach mir eine Schule Title ✜ **Exhibition** | Ausstellung Medium
✜ 3 - 5 Study Year ❖ **Hochschule für Grafik und Buchkunst Leipzig** College ✳
Germany Country ✰ **Ruedi Baur** Professor

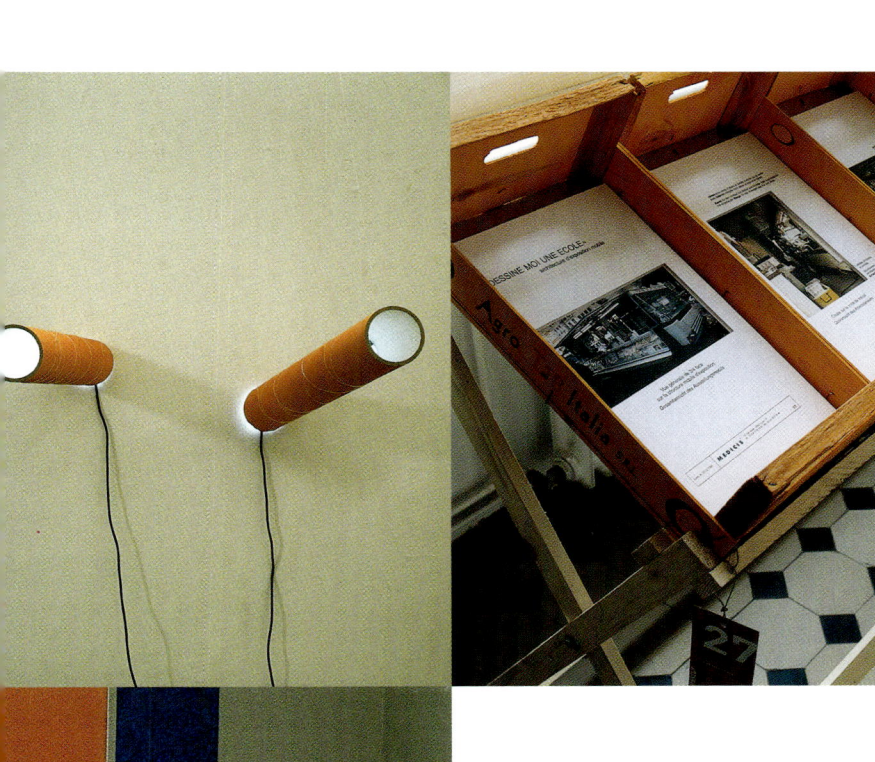

Fachklasse Grafik Design Students **113**

✜ *The prensentation format is supposed to reflect the contributions' conceptual content, which is concerned with the mobility and use of already available structures. The idea was to show the market situation in form of a fruit stand: the fruit crates carry the fruits of thought.*
✜ *Die Form der Präsentation soll den Inhalt der Überlegungen des Beitrages widerspiegeln, der sich mit Mobilität und Nutzung bereits vorhandener Strukturen beschäftigt. Die Idee war, die Marktsituation in Form von Obstkistenständern darzustellen: die Obstkisten tragen die Früchte des Denkens.*

⌒ Für die Ausstellung »Mach mir eine Schule« wurden Persönlichkeiten aus Kunst, Design, Wissenschaft und Architektur aufgefordert, Ideen zur Veränderung der Akademie einzureichen, die gleichzeitig Anregungen für eine Kunsthochschule der Zukunft sein könnten. Die Ergebnisse des Aufrufs wurden in einer Ausstellung präsentiert. Das Ausstellungsdesign entstand in Zusammenarbeit mit Studierenden der Hochschule für Gestaltung in Halle, Burg Giebichenstein.

Tour de France Title ◆ Poster Series | Plakatserie Project ❋
3 Study Year ⊠ FH Münster College ▪ Germany Country 🏛
Hartmut Brückner Professor

Stephanie Kluck Student

114

❖ In this project the phenomenon of time is examined, worked through and demonstrated in all its dimensions and complex applications. Each poster is one stage of the Tour de France. It shows the overall position of each competitor; it shows who wore the yellow, green and white-red shirts; and, it also shows a detailed route. ⌒ In diesem Projekt soll das Phänomen Zeit in all seinen Dimensionen und komplexen Anwendungen untersucht, bearbeitet und visualisiert werden. Jedes Plakat der Serie bezieht sich auf eine Etappe der Tour de France. Es wird gezeigt, wo sich die Fahrer im Gesamtklassement vor und nach der jeweiligen Etappe befinden, wer das gelbe, grüne bzw. weiss-rote Trikot trägt und wie die Strecke verläuft.

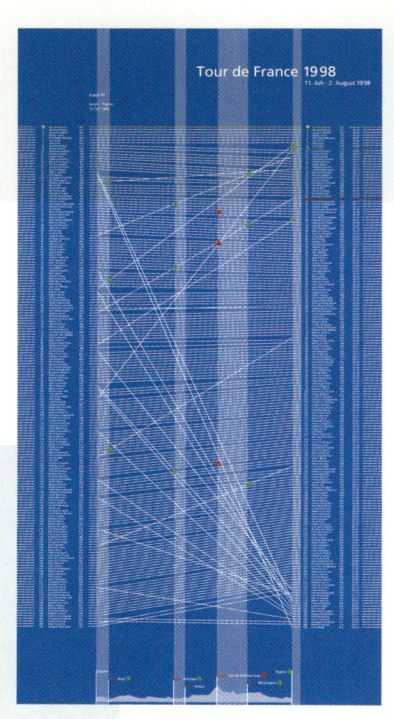

✪ *Stage 1 (Lowland)*
✳ *Etappe 1 (Flachland)*

✳ *Complete poster*
❖ *Gesamtplakat*

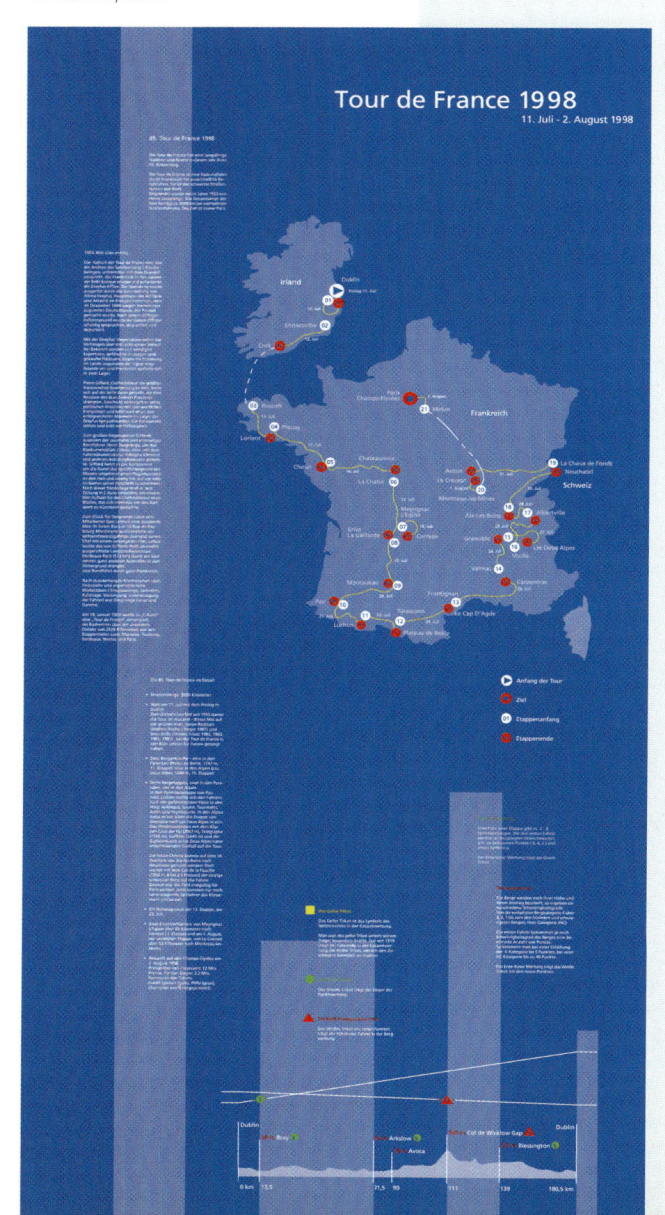

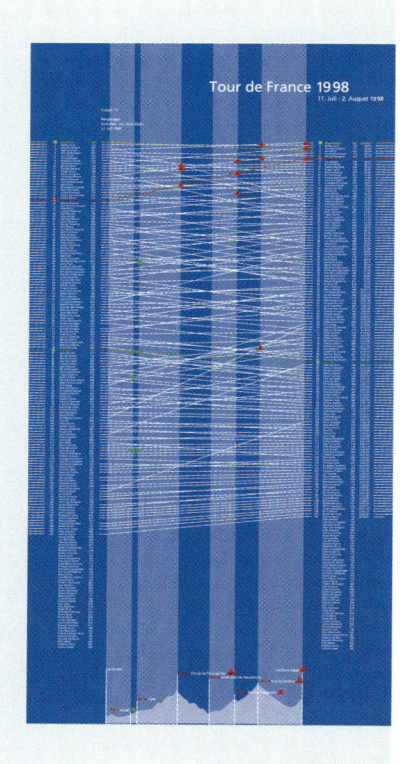

◆ *Stage 15 (Alpine)*
★ *Etappe 15 (Bergland)*

Sonja Köhler Student

115

The Post-Mortem Examination | Die klinische Obduktion Title
Faltblatt | Folder Medium   6 Study Year   FH Münster College
Germany Country   Hartmut Brückner Professor

✤ In order to better their understanding of the post-mortem examination process and its background, this system of folding pages gives medical students a chronological overview in three layers. ✦ Zur besseren Veranschaulichung von klinischen Obduktionsvorgängen und deren Hintergründen wurde ein Faltsystem entwickelt, das Medizinstudenten in drei Ebenen einen Gesamtüberblick über die chronologische Abfolge der Obduktion geben soll.

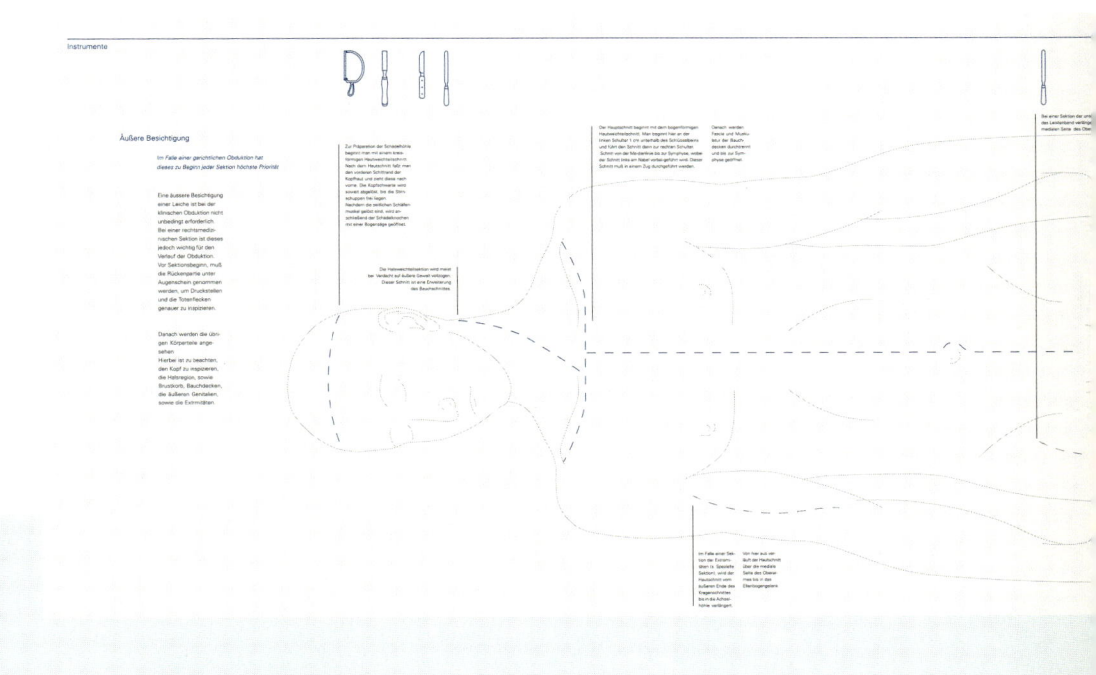

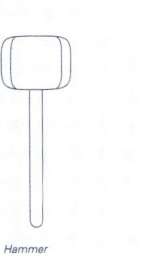

| Hammer | Parenchymmesser | Rippenschere | Darmschere | Metalllineal | Sektionsmesser | Meissel |

Der Hammer wird hauptsächlich in Verbindung mit dem Meissel benutzt, wenn damit die Schädeldecke geöffnet wird.

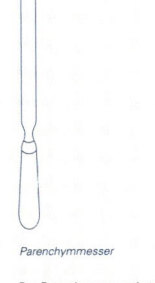

Das Parenchymmesser hat ein schmales Klingenblatt, welches glatte, stufenlose, schmale Schnitte aller Organe gewährleistet.

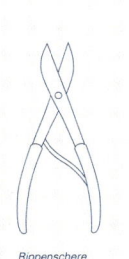

Die Rippenschere kommt dann zum Einsatz, wenn der knöcherne Thorax geöffnet wird.

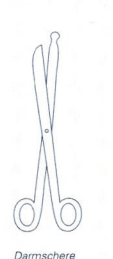

Die Darmschere wird mit ihrem runden Kopf zur Öffnung des Darmes, sowie anderer Hohlorgane benötigt.

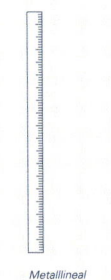

Mit dem Metalllineal werden Abweichungen bezüglich der Grösse der verschiedenen Organe gemessen.

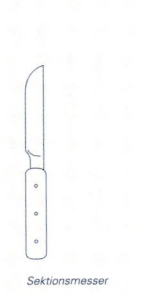

Das Sektionsmesser wird zur Anlage der Hautschnitte, sowie zur Entnahme der Brust- und Bauchorgane verwendet.

Die schmale Meissel wird im Bereich der Schädelbasis eingesetzt, u.a. auch zur Entnahme der Wirbelsäule.

Hatem Imam Student **116**

Built To Last Title ✦ Poster Series | Plakatserie Medium ❦ American University of Beirut College ✎ Lebanon Country ★ Leila Musfy Professor

★ This poster series connects typeface (Franklin Gothic) with furniture design (barber's chair). It shows the structural similarities of both design objects: The stringency of each design makes them last a long time. ✦ Diese Plakatserie stellt einen Zusammenhang zwischen Schriftgestaltung (Franklin Gothic) und Möbeldesign (ein Friseurstuhl) her. Dabei sollen die strukturellen Ähnlichkeiten beider Gestaltungsobjekte herausgearbeitet werden: Die Strenge der Gestaltung, die beide für eine lange Zeit haltbar macht.

Eleonore ^{Title} ✦ Illustrations ^{Project} ✦ 5 ^{Study Year}
Muthesius Hochschule Kiel ^{College} Germany ^{Country}
Peetsche Peelmöller ^{Professor}

117

Doreen Kiepsel, Marlena Sang ^{Students}

❖ »We worked on the text of this story one after another without talking about it beforehand. The reader follows a female through the night. It plays with words and sentences, adding up to a strange story. While I was drawing, I couldn't imagine what Marlena was writing down. Finally we brought our two stories together in ›Eleonore.‹ The story appears as a collection of pictures and texts, leaving enough space for one's own thoughts.« ✦
»Wir haben nacheinander an einer Geschichte gearbeitet, ohne uns vorher auszutauschen. Der Leser begleitet eine weibliche Person auf einem Weg durch die Nacht. Es ist ein Spiel mit Worten und Sätzen, die sich aufeinanderfolgend zu einer seltsamen Geschichte ergänzen. Beim Zeichnen meiner Geschichte wusste ich nicht, was sich Marlena beim Schreiben vorgestellt haben könnte. Am Ende haben wir unsere zwei Geschichten in ›Eleonore‹ vereint. Für den Betrachter ist die Geschichte eine Folge von Text- und Bildseiten. Ihm bleibt Raum für eigene Gedanken.«

False Words/Failed Words | Falsche Worte/Fehlende Worte Title ✜ Book Medium
✜ 2 Study Year ⚊ FH Darmstadt College ✱ Germany Country ⚒ Kai Krippner Professor

Charalampos Lazos Student 118

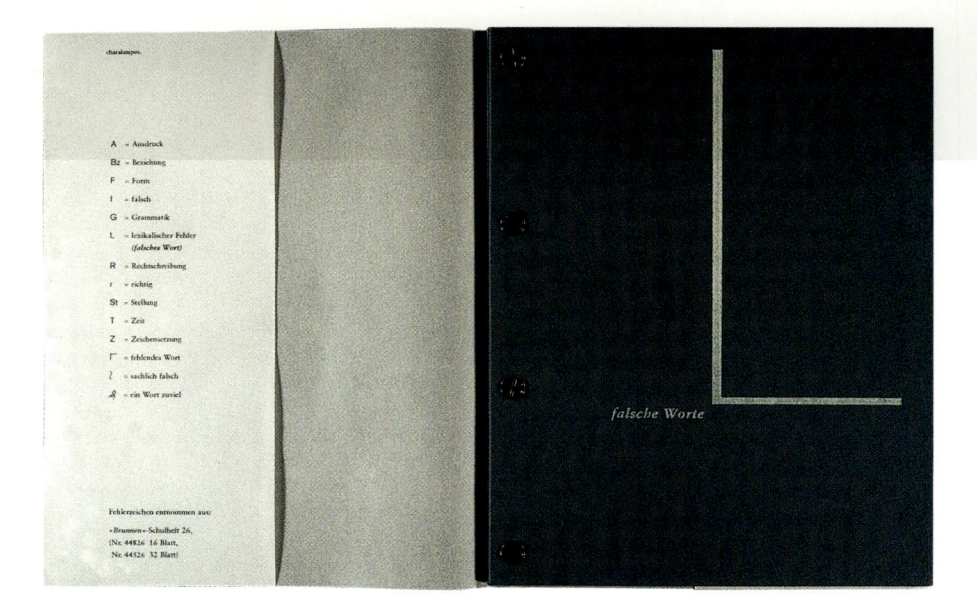

) The title of the book alludes to the »false,« or wrong words, that the translator of a text used and those words that »failed« him in translation. So the theme of the book is failure. The book compares false translations with the original texts. The book has two title pages, »False Words« and »Failed Words.« ✣ Mit dem Titel der Arbeit sind die »falschen« Worte gemeint, die der Übersetzer eines Textes benutzt, beziehungsweise Worte, die ihm bei der Übersetzung fehlen. Damit ist das Thema des Buches definiert: Das Scheitern. Im Buch werden »gescheiterte« Übersetzungen den »richtigen Texten« gegenübergestellt. Das Buch hat zwei Titelseiten »Falsche Worte« und »Fehlende Worte«.

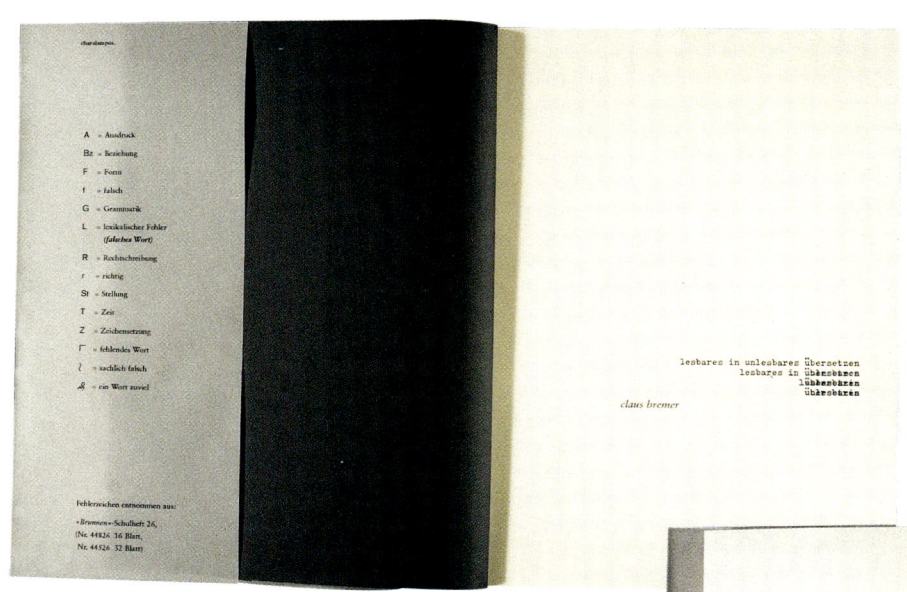

Christina Gschwantner Student **119**

Personal Stationery | Persönliches Briefpapier Title + 2 Study Year
Universität für angewandte Kunst Wien College ✎ Austria Country
G.G. Lange Professor

christina gschwantner
mittersteig 7|21
1040 wien
58.51.843

christina gschwantner
mittersteig 7|21
1040 wien
58.51.843

January 19th 1998

My name is Eva Heibl and I´m in the second year of
Graphic Design (emphasis on advertising) - Mastercl
at the University of Applied Arts, Vienna

As I´m interested how Visual Communication can work
want to take advantage of my exchange semester to
different ways of communication in different cultures
inspirations.

Mexico especially appeals to me with the
Pre-Columbian Codices. Studying at the
Puebla it would be great for me to find
Graphic Design today in Mexico. Of

expressive symbolism in the

Eva Heibl

christina gschwantner
mittersteig 7|21
1040 wien
58.51.843

Identity system for an art school | Erscheinungsbild für eine Kunsthochschule Title
2 Study Year Higher Academic School of Graphic Design Moscow College
Russia Country Boris Trofimov Professor

120 Elena Tolokonia Student

121

Bettina Berg, Chae Lee Students

Information Overlaod Title ☒ University of the Arts, Philadelphia College
USA Country ✱ Debra Drodvillo Professor

♥ Debra Drodvillo Contributing Editor

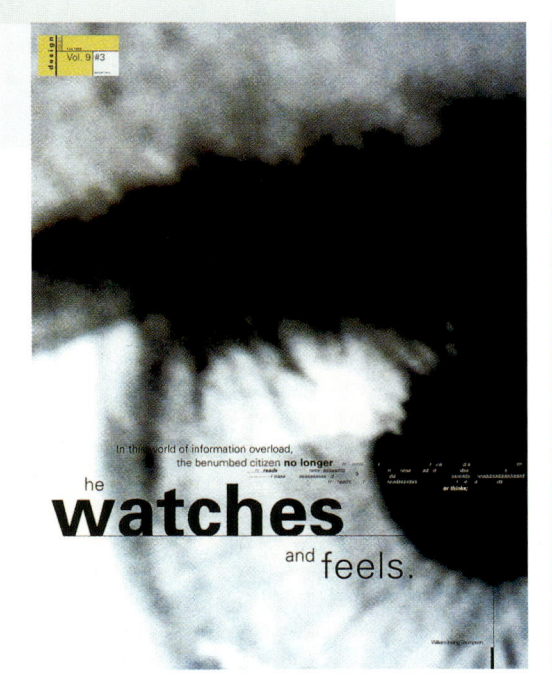

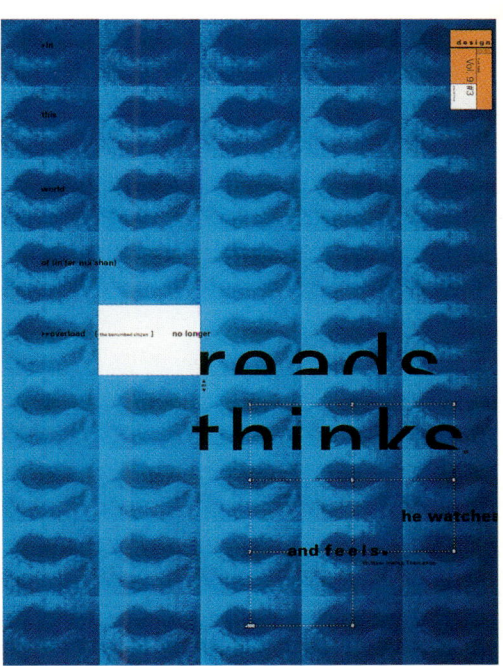

✤ »In this world of information overload, the benumbed citizen no longer reads or thinks; he watches and feels.« (William Irwin Thompson) This quote was the starting point for the development of visual forms. ✱ »In dieser Welt des totalen Informationsüberflusses kann der benommene Einwohner nur noch sehen und fühlen, denn er ist nicht mehr in der Lage, zu lesen und zu denken.« (William Irwin Thompson) Dieses Zitat war der Ausgangspunkt für die Entwicklung von visuellen Formen.

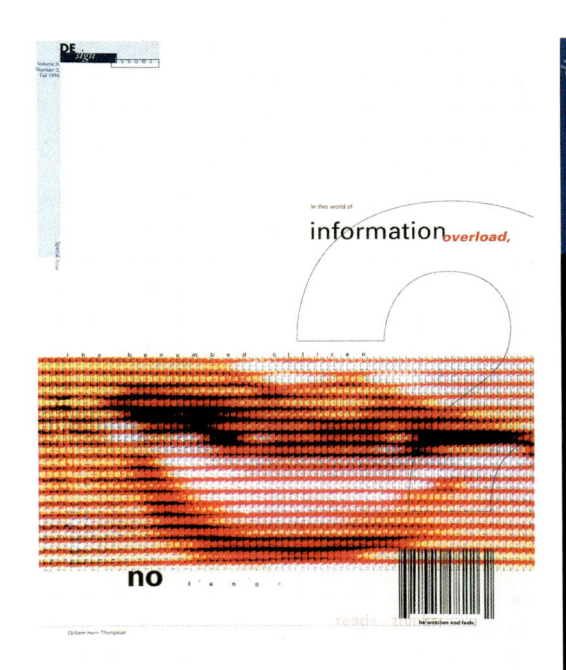

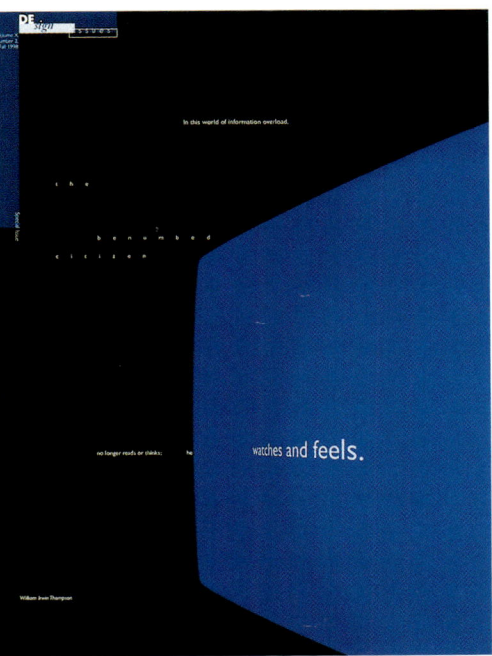

IIC Beginner Course 1 – Murder Manual | IIC Grundkurs 1 – der Auftragsmord
Title ✦ **Book** Medium ✳ **3** Study Year ✤ **FH Darmstadt** College ✦ **Germany** Country ✤
Sandra Hoffmann Professor

122

Tobias Bender, Stephan Trischler, Martin Lorenz, Sebastian Puhze Students

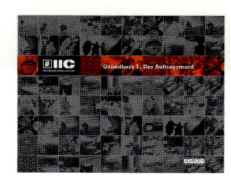

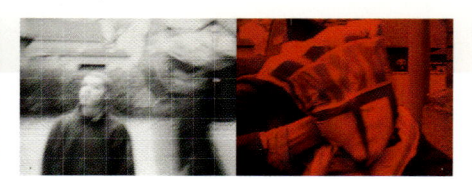

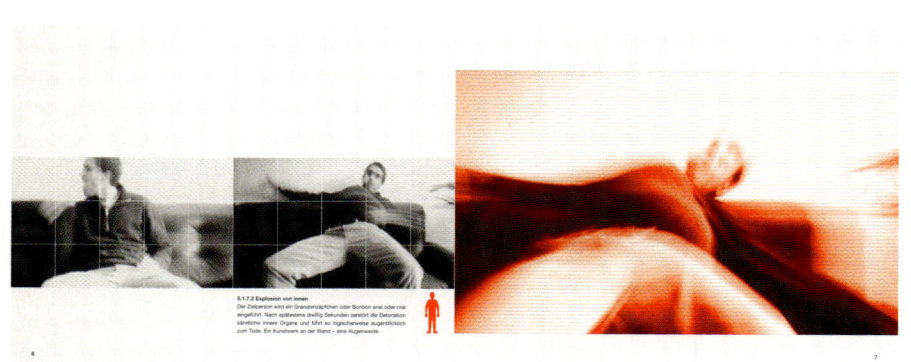

✦ *An art of killing: blow 'em up*
▮ *Tötungsarten: Platzen lassen*

● »*The price for a job: ... Take more if you're not sure. The clients will always pay.*«
✦ »*Der Preis eines Auftrages: ... Wenn Sie Zweifel haben, bewerten Sie immer zu hoch, denn die Auftraggeber zahlen immer.*«

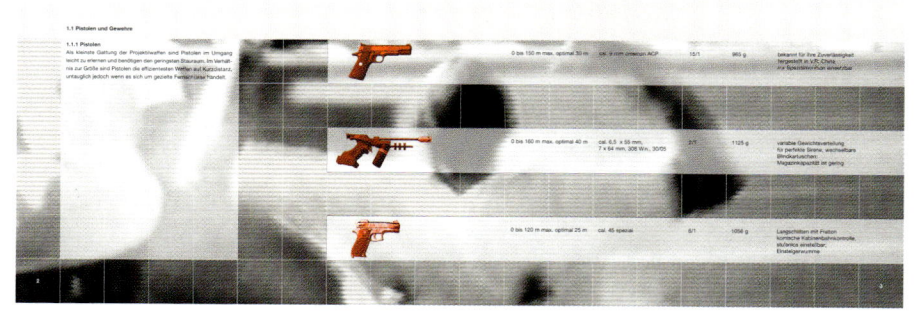

✦ *Weapons*
✳ *Waffen*

✳ *Location and surveillance*
● *Aufsuchen und Observieren*

✳ This is the schoolbook of a fictitious, federally and internationally accepted academy (IIC – International Institute of Crime). It is a dark view on the public legitimization of violence, a satire on the increasing violence in media and the growing propensity of the public to violence.

✳ Das Buch ist ein seminarbegleitendes Schulbuch einer fiktiven, staatlichen, weltweit anerkannten Schule (IIC – International Institute of Crime). Es soll mit schwarzem Humor eine gesellschaftliche Legitimierung der Gewalt darstellen. Es ist eine Satire über zunehmende Gewalt in den Medien und Gewaltbereitschaft in der Gesellschaft.

Crime Scene: College – on the trail | Tatort FH – eine Spurensuche Title
Concept for Student Orientation | Begrüßungskonzept für Studienanfänger Project
5 Study Year ❄ FH Mainz College ✻ Germany Country ❄ Charlotte Schröner, Thomas Daum Professors

Tanja Kirschner, Annette Forsch Students

✱ **123**

✻ Brochure
✻ Broschüre

»Crime Scene: College« is the overall concept for welcoming the first-year students of design to FH Mainz. The German word »Tat« (action) is part of the word »Tatort« (crime scene) – there is always action at the scene of a crime, it is always scary and full of secrets. Addressing the new students in a humorous way makes them think and changes their point of view. For this reason a brochure and a CD-ROM were given to the students to lead them through the college. Bags with pieces of circumstantial evidence made by professional designers were also given out to motivate and inform them, to broaden their minds or to sober them up. »Tatort FH« ist ein Gesamtkonzept für die Begrüßung der Studienanfänger im Studiengang Design an der FH Mainz. Ein »Tatort« ist im wahrsten Sinne ein Ort der Tat aber auch ein unheimlicher Ort, der etwas Geheimnisvolles verströmt. Durch eine humorvolle Ansprache sollen die Erstsemester zum Neudenken und Umdenken bewegt werden. Zu diesem Zweck gibt es eine Broschüre, eine CD-ROM, die durch die Räumlichkeiten der FH führt und Indizientüten mit Beiträgen von professionellen, erfahrenen Gestaltern, die motivieren, informieren, den Horizont erweitern oder ernüchtern sollen.

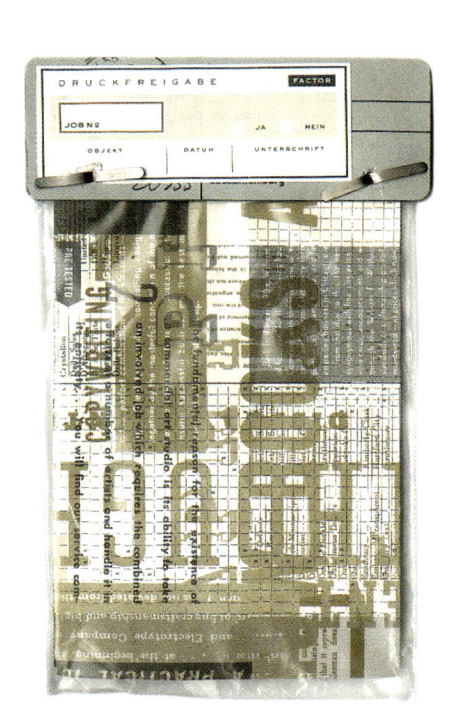

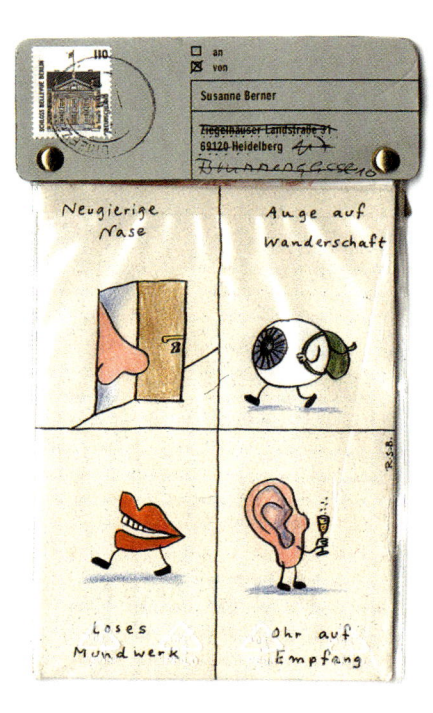

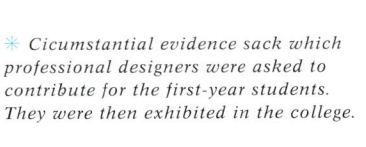

✻ Cicumstantial evidence sack which professional designers were asked to contribute for the first-year students. They were then exhibited in the college.

✻ Indizientüten: Professionelle und erfahrene Designer wurden angeschrieben mit der Bitte, einen Beitrag für die Studienanfänger zurückzuschicken. Die Indizientüten wurden in der Fachhochschule ausgestellt.

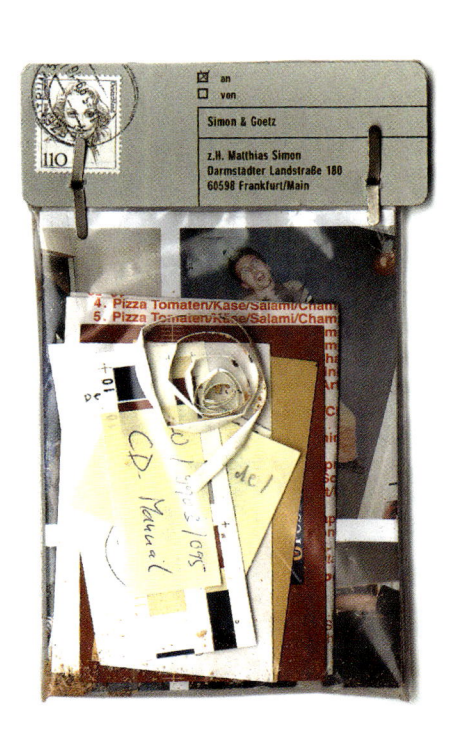

Robert Schäfer Student **124**

The Book Object | Das Buchobjekt Title ✿ 4 Study Year ✣ Freie Kunstschule Ravensburg College ◆ Germany Country ✳ Roland Wagner Professor

✤ »The Book Object« tells the story of the design and production of a book. Each element of the book object is directly labeled with the terminology of the bookbinder. Photos show what content may be transferred by books, and also how they can be »misused.« The work shows that a book is an unique object. For that reason the traditions of book design are made apparent but then also broken.

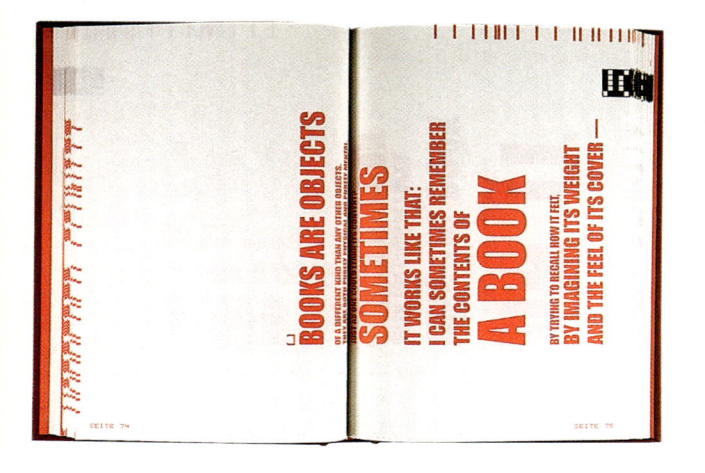

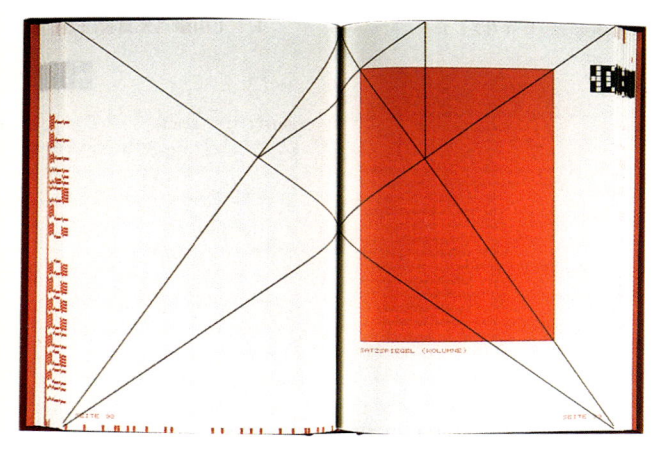

◆ »Das Buchobjekt« erzählt etwas über Buchgestaltung und -herstellung. Begriffe aus der Sprache der Buchbinder finden sich an genau den Stellen wieder, die sie beschreiben. Eine Fotostrecke zeigt, welche unterschiedlichen Inhalte Bücher transportieren können und wofür Bücher »missbraucht« werden. Die Arbeit soll das Buch als eigenständiges Objekt begreifbar machen. Dazu werden die spezifischen Eigenheiten eines Buches als Gestaltungsmittel genutzt – aber auch gebrochen.

♥ Bill Longhauser Contributing Editor

Jayme Smith Student

125

Studies Title ✦ 3 Study Year ⊠ University of the Arts, Philadelphia College
USA Country Bill Longhauser Professor

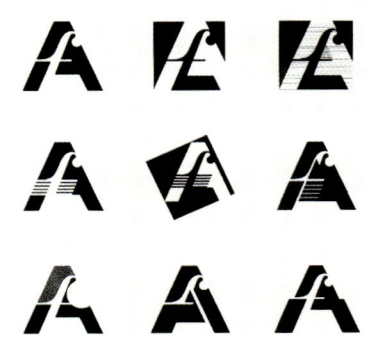

⌢ *Formal investigations of the basic combination in search of new formulations that may evoke a specific theme.*
⌢ *Formale Untersuchungen mit den original Kombinationen, mit dem Ziel neue Formulierungen zu finden die an spezifische Themen erinnern.*

✌ *Using variations developed in the exploratory process, the studies are then combined with photography.*
▲ *Unter Verwendung der Variationen die im Forschungsprozess entstanden, sind die Studien mit Fotos kombiniert.*

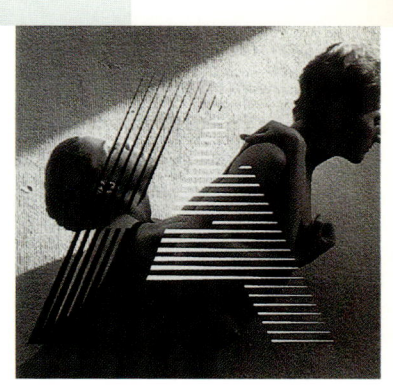

✦ Project: Combine two letterforms that, while retaining the original identity of each letter, merge into a new single unit sharing equally the unique formal characteristics of the other. Then each student explores a variety of formal mutations. During this exploration, generic subject matter such as music, architecture and technology is identified and appropriate formal adjustments are made to enhance the meaning. ✳ Das Projekt: Kombiniere zwei Buchstaben, damit sie in einer neuen Einheit verschmelzen, wobei die Identität der beiden Buchstaben und deren einzigartiger formaler Charakter erhalten bleiben sollen. Danach experiementiert jeder Student mit einer Anzahl formaler Veränderungen. Während dieser »Erforschung«, werden gattungsbezogene Inhalte wie Musik, Architektur und Technologie in die Gestaltung integriert.

✎ *Final series on the integration of photography, typography and abstract visual language. The goal is to experience how form and content are qualified and enhanced by creating specific content.*
✿ *Serie über die Integration von Fotografie, Typografie und abstrakter visueller Sprache. Das Ziel ist es, herauszufinden, in wie weit Form und Inhalt durch die Kreation eines spezifischen Inhalts mehr Qualität erlangen und erhöht werden.*

♥ Teal Triggs Contributing Editor

Niall Sweeney Student   **126**

Bastard Metropolis Title ★ Installation Medium
✱ London College of Printing College ✱ Great Britain Country
✱ Teal Triggs Professor

✳ The city is a vessel of memory and the city is a labyrinth of ritualized space. We make maps to help us remember and navigate these spaces. This project investigates the symbiotic relationship between this collection of maps that is the city, and those who journey through it. The visual outcome of the »Bastard Metropolis« was installation-based. It uses five slide projectors, cycling at various speeds, together with objects and video derived and constructed from the results of primary research. While the content and sequence of each projector was contrived, the combinations of the 5 projected images at any moment remained random and almost infinitely variable (3,276,800,000 possible combinations). ✤ Die Stadt ist ein Behälter für Erinnerungen, ein Labyrinth aus ritualisiertem Raum. Wir brauchen Pläne, um uns zurechtzufinden und uns zu erinnern. Dieses Projekt untersucht die symbiotische Beziehung zwischen den Plänen, den Städten und den Menschen, die durch sie reisen. Die visuellen Ergebnisse von »Bastard Metropolis« wurden in einer Video-Dia-Collage gezeigt. Fünf Dia-Projektionen, die sich in verschiedenen Geschwindigkeiten bewegten, wurden mit Objekten und Videos kombiniert und überlagert. Dadurch entstanden 3.276.800.000 mögliche Bildkombinationen.

Nagisa Otsubo Student **127**

♥ Hans van Dijk Contributing Editor

Waterfire Title ✱ Poster Medium ✤ Rhode Island School of Design College ✿
USA Country ✤ Nancy Skolo Professor

Childhood | Kinderjahre Title ❖ Map | Plan Medium ‖ 4 Study Year
GH Kassel College ✳ Germany Country ☆ Uta Schneider Professor

Petra Schultze Student 128

✳ »The aim of this work is to reconstruct childhood – the first eight years
of life that you no longer have a clear picture of. The material for this search
comes from family photos, magazines and dictionaries from these years.
The pictures and words I found form a timeless landscape. The associative
interaction of the components is the decisive moment.«

❖ »Ausgangspunkt dieser Arbeit ist die Suche nach der Kindheit, den ersten acht
Lebensjahren, von denen man kein klares Bild mehr hat. Das Material für diese
Suche sind Fotos meiner Familie, Zeitschriften, Magazine und Wörterbücher dieser
Jahre. Die gefundenen Bilder und Begriffe bilden eine Erinnerungslandschaft, die
sich nicht zeitlich oder thematisch gliedern lässt. Das assoziative Zusammenspiel der
Komponenten ist das entscheidende Moment.«

Pictograms for a Zoo | Piktogramme für einen Zoo Title ◆ **Illustration** Project
✳ 2 Study Year ✳ **Notre Dame University, Beirut** College ✧ **Lebanon** Country
◇ **John Kortbawi, Yara Khoury** Professors

129

Hala Bou Akl Student

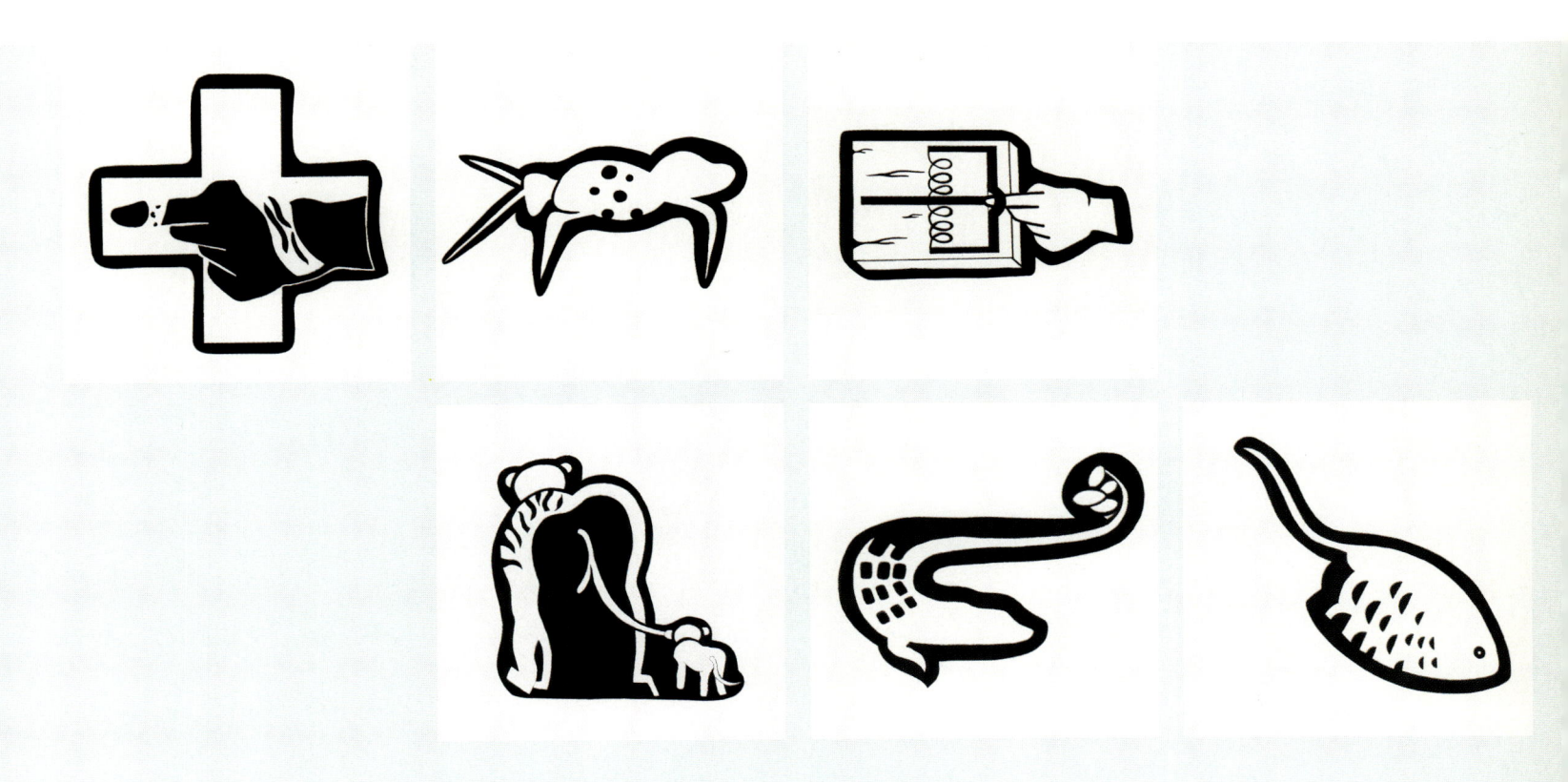

◇ The aim was to develop pictograms for a zoo's signage system. The texture of the animals' skin or fur became the common design element between the illustrations. ✳ Aufgabe war es, Piktogramme für ein Orientierungssystem für einen Zoo zu entwerfen. Als gemeinsames Gestaltungselement für die Zeichen wurde die Oberfläche der Haut bzw. des Fells der Tiere gewählt.

Ole Kaleschke, Martin Rollmann, Jan Schmitt Students

Dispatch | Nachschub Title ✜ **Instant Newspaper** | Instant Zeitung
Projekt ✦ **3** Study Year ✦ **HfK Bremen** College ✡ **Germany** Country ✳
Peter Rea, Nick Kapica Professors

✳ For the three-day design and art conference »profile intermedia 2« in Bremen, a documentation was produced of events and contributions. Each issue was made at the visitors' disposal within just a few hours of inception. All of the 1,500 participants received a »dispatch box« at the beginning of the conference that was to be filled over the course of the event. Individual issues of the conference newspaper could be picked up directly from their point of production in the conference hall's foyer. While one issue was being produced and printed, the editorial content of the next edition was already being prepared. ✜ Für die dreitägige Design- und Kunstkonferenz »profile intermedia 2« in Bremen sollte eine Dokumentation der Beiträge und Veranstaltungen erstellt werden, die den Besuchern bereits nach wenigen Stunden zur Verfügung stehen sollte. Jeder der 1.500 Teilnehmer erhielt zu Beginn der Konferenz eine »Nachschub-Box«, die es im Laufe der Veranstaltung zu füllen galt. Die einzelnen Ausgaben der Konferenzzeitung konnten direkt am Produktionsstandort im Foyer der Messehalle abgeholt werden. Während eine Ausgabe produziert und gedruckt wurde, wurde die folgende Ausgabe bereits redaktionell vorbereitet.

CD Desktop Soundspace *Title* ❖ Interactive *Medium* ◆
3 *Study Year* ◆ Cranbrook Academy of Art *College* ✿ USA *Country* ✽
Laurie Haycock Makela *Professor*

✢ Desktop CD-player interface
🏛 Interface zum Abspielen von Musik-CD's auf dem Computer
○ more on the CD :output screen design
🏛 mehr auf der CD :output screen design

131 Carla Y. Diana *Student*

Journey *Title* ✳ Interactive *Medium* ✿ 3 *Study Year* ◆
Manchester Metropolitan University *College* ✳ Great Britain *Country* ✯
Eric Gristwood *Professor*

◆ Text/image/sound collage with personal imagery, using text from tomato and music off the »Romeo and Juliet« soundtrack.
❖ Text-Bild-Ton-Collage mit eigenen Bildern, Texten von tomato und Musik aus dem Soundtrack zu dem Film »Romeo und Julia«.
🏛 more on the CD :output screen design
✶ mehr auf der CD :output screen design

132

Robert Chiu *Student*

133

Maya C. Drodz *Student*

❖ Two Websites for the Cranbrook Academy of Art
✧ Zwei Websites für die Cranbrook Academy of Art
▶ more on the CD :output screen design
⛿ mehr auf der CD :output screen design

Cranbrook | 2D Design | Paper | Cathode, 4817 Concord *Titles* ✳ Website *Medium*
❖ 2 *Study Year* ● Cranbrook Academy of Art *College* ▶ USA *Country* ✿
Laurie Haycock Makela *Professor*

Goldfischbar Title ✴ **Trailer Design** Project ✦ 5 Study Year ✦
FH Wiesbaden College ✴ **Germany** Country ✦ **Rolf Schubert** Professor

✴ Sound and image installation for a bar
✦ Ton- und Bild-Installation für eine Bar
▶ more on the CD :output screen design
♯ mehr auf der CD :output screen design

Constanze Fries Student

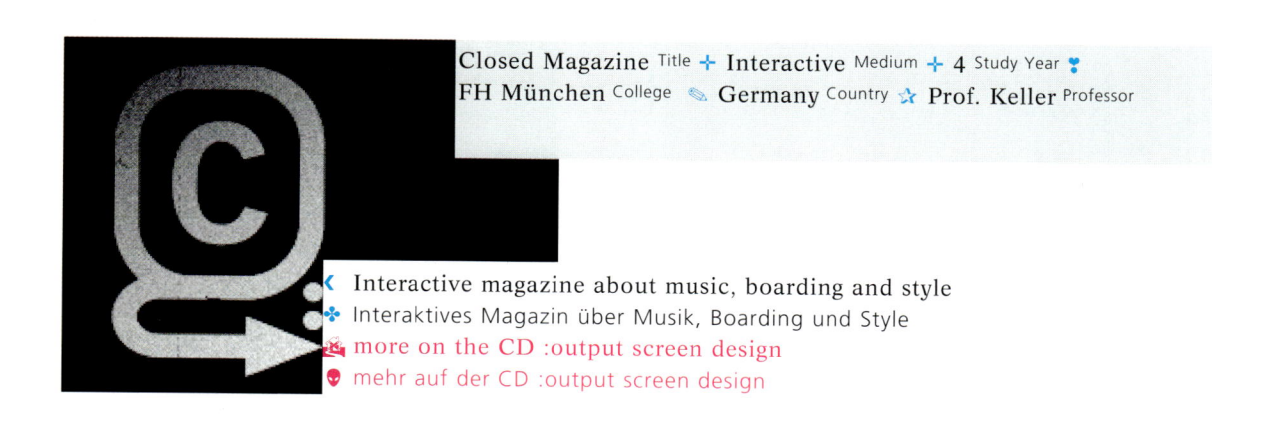

134

Peter Nitsch Student **135**

Closed Magazine Title ✦ **Interactive** Medium ✦ 4 Study Year ✦
FH München College ✦ **Germany** Country ✦ **Prof. Keller** Professor

◀ Interactive magazine about music, boarding and style
✦ Interaktives Magazin über Musik, Boarding und Style
▶ more on the CD :output screen design
♥ mehr auf der CD :output screen design

One Moment ^{Title} ❖ Interactive ^{Medium} ✲ University of Technology, Sydney ^{College} ❖ Australia ^{Country} ✶ Chris Browman ^{Professor}

James Hancock ^{Student} **136**

✴ Interactive CD-ROM about the experience of the fictional figure Martin, who is a metaphor for all human consciousness.
✳ Interaktive CD-ROM über die Erlebnisse der fiktiven Figur Martin, die eine Metapher für das menschliche Bewusstsein ist.
▸ more on the CD :output screen design
☃ mehr auf der CD :output screen design

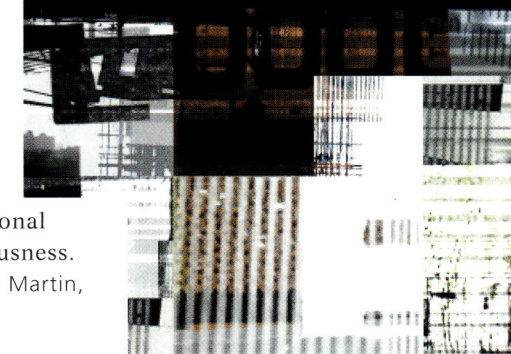

137 **Stefanie Barth** ^{Student}

✴ Music Visual is a graphic approach to minimal electronic music.
◆ Music Visual ist eine grafische Annäherung an minimalistische elektronische Musik.
🎥 more on the CD :output screen design
👽 mehr auf der CD :output screen design

Music Visual ^{Title} ✚ Moving Image ^{Medium} ✚ 4 ^{Study Year} ❣ HfG Offenbach ^{College} 🍃 Germany ^{Country} ✰ Lars Müller ^{Professor}

♥ Robyn Stacey Contributing Editor

Re: design Title (Interactive Medium ✶ 4 Study Year ❑
University of Western Sydney College ▲ Australia Country ❑
Robyn Stacey Professor

) Educational interactive and website developed to be integrated into the graphic design sector of the Visual Design Course for high school students in the 12th grade.
✧ Interaktives Lernprogramm und Website über Grafik-Design für High School Studenten in der 12. Klasse
▶ more on the CD :output screen design
⚥ mehr auf der CD :output screen design

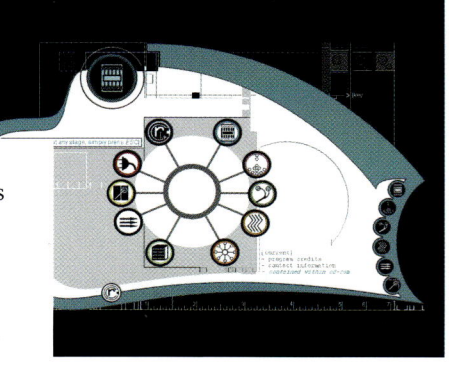

Melanie Halliwell Student

138

139

Carla Y. Diana Student

Wide Open Title ✚ Interactive Medium ✧ 3 Study Year ✧
Cranbrook Academy of Art College ❦ USA Country ✤
Laurie Haycock Makela Professor

✶ Dynamic, graphical interpretation of the music from the Wide Open music CD by Laurie Haycock Makela and Skooby
✤ Dynamische, grafische Interpretation der Musik der Wide Open Musik-CD von Laurie Haycock Makela und Skooby
▶ more on the CD :output screen design
⚥ mehr auf der CD :output screen design

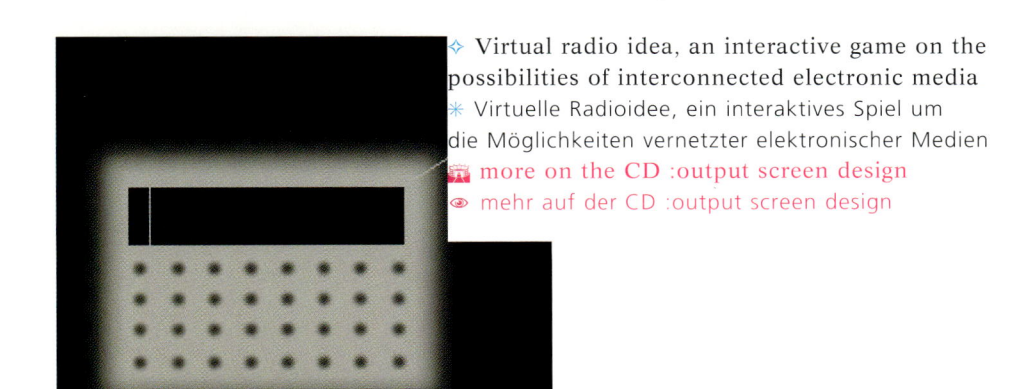

◇ Virtual radio idea, an interactive game on the possibilities of interconnected electronic media
✳ Virtuelle Radioidee, ein interaktives Spiel um die Möglichkeiten vernetzter elektronischer Medien
🎦 more on the CD :output screen design
👁 mehr auf der CD :output screen design

Dominik Mycielski Student

140

Audible | Hörbar Title ✛ Interactive Medium ✛ 6 Study Year ❣ FH Düsseldorf College ✎ Germany Country ✯ Philipp Teufel, Stefan Nowak Professor

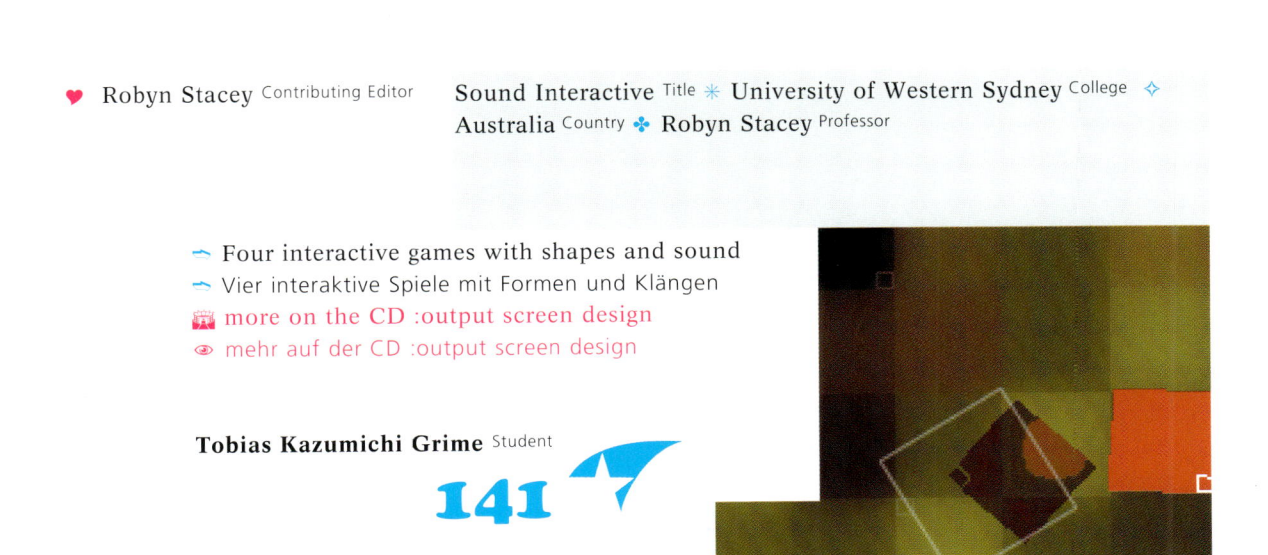

♥ Robyn Stacey Contributing Editor   Sound Interactive Title ✳ University of Western Sydney College ◇ Australia Country ✤ Robyn Stacey Professor

⌒ Four interactive games with shapes and sound
⌒ Vier interaktive Spiele mit Formen und Klängen
🎦 more on the CD :output screen design
👁 mehr auf der CD :output screen design

Tobias Kazumichi Grime Student

141

Vanessa K. Enriquez Student

142

Intersections, Nothing To Say Titles ✴ Interactive Medium
2 Study Year ❤ Yale School of Art College ✯ USA Country ✳
Paul Elliman, Michael Rock Professors

don't fight forces
use them

➷ Interactive poetry
✴ Interaktive Gedichte
🎬 more on the CD :output screen design
👁 mehr auf der CD :output screen design

143

Hide and Seek | Verstecken und Suchen Title ✺ Interactive Medium
✚ 4 Study Year ✤ Minneapolis College of Art and Design College ✺ USA Country ✳
Piotr Szyhalski, Sean McKay Professor

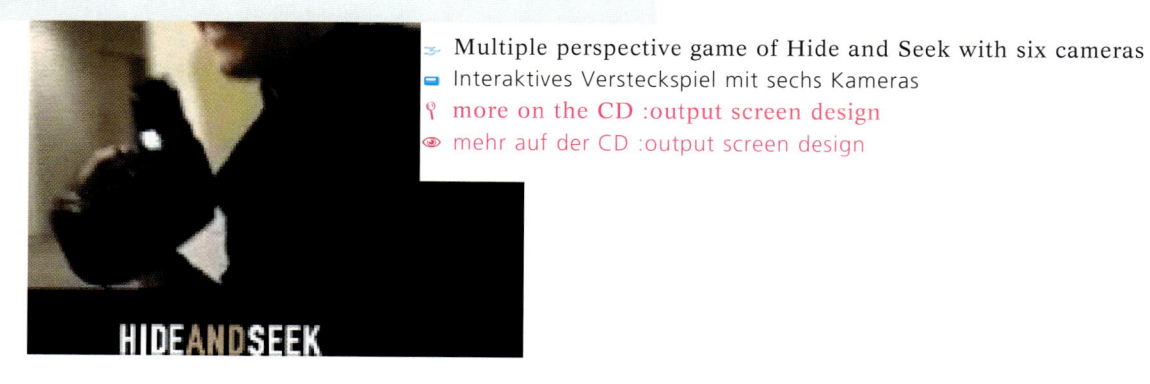

Jon Thomas, Kai-Roman Schöttle Students

Multiple perspective game of Hide and Seek with six cameras
Interaktives Versteckspiel mit sechs Kameras
more on the CD :output screen design
mehr auf der CD :output screen design

HIDEANDSEEK

f.i.n.d.[x]. Title Databank User Interface Project ‖ 6 Study Year
FH Schwäbisch Gmünd College Germany Country Jürgen Hofmann Professor

* Beta-versions of a user interface for research software
◇ Beta Version einer grafisch gestützen Recherchesoftware
 more on the CD :output screen design
•• mehr auf der CD :output screen design

144

Andreas Zeischegg, Dirk Bader, Gerd Häußler Students

145 Sebastian Lemm Student

* Cinematic Light/Letterform Installation
* Filmische Licht-Buchstaben Installation
 more on the CD :output screen design
 mehr auf der CD :output screen design

Between Spatial and Planar View | Zwischen Raum- und Bildansicht Title
Moving Image Medium 6 Study Year HfK Berlin College Germany Country
Holger Matthies Professor

>>>>>>>>>>>>>>>>>>>>>>>>>>>>>>>>>>>>>>>Advertising>>Werbung>>>>>>>>>>>>>
<<<<Works<<Arbeiten<<<<<<<<<<<<<<<<<<<<<<<<<<<<<<<<<<<<<<<<<<<<<

profile intermedia 3

the international conference on the crossover in design, art, architecture, photography, film, video, performance and music

1 2 3 dezember 2000
messe centrum bremen

fusion:
integration von x + y = formel für veränderung

gäste bereits zugesagt:
- **gert dumbar** opening speaker (nl) mensch + maschine – specially early french motorcycles + the dumbar ideology
- **studio dumbar** (nl) architektur + graphik
- **diane gromala** (usa) virtual reality + die nächste dimension
- **ken and eleanor hiebert** (usa) emotionen + computer
- **stanislaus kadingdi**
- **kwame sam** (ghana, africa) erziehung + zukunft
- **tadanori nagasawa** (jp) 'cultural engineering' + medien
- **raman v raman** (india) bollywood + fusion + musik
- **jeffrey shaw** (d) musik + farben + computer
- **sara saba** (lebanon) orient + okzident
- **tomato** (gb) under (the) world + video

young blood, new innovators:
- **die jüngeren** (hamburg) curiosity + sub-cultures
- **the internet and your net** (berlin)
- **artificial environments** (london)
- **integrated design** (hfk bremen)

special guest:
wolfgang weingart (ch) zweideutigkeit + kommunikation – the most influential typographic design teacher of the 1970s and 80s – prepared the ground for the new type + image of europe and north america

'eye to eye' interview:
- **yvonne schwemer-scheddin**
- **anna berkenbusch** (d) journalistin + lehrerin

special events:
1 2 3 dezember 2000
profile fair intermedia messe in bremen
profile revelation kunst + design exhibition: persönliche visionen + neue ideen
profile kino forum für film + video
media lounge profile relax + workshops

1. bis 10. dezember 2000: profile festival
profile filmfest bremer filmkunstkinos präsentieren ein filmprogramm zum thema 'fusion'
profile concert performance + musik 'live on stage'

tickets + info:
ab 28 11 00 professionelle dm 750/studenten dm 350
reduced prices for early bookers:
bis 29 10 00 professionelle dm 480/studenten dm 180
30 10 00 bis 27 11 00 professionelle dm 580/studenten dm 250
spezielle gruppenpreise erfahren sie über die hotline
simultanübersetzung deutsch + englisch

kontakt:
hotline +49 (0)421 791 88 13
infofax +49 (0)421 70 10 13
info@profile-intermedia.de
www.profile-intermedia.de

konzept + planung + design:
evhide aydogdu, kathrin natterer, katrin wellmitz, patrick woiciechowski
prof. peter rea
doz. nick kapica
kanzler klaus güse

veranstalter: Hochschule für Künste Bremen
unterstützt von: Rat für Formgebung / German Design Council
mit freundlicher unterstützung von: MESSE BREMEN GMBH, Deutsche Telekom, SCHNEIDERSÖHNE PAPIER, ASCO, HEADLINE

obwohl vom veranstalter nicht beabsichtigt, behält dieser sich vor, unvorangekündigte änderungen im programm und im programmablauf vorzunehmen.

MetaDesign | create | future | value

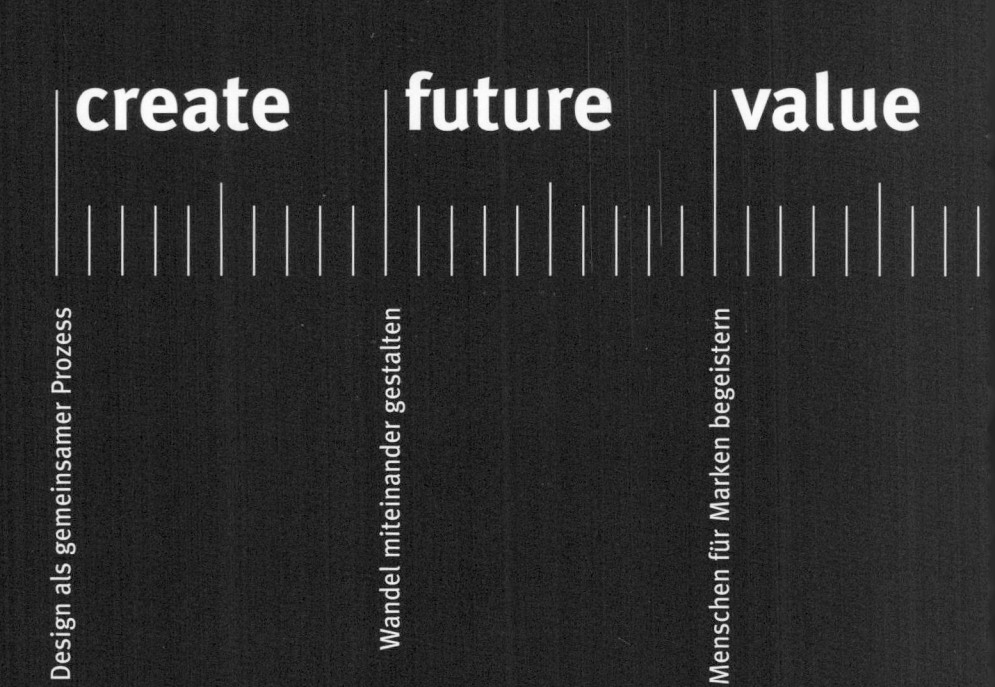

Design als gemeinsamer Prozess

Wandel miteinander gestalten

Menschen für Marken begeistern

MetaDesign AG
Berlin San Francisco Zürich
+49 · 30 · 695 79 · 236
fax +49 · 30 · 695 79 · 311
query@metadesign.de
www.metadesign.com

Creativity, Ideas, Innovation

2nd Leitz Innovation Design Award

Interested in letting your fantasy run wild, without limitations or constraints? Would you like to win an award or, at the very least, gain experience in competitions? If so, then it's time for you to participate in the 2nd Leitz Innovation & Design Award.

We're looking for new product ideas: products to optimise and facilitate organisation, filing, searching, archiving and presenting. Solutions that will positively influence the entire working process. Creative ideas that will serve to improve organisation while enhancing motivation.

You can submit ideas for products, product lines, whole organisational systems or even suggestions for relevant services. New products can be designed, or existing products and designs can be optimised. As long as truly innovative thinking is the take-off point. Unrestricted in terms of category and free to roam within the boundaries of an all-encompassing theme: today's and tomorrow's office world (corporate, home or mobile).

Students and young professionals are eligible to participate in the competition. Monetary awards amounting to DM 50,000 will be available to reward your efforts. We'll be pleased to send you further information and a complete participation documentation package.

Deadline for submissions is February 28th, 2001.

Our partners are:

Rat für Formgebung
German Design Council

Fraunhofer Institut Arbeitswirtschaft und Organisation

To order more detailed information and participation documentation, please contact:

Roth Lohre Lorenz GmbH
2nd Leitz Innovation & Design Award
Waldburgstrasse 17/19
D-70563 Stuttgart
Telephone hotline: +49 (0) 711 / 901 40 39
e-mail: leitz@rll.de
Internet: www.leitz.com

LEITZ®

godz

Z.
ZANDERS

INTERNATIONAL PAPER

Hier sehen Sie,
womit wir uns täglich beschäftigen: mit herausragenden Feinpapieren. Mit Werkstoffen, die Kreative gerne veredeln. Und wir beschäftigen uns mit Ihnen. Ihre Anregungen helfen uns, gutes Feinpapier noch besser zu machen. Mailen Sie uns: info@zanders.de.
Erwarten Sie etwas mehr von uns.

Thank you ... ♥)

♥) :output 03 wurde
gedruckt auf
ZANDERS Mega matt
und ikono silk

www.zanders.de

>>>Happy End>>>>>>>>>>>

<<<<<<Advertising<<Werbung<<<<<<<<<<<<<<<<<<<<<<<<<<<<<<<<<<<<<<<<<<<

www.german-design-council.de

Leading to Design.

Rat für Formgebung
German Design Council

Frankfurt   Berlin   New York   Nagoya   St. Moritz   Tampere   Daressalam   Perth   St. Petersburg   Montevideo

This / Dieses has been / wurde planned / geplant

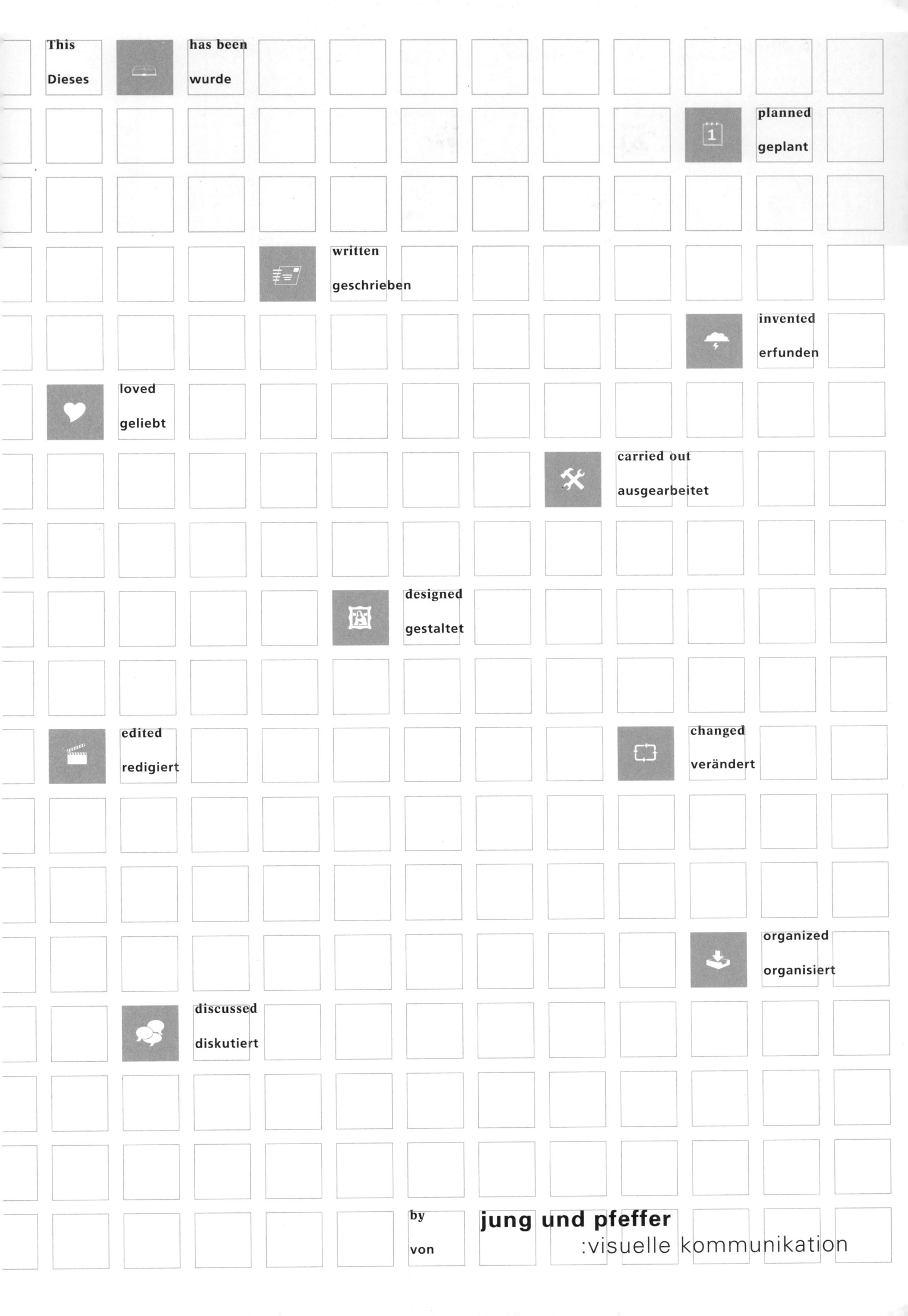

written / geschrieben

invented / erfunden

loved / geliebt

carried out / ausgearbeitet

designed / gestaltet

edited / redigiert changed / verändert

organized / organisiert

discussed / diskutiert

by / von **jung und pfeffer**
:visuelle kommunikation

Student List

Christine Akmakji 95
Fanar Main Street
Fanar, Lebanon
fon +961 (0)3 34 48 66
tentoun@hotmail.com

Doreen Ambrosius 91
Randersackererstr. 16
97072 Würzburg
Germany
fon/fax +49 (0)931 78 14 41
doram@01019freenet.de

Paul Arnot 39
c/o **University of Reading**

Claudia Atencia 6, 76
48 Ft. Greene Fl., Apt. 4
Brooklyn NY
11217 USA
fon +1 718 62 56 889
catencia@hotmail.com

Tarek Atrissi 77
c/o **American University of Beirut**

Dirk Bader 144
Bruchweisenstr. 22
73110 Hattenhofen
Germany
fon +49 (0)7164 43 73
dirkbader@web.de

Julia Baier 16
Herzberger Str. 21
28205 Bremen
Germany
fon +49 (0)421 4 98 43 36
maybe_mail@gmx.de

Fadi Baki 71
P.O. Box 11-0236/2107
American University of Beirut
Department of Architecture and Design
Beirut, Lebanon
fon +961 (3) 68 97 25
dyezer@yahoo.com

Ludovic Balland 82
Klybeckstr. 58
4057 Basel
Switzerland
fon/fax +41 (0)61 6 92 59 62
l.balland@datacomm.ch

Rania Baltagi 3
c/o **American University of Beirut**
fon +961 (0)1 74 15 16
rania_baltagi@hotmail.com

Stefanie Barth 137
Windmühlstr. 4
60329 Frankfurt a.M.
Germany
mobile +49 (0)172 69 28 158
fon/fax +49 (0)69 23 29 02
stefaniebarth@iname.com

Markus Baude 57
c/o **Kunsthochschule Kassel**

Kirstin Bauer 46
Brehmstr. 3
81543 München
Germany
mobile +49 (0)179 5 94 13 35
fon/fax +49 (0)89 65 11 31 19
k.bauer@argonauten.de

Norbert Bayer 57
c/o **Kunsthochschule Kassel**

Jana Behrendt 10
c/o **FH Düsseldorf**

Tobias Bender 122
c/o krænk
spezialklinik für gestaltung
Ober-Ramstädter Str. 96g
64367 Mühltal
Germany
fon +49 (0)6151 60 63 36
fax +49 (0)6151 60 63 37
bender@kraenk.de
www.kraenk.de

Bettina Berg 121
c/o **University of the Arts, Philadelphia**

Liu Bin 80
c/o Shanghai Light Industry College
fon +86 20 83 59 98 59
fax +86 20 83 59 62 34
xu@wangxu.com.cn

Nikolaus Birk 57
c/o **Kunsthochschule Kassel**

Cosima Böck 14
Kemmelbergstr. 8
70374 Stuttgart
Germany
fon +49 (0)711 5 28 36 51
cosima.boeck@abk-stuttgart.de

Guido Böhm 59
Kaiser-Wilhelm-Ring 61
55118 Mainz
Germany
fon/fax +49 (0)6131 67 57 10
guidoboehm@coffein.de

Hala Bou Akl 129
Achrafie, Sassine St., Jaqueese Bd.
Beirut, Lebanon
fon +961 (0)3 69 23 38
eyecon@xnet.com.lb

Nicola Brandt 10
c/o **FH Düsseldorf**

Anne Breucha 90
Rhinowerstr. 1
10437 Berlin
Germany
fon +49 (0)30 47 37 48 36
anne@grotesk.de

Karen Buermann 44
Werderstr. 57
68165 Mannheim
Germany
fon +49 (0)621 41 86 0 37
k.buermann@t-online.de

Gisela Burkhalter 53
Hebelstr. 104
4056 Basel
Switzerland
fon/fax +41 (0)61 3 21 60 47
gisela.burkhalter@unibas.ch

Heike Burkhardt 37
Birkenstr. 30
28816 Stuhr
Germany
fon +49 (0)421 80 30 30
burkhardt@incorporate.de

David Cabianca 2
c/o **Cranbrook Academy of Art**
fon +1 248 645 3365
fax +1 734 763 2322
cabianca@umich.edu

Nadine Chahine 79
P.O. Box 11-0236/073
American University of Beirut
Department of Architecture and Design
Beirut, Lebanon
fon +961 (0)1 56 00 97
nchahine@excite.com

Ali Cherry 89
c/o **American University of Beirut**

Robert Chiu 132
77 Norwood Road
Birkby
Huddersfield, HD2 2YD
Great Britain
mobile +44 (0)958 975 046
fon +44 (0)1484 534 067
ronin@xmail.com

P.J. Chmiel 27
622 Raleigh Ave. #2
Norfolk VA
23507 USA
fon +1 757 622 6069
pj_chmiel@usa.net

So-Hyon Choe 63
c/o **HdK Berlin**

Rena Chrysikopoulou 57
c/o **Kunsthochschule Kassel**

Candice S. Davidian 87
Jonieh
P.O. Box 1174
Beirut, Lebanon
fon +961 (0)3 60 18 75
candice@dm.net.lb

Katrin Degenkolb 42
Adlerstr. 7
88212 Ravensburg
Germany
fon +49 (0)751 3 54 14 88
k_degenkolb@hotmail.com

Carla Y. Diana 131, 139
c/o **Cranbrook Academy of Art**
fon +1 248 842 7523
carla_diana@hotmail.com

Anke Dievernich 10
c/o **FH Düsseldorf**

Maya C. Drodz 133
c/o **Cranbrook Academy of Art**
fon +1 248 645 3336
maya@specula.org

Simona El Khoury 18, 55
Slave Dekouaneh
Beirut, Lebanon
fon +961 (0)1 69 22 20
fax +961 (0)1 69 22 21

Ziad El Khoury 67
P.O. Box 11-0236/1611
American University of Beirut
Department of Architecture and Design
Beirut, Lebanon
fon +961 (0)4 9 25 92
revolution@hotmail.com

Vanessa K. Enriquez 142
265 College Street 7A
New Haven CT
06510 USA
fon +1 203 865 52 85
vankare@yahoo.com

Susanne Erdmann 10
c/o **FH Düsseldorf**

Ozan Erdogan 94
c/o **Mimar Sinan Üniversitesi, Istanbul**
fon +90 212 252 16 00/265

Katharina Fiedler 57
c/o **Kunsthochschule Kassel**

Annette Forsch 123
Bahnhofstr. 2b
55116 Mainz
Germany
fon +49 (0)6131 23 72 24
forsch@km-net.de

Constanze Fries 134
Sandgasse 28
63739 Aschaffenburg
Germany
mobile +49 (0)177 6 62 27 75
fon/fax +49 (0)6021 58 12 82
constanze@variovision.de

Christiane Grauert 20
1501 N. Farwell Ave., Apt. 5
Milwaukee WI
53202 USA
fon +1 414 273 4538
c_grauert@hotmail.com

Isabell Große Holtforth 74, 103
Buschfeld 36
46499 Hamminkeln
Germany
i.grosseholtforth@gmx.de

Ilona Grunau 84
Kirchstr. 56
40227 Düsseldorf
Germany
mobile +49 (0)170 4 22 59 03
fon +49 (0)211 7 88 15 31
dreihexen@hotmail.com

Christina Gschwantner 68, 119
Kaiserstr. 64/8
1070 Wien
Austria
fon +43 (0)1 5 24 79 55
weichtier@hotmail.com

Julia Guther 29
Rosenthaler Str. 19
10119 Berlin
Germany
fon +49 (0)30 28 09 07 01
julia.guther@fhtw-berlin.de

Melanie Halliwell 138
CADRE Design
P.O. Box 305
Westmead NSW
2145 Australia
fon +61 2 9685 9743
mobile +61 (0)407 92 82 83
melanie@cadre.com.au

James Hancock 136
7 Stack St. Balmain
Sydney NSW
2041 Australia
fon +61 2 9818 1129
fax +61 2 9555 1157
hancockjames@hotmail.com

Ingrid Haug 56
Münchener Str. 10
60329 Frankfurt a.M.
Germany
fon +49 (0)69 24 24 95 58
fax +49 (0)69 24 24 66 83
ingrid@surface.de

Gerd Häußler 144
Ortsstr. 62
89081 Ulm
Germany
fon +49 (0)7304 79 84
haeussler-g@hfg-gmuend.de

Jan Haux 83
Kriegsstr. 274
76135 Karlsruhe
Germany
fon +49 (0)721 85 45 00
fax +49 (0)721 8 20 32 00
jhaux@hfg-karlsruhe.de

Eva Heibl 15, 111
Seidengasse 27/1/6
1070 Wien
Austria
fon +43 (0)1 5 22 88 02
efricola@hotmail.com

Julia Henning 57
c/o **Kunsthochschule Kassel**

Willem Heskes 102
c/o **London College of Printing**

Kazem Heydari 10
c/o **FH Düsseldorf**

Meike Hoffmann 84
Fürstenwall 37
40219 Düsseldorf
Germany
fon +49 (0)211 3 17 94 83
dreihexen@hotmail.com

Cornelia Hofmann 97
Ziegeleiweg 11
09355 Gersdorf
Germany
fon +49 (0)37203 46 49
c_hofmann@hotmail.com

Stefanie Hofmann 12
Fasanenstr. 13
71131 Jettingen
Germany
fon +49 (0)7452 7 63 93
stefanie.hofmann@merz-akademie.de

Daniel Holmes 11
4737 Orion Ave. 21
Sherman Oaks CA
91403 USA
danielholmes@hotmail.com

Simone Holzberg 10
c/o **FH Düsseldorf**

Stefanie Huber 1, 31
Ritterstr. 170
47805 Krefeld
Germany
fon +49 (0)2151 61 17 65
hust0001@fh-niederrhein.de

Sohn Ik-Weon 64
#2-301, Baekcho Apt., 859-3(24/2)
Chakchon-dong, Kyeyang-gu
Inchon 407-062
Korea
fon +82 2 320 1214
fon +82 32 544 8303
fax +82 2 744 3251
shon95@chollian.net

Hatem Imam 35, 116
P.O. Box 11-0236/1321
American University of Beirut
Department of Architecture and Design
Beirut, Lebanon
fon +961 (0)3 83 86 72
hawzers@hotmail.com

Elena Isaeva 60
c/o **Alexandra Ostrovskaya**

Ellen Jacoby 81
ellenjacoby@hotmail.com

Lembu Wiworo Jati 72
Jl. Jembatan II/5 Condet Balekambang
Jakarta
13530 Indonesia
fon +62 (0)21 800 0291
fax +62 (0)21 3190 0279
lembulucu@hotmail.com

Jennifer Jenkins 21
2310 Harriet Ave. #106
Minneapolis MN
55405 USA
fon +1 612 870 8307
jennyjenkins@earthlink.net

Berit Kaiser 37, 108
Brunnenstr. 25b
10119 Berlin
Germany
fon +49 (0)30 44 04 14 89
berit@moniteurs.de

Ole Kaleschke 47, 130
Uhlandstr. 1d
28211 Bremen
Germany
fon +49 (0)421 7 94 89 96
ole@kaleschke.de

Tobias Kazumichi Grime 141
P.O. Box A2384
Sydney South NSW
2000 Australia
mobile +61 (0)412 030 177
fon +61 2 9383 4800
fax +61 2 9383 4801
toby@ebom.org

Peter Kienzle 109
33 Lexington Ave., Apt. 1
Brooklyn NY
11238 USA
fon +1 917 202 3243
peter_kie@hotmail.com

Doreen Kiepsel 70, 117
Werftstr. 214
24134 Kiel
Germany
fon +49 (0)431 70 29 98 24
fax +49 (0)431 70 29 98 88
d.kiepsel@comcity.de
www.comcity.de

Hyun-Soo Kim 40
310 E23 St. #7H
New York NY
10010 USA
fon +1 646 602 2102
empirewindow@hotmail.com

Tanja Kirschner 123
Mittenwalderstr. 57
10961 Berlin
Germany
fon +49 (0)40 22 52 16
fon +49 (0)40 43 21 20 19
tanja_kirschner@jvm.de

Thomas Klöß 30
Florastr. 3
97072 Würzburg
Germany
fon +49 (0)931 7 84 55 42
scholle2000@hotmail.com

Stephanie Kluck 114
Kettelerstr. 48
48147 Münster
Germany
fon +49 (0)251 29 65 96
stkluck@gmx.de

Bethany Koby 107, 110
11 Arnold Street
Providence RI
02903 USA
fon +1 401 954 8361
fax +1 909 595 9631
bkoby@risd.edu

Sonja Köhler 115
Weseler Str. 50
48151 Münster
Germany
fon +49 (0)251 6 74 28 60
fax +49 (0)251 6 74 29 08
madels@xoommail.com

Anita Kolb 33
Robertstr. 15
51105 Köln
Germany
fon +49 (0)221 87 99 37
anitakolb@hotmail.com

Stefani Konrad 25
Plateniusstr. 18
42105 Wuppertal
Germany
fon +49 (0)202 3 09 63 42
stefani.konrad@t-online.de

Daniela Koza 10
c/o **FH Düsseldorf**

Anja Kramps 10
c/o **FH Düsseldorf**

Adrian Krell 83
c/o **Jan Haux**

Uta Krogmann 51
Werderstr. 70
76137 Karlsruhe
Germany
fon +49 (0)721 3 84 16 18
ukro@gmx.de

Kristiane Krüger 57
c/o **Kunsthochschule Kassel**

Jan Kruse 75
Eppendorfer Weg 117
20259 Hamburg
Germany
fon +49 (0)40 4 91 81 08
jan@factordesign.com

Henrik Kubel 34
c/o **Royal College of Art**
fon +44 (0)171 59 04 122
fax +44 (0)171 59 04 500
h.kubel@rca.ac.uk

Joana Lai 28
Rm 3, 20/F Hin Tsui Hse
Kai Tsui Court, 16 Siu Sai Wan Rd.
Chai Wan, Hong Kong
fon +852 25 05 92 81
joanna@hphk.com

Friederike Lambers 85
Ostendorpstr. 26
28203 Bremen
Germany
fon +49 (0)421 7 94 83 72
fredlambers@hotmail.com

Viola Läufer 92
c/o Atelier Krippner
Ober-Ramstädter Str. 96 / F3
64367 Mühltal-Darmstadt
Germany
fon +49 (0)6151 14 71 25
violal@stud.fh-frankfurt.de

Charalampos Lazos 118
Hügelstr. 24a
64283 Darmstadt
Germany
fon +49 (0)6151 29 38 27

Michael Lechner 7
1206 3rd St. NE
Minneapolis MN
55413 USA
fon +1 612 623 8862

Cass Lee 8
Rm 204 Hang On House
Wo Lok Est, Kwn Tong
Hong Kong
fon +852 23 43 00 59
casslee@netrigator.com

Chae Lee 121
c/o **University of the Arts, Philadelphia**

Pion Lee 19
Flat 3206, Kam Ling House
Kam Fung Court
Man On Shan NT
Hong Kong
fon +852 26 92 33 74
sbb@innocent.com

Birgit Lehner 10
c/o **FH Düsseldorf**

Kristin Leichtl 57
c/o **Kunsthochschule Kassel**

Sebastian Lemm 145
c/o atelier 41
Bundesallee 89
12161 Berlin
Germany
mobile +49 (0)171 6 81 90 52
fon +49 (0)30 85 99 61 12
fax +49 (0)39 85 99 61 20
atelier41@aol.com

Sibylle Lenz 44
Rosinenstr. 18
49201 Dissen
Germany
fon +49 (0)5421 93 34 44
fax +49 (0)5421 93 34 46
Lenz@lichtweisz.de

Daniel Leung 41
Rm 2814, Wan Lai House
Wan Tau Tong Est, Tai Po
Hong Kong
fon +852 26 56 03 83
papadaniel@netscape.net

Nicole Liekenbröcker 10
c/o **FH Düsseldorf**

Dionysios Livanis 102
c/o **London College of Printing**

Britta Lorch 57
c/o **Kunsthochschule Kassel**

Martin Lorenz 122
malo2000@hotmail.com

Zhi-Zhong Lue 98
3F-3, #2, Lane 204, Kuangfu S. Rd.
Taipei 106
Taiwan
fon +886 2 274 8489
fax +886 2 2731 9318
ashit1207@kimo.com.tw

Cecil Mariani 23
Lebak Lestari Indah N/32
Jakarta 12440
Indonesia
fon +62 (0)21 750 1697
Plato@indosat.net.id

Nadim Matta 102
c/o **London College of Printing**

Stefanie Matter 73
Muldenweg 23
99099 Erfurt
Germany
fon +49 (0)30 88 67 95 81
1stmatter@gmx.de

Matthias Megyeri 83
c/o **Jan Haux**

Marcus Meyer 16
Kurfürstenalle 32
28211 Bremen
Germany
mobile +49 (0)177 32 62 450
fon/fax +49 (0)421 4 99 26 64
maybe_mail@gmx.de

Susanne Meyer-Götz 10
Hüttenstr. 29
40215 Düsseldorf
Germany
mobile +49 (0)170 9 82 03 14
su_meyergoetz@hotmail.com

Natascha Miteva-Efremova 10
c/o **FH Düsseldorf**

Christiane Möller 88
Liebigstr. 42
44139 Dortmund
Germany
fon +49 (0)231 1 06 03 02
chmoelle@fasta.fh-dortmund.de

Marco Morosini 4
c/o **Fabrica**

Jörg Morsbach 106
Corneliusstr. 88
40215 Düsseldorf
Germany
fon/fax +49 (0)211 5 14 26 85
Joerg.Morsbach@t-online.de

Dominik Mycielski 140
Grüner Brunnenweg 54
50827 Köln
Germany
fon +49 (0)221 5 30 53 01
dom@grafikbuero.net

Claudia Nachtmann 9
Nunnenbeckstr. 28
90489 Nürnberg
Germany
fon +49 (0)911 5 81 99 59

László Nagy 112
Hősök út 15
2119 Pécel
Hungary
fon +36 6 28 45 40 36

Peter Nitsch 135
Schleißheimer Str. 34
80333 München
Germany
fon +49 (0)89 52 38 98 48
peter@wortkommission.de

Vera Nowottny 65
Daiser Str. 18
81371 München
Germany
fon +49 (0)89 72 05 97 70
fax +49 (0)89 72 05 97 91

Michael David Ochs 57
c/o **Kunsthochschule Kassel**

Alexandra Ostrovskaya 60
Dmitrovskoye Chaussee 43-1-291
Moscow, Russia
fon +7 (0)95 97 69 549
fon +7 (0)95 97 60 557
ostrow@dataforce.net

Nagisa Otsubo 127
c/o **Rhode Island School of Design**

Paolo Palma 17
c/o **Fabrica**

Björn Börris Peters 50
Schubartstr. 29
70190 Stuttgart
Germany
mobile +49 (0)174 9 21 65 88
fon +49 (0)711 6 36 80 00
designklinik@gmx.de

Tanya Pike 66
7 Brereton St. Gladesville
Sydney NSW
2111 Australia
fon +61 (0)410 438 266
tanyapike@hotmail.com

Sebastian Puhze 122
spuhze@hotmail.com

Alejandro Quinto 48
2537 Stevens Ave. S, Apt. 10
Minneapolis MN
55404 USA
fon +1 612 874 3560
alex_quinto@hotmail.com

Aline Raab 10
c/o **FH Düsseldorf**

Maren Rache 47
Kantstr. 107
28201 Bremen
Germany
fon +49 (0)421 53 19 70
fax +49 (0)421 53 20 55

Steffi Rall 57
c/o **Kunsthochschule Kassel**

Martin Rollmann 130
Friedrich-Willhelm-Str. 10
28199 Bremen
Germany
fon +49 (0)421 5 97 75 62
frikassee@hotmail.com

Wattanapol Ruenroeng 100
c/o **University of the Arts, Philadelphia**

Carla Salem 43, 54
P.O. Box 11-0236/0619
American University of Beirut
Department of Architecture and Design
Beirut, Lebanon
fon +961 (0)4 41 13 70
carlasalem@hotmail.com

Marlena Sang 117
Behmstr. 73
10439 Berlin
Germany
mobile +49 (0)179 2 02 13 82
fon +49 (0)30 43 73 48 10
marsang@muthesius.de

Lena Schalén 96
c/o Scherwall
Malmskillnadsgatan 47a
Stockholm 11138
Sweden
fon +46 (0)8 4 11 22 35
lenaschalen@hotmail.com

Natascha Schäfer 44
Bundesstr. 41
33775 Versmold
Germany
fon +49 (0)5421 93 34 44
fax +49 (0)5421 93 34 46
schaefer@lichtweisz.de

Robert Schäfer 124
Friedrichstr. 211-212
10969 Berlin
Germany
fon +49 (0)30 25 29 67 25
fax +49 (0)30 25 29 67 26
robert.schaefer@web.de

Regina Schauerte 30
Julius-Echter-Str. 32
97232 Giebelstadt
Germany
fon +49 (0)9337 9 98 46
reginaschauerte@hotmail.com

Katrin Schlüsener 26
Alexanderstr. 170
70180 Stuttgart
Germany
fon/fax +49 (0)711 60 40 20
k.schluesener@abk-stuttgart.de

Jan Schmitt 130
Schwachhauser Heerstr. 5
28203 Bremen
Germany
fon +49 (0)421 7 94 83 79

Stephan Schmotz 10
c/o **FH Düsseldorf**

Sandra Schmutzenhofer 10
c/o **FH Düsseldorf**

Dima Schneider 102
c/o **London College of Printing**

Kai-Roman Schöttle 143
Frauentorstr. 17
99423 Weimar
Germany
mobile +49 (0)170 78 95 75 86
fon/fax +49 (0)3643 77 18 14
kai@effektschmiede.de

Nils Schrader 10
c/o **FH Düsseldorf**

Sarah Schroeder 84
Kronprinzenstr. 76
40217 Düsseldorf
Germany
mobile +49 (0)170 2 82 02 35
fon +49 (0)211 34 93 60
sarahaudrey@gmx.de
dreihexen@hotmail.com

Petra Schultze 57, 128
Töpfenmarkt 12
34117 Kassel
Germany
fon +49 (0)561 71 98 41

Shau Chung Shin 93
Nieder-Ramstädter Str. 185c
64285 Darmstadt
Germany
fon +49 (0)6151 42 55 88
shauchung@yahoo.com

Kutlay Sindirgi 78
c/o **Mimar Sinan University, Istanbul**

Jayme Smith 125
c/o **University of the Arts, Philadelphia**

Nadine Spachtholz 32
Kämpenstr. 44
45147 Essen
Germany
fon +49 (0)201 73 36 67
fax +49 (0)73 61 57
nadine.spachtholz@uni-essen.de

Anke Stache 13
Hansaring 151
50670 Köln
Germany
fon +49 (0)221 72 62 97
ankestache@aol.com

Ethel Strugalla 10
c/o **FH Düsseldorf**

Niall Sweeney 102, 126
c/o **London College of Printing**

Maike Taddicken 44
Zollweg 3
26446 Friedeburg
Germany
fon +49 (0)4956 99 09 10
helmai@t-online.de

Jon Thomas 143
6566 France Ave. S, Apt. 1101
Edina MN
55435 USA
jonmaichelthomas@hotmail.com

Jan Tittelbach 106
Tußmannstr. 19
40477 Düsseldorf
Germany
fon +49 (0)211 9 35 71 10
fax +49 (0)211 9 35 71 14
jan.tittelbach@permanent.de

Elena Tolokonina 38, 58, 120
Zelenograd 1004-181
Moscow, Russia
fon +7 (0)95 53 20 004

Minja Töniges 10
c/o **FH Düsseldorf**

Jana Traboulsi 86
P.O.Box 11-0236/794
American University of Beirut
Department of Architecture and Design
Beirut, Lebanon
fon +961 (0)3 45 30 19
fax +961 (0)1 73 66 35
jana79@hotmail.com

Stephan Trischler 122
c/o krænk
spezialklinik für gestaltung
Ober-Ramstädter Str. 96g
64367 Mühltal
Germany
fon +49 (0)6151 60 63 36
fax +49 (0)6151 60 63 37
trischler@kraenk.de
www.kraenk.de

Erika Usselmann 5
usselmann-e@hfg-gmuend.de

Sabine Veerkamp 24
Erlenstr. 70
28199 Bremen
Germany
fon +49 (0)421 5 97 89 97

Rasik Versani 22
c/o **University of Reading**

Britta Waldmann 10
c/o **FH Düsseldorf**

Ricarda Wallhäuser 57
c/o **Kunsthochschule Kassel**

Stefan Walz 99
Fangelsbachstr. 12
70178 Stuttgart
Germany
fon +49 (0)711 6 49 91 85
stefan.walz@merz-akademie.de

Ina Watermann 10
c/o **FH Düsseldorf**

Max Weber 10
c/o **FH Düsseldorf**

Svenja Weber 29
c/o **Julia Guther**

Li Wei 62, 69, 104
100 Howe St., Apt. 205
New Haven CT
06511 USA
fon/fax +1 203 787 3498
liannwei@aol.com

Stephanie Westmeyer 10
c/o **FH Düsseldorf**

Anne Wichmann 37
Sophienstr. 23
60487 Frankfurt a.M.
Germany
fon +49 (0)69 70 79 32 77
annewichmann@gmx.de

Jennifer Wiefel 5
Sebaldstr. 7
D-73525 Schwäbisch Gmünd
fon +49 (0)7171 18 15 67
wiefel-j@hfg-gmuend.de

Petra Wierzchula 57
c/o **Kunsthochschule Kassel**

Scott Williams 34
c/o **Royal College of Art**

Sarah Winter 105
Richard-Wagner-Str. 13
34277 Fuldabrück
Germany
fon +49 (0)561 4 46 98
swinter@student.uni-kassel.de

Lap-yan Wong 101
Rm 3, 4/F Man Hoi House
Chun Man Court, Homantin
Hong Kong
fon +852 27 15 31 40
lywong@chickmail.com

Fang Yi 80
c/o **Shanghai Light Industry College**
fon +86 20 83 59 98 59
fax +86 20 83 59 62 34
xu@wangxu.com.cn

Avital Josef Yosef 52
c/o **Vital – The Tel Aviv Center
for Design Studies**

Noriko Yuasa 61
4633 Dahlia St.
St. Louis MO
63116 USA
fon +1 314 832 7151
nyuasa@hotmail.com

Alan Zaruba 102
c/o **London College of Printing**

Amanda Zaslow 49
c/o **Rhode Island School of Design**

Andreas Zeischegg 144
Oblatterwallstr. 22h
86153 Augsburg
Germany
fon +49 (0)821 51 91 07
zeischegg@web.de

Thomas Zika 45
Gronaustr. 49
Germany
42285 Wuppertal
fon +49 (0)202 88 45 50
fax +49 (0)202 8 90 49 06

Nelli Zwirner 36
Bäckergasse 20
86150 Augsburg
Germany
fon +49 (0)821 15 27 17
nellizwi@hotmail.com

College List

Australia

University of Technology
P.O. Box 123
Broadway NSW
2007 Australia
fon +61 (02) 9514 2000
www.uts.edu.au

University of Western Sydney
P.O. Box 10
Kingswood NSW
2747 Australia
fon +61 (0)2 2736 0222
www.nepean.uws.edu.au

Austria

Universität für angewandte Kunst Wien
1. Bezirk Oskar-Kokoschka-Platz 2
1010 Wien
fon +43 (0)1 7 12 10 29

China

Hong Kong Baptist University
Kowloon Tong, Hong Kong
fon (852) 2339 7400
www.hkbu.edu.hk

Shanghai Light Industry College
No. 440, Hangdan Road
Shanghai 200433
China

Germany

Staatliche Akademie der Bildenden Künste Stuttgart
Am Weißenhof 1
70191 Stuttgart
fon +49 (0)711 25 75 0
fax +49 (0)711 25 75 225
www.abk-stuttgart.de

FH Anhalt
Abteilung Dessau/FB Grafik-Design
Bernburger Straße 55
06366 Köthen
fon +49 (0)3496 67 223 oder 67 251
fax +49 (0)3496 67 208
www.hs-anhalt.de

FH Augsburg
Baumgartnerstr. 16
86161 Augsburg
fon +49 (0)821 5586 0
fax +49 (0)821 5586 222
www.fh-augsburg.de

Fachhochshule für Technik und Wirtschaft Berlin
Treskowallee 8
10313 Berlin
fon +49 (0)30 50 19 24 42
fax +49 (0)30 50 19 22 50
www.fhtw-berlin.de

HdK Berlin
Ernst-Reuter-Platz 10
10595 Berlin
fon +49 (0)30 31 85 24 50
fax +49 (0)30 31 85 26 35
www.hdk-berlin.de

HfK Bremen
Am Wandrahm 23
28195 Bremen
fon +49 (0)421 30 19 0
fax +49 (0)421 30 19 119
www.hfk-bremen.de

FH Darmstadt
Haardtring 100
64295 Darmstadt
fon +49 (0)6151 16 80 43
fax +49 (0)6151 16 80 43
www.fh-darmstadt.de

FH Dortmund
Postfach 10 50 18
44047 Dortmund
fon +49 (0)231 91 12 0
www.fh-dortmund.de

FH Düsseldorf
Universitätsstraße
40225 Düsseldorf
fon +49 (0)211 8 11 49 15
fax+49 (0)211 8 11 49 16
www.fh-duesseldorf.de

Universität GH Essen
Universitätsstr. 2
45141 Essen
fon +49 (0)201 1 83 1
fax +49 (0)201 1 83 21 51
www.uni-essen.de

FH Hamburg
Winterhuder Weg 29
22085 Hamburg
fon +49 (0)40 428 63 36 45 oder 36 44
fax +49 (0)40 428 63 32 17
www.fh-hamburg.de

FH Hannover
Ricklinger Stadtweg 118
30459 Hannover
fon +49 (0)511 9 29 60
fax +49 (0)511 9 29 61 20
www.fh-hannover.de

Universität GH Kassel
Mönchebergstrasse 19
34125 Kassel
fon +49 (0)561 8 04 22 06
fax +49 (0)561 8 04 72 16
www.uni-kassel.de

HfG Karlsruhe
Durmersheimer Str. 55
76185 Karlsruhe
fon +49 (0)721 9 54 10
www.hfg-karlsruhe.de

Muthesius-Hochschule Kiel
Lorentzendamm 6-8
24103 Liel
+49 (0)431 5 19 84 00
+49 (0)431 5 19 84 08
www.muthesius.de

Hochschule für Grafik und Buchkunst Leipzig
Wächterstraße 11
04107 Leipzig
fon +49 (0) 341 2 13 50
fax +49 (0) 341 2 13 51 66
www.hgb-leipzig.de

FH Mainz
Seppel-Glückert-Passage 10
55116 Mainz
fon +49 (0)6131 2 39 20
www.fh-mainz.de

FH München
Lothstraße 34
80335 München
fon +49 (0)89 12 65 0
fax +49 (0)89 12 65 14 90
www.fh-muenchen.de

FH Münster
Hüfferstraße 27
48149 Münster
fon +49 (0)251 8 30
fax +49 (0)251 8 36 40 15
www.fh-muenster.de

FH Niederrhein
Reinarzstraße 49
47805 Krefeld
fon +49 (0)2151 82 20
fax +49 (0)2151 82 25 55
www.fh-niederrhein.de

FH Nürnberg
Keßlerstraße 16
90489 Nürnberg
fon +49 (0)911 58 80 43 27
fax +49 (0)911 58 80 83 27
www.fh-nuernberg.de

HfG Offenbach
Schlossstrasse 31
63065 Offenbach am Main
fon +49 (0)69 80 05 90
www.hfg-offenbach.de

FH Pforzheim
Tiefenbronner Straße 65
75175 Pforzheim
fon +49 (0)7231 28 67 24
fax +49 (0)7231 28 67 26
www.fh-pforzheim.de

Freie Kunstschule Ravensburg
Kapuzinerstr. 27
88212 Ravensburg
fon +49 (0)751 1 53 13

FH Schwäbisch Gmünd
Rektor-Klaus-Straße 100
073525 Schwäbisch Gmünd
fon +49 (0)7171 6 02 60 0
fax +49 (0)7171 6 92 59
www.hfg-gmuend.de

Merz Akademie Stuttgart
Staatlich anerkannte FH für Gestaltung
Teckstraße 58
70190 Stuttgart
fon +49 (0)711 26 86 60
fax +49 (0)711 26 86 621
www.merz-akademie.de

FH Wiesbaden
Fachhochschule Wiesbaden
Kurt-Schumacher-Ring 18
65197 Wiesbaden
fon: +49 (0)611 94 95 01
fax: +49 (0)611 44 46 96

Bergische Universität
GH Wuppertal
Gaußstraße 20
42097 Wuppertal
fon +49 (0)202 4 39 0
fax +49 (0)202 4 39 29 01
www.uni-wuppertal.de

FH Würzburg
Sanderring 8
97070 Würzburg
fon +49 (0)931 35 11 0
www.fh-wuerzburg.de

Great Britain

Royal College of Art
Kensington Gore
London SW7 2EU
Great Britain
fon +44 (0)20 7590 4444
fax +44 (0)20 7590 4500
www.rca.ac.uk

London College of Printing
Elephant & Castle
London SE1 6SB
Great Britain
fon +44(0)20 75146569
www.lcp.linst.ac.uk

Manchester Metropolitan University
All Saints Building
All Saints
Manchester M15 6BH
Great Britain
fon +44 (0)161 247 2000
fax +44 (0)161 247 6390
www.mmu.ac.uk

University of Reading
Department of Typography and Graphic Communication
2 Earley gate
Reading RG6 6AU
Great Britain
fon +44 (0) 118 931 8081
fax +44 (0) 118 935 1680
www.reading.ac.uk

Hungary

Hungarian Academy of Craft and Design
Magyar Iparmuvészeti Egyetem
Zugligeti út 11-25
H-1121 Budapest
Hungary
fon +36 1 394 1722
fax +36 1 2008 726
www.mif.hu

Israel

Vital - The Tel Aviv Center for Design Studies
12 Vital St.
Tel Aviv
66088 Israel
fon +972 3 6812175
fax +972 3 6812716
www.vital.co.il

Italy

Fabrica
via Ferrarezza
Catena di Villorba TV
31050 Italy
fon +39 0422 616235
fax +39 0422 616251
www.fabrica.it

Korea

Hong-Ik University
72-1 Sangsu-dong, Mapo-gu
Seoul 121-791
Korea
fon +82 02 320 1114
fax +82 02 320 1122
www.hongik.ac.kr

Lebanon

American University of Beirut
Department of Architecture and Design
P.O. Box 11-0236
Beirut, Lebanon
fon +961 1 354911
fax +961 1 744462
www.aub.edu.lb

Notre Dame University
P.O. Box 72
Zouk Mikael, Lebanon
fon +961 9 218950
fax +961 9 218771
www.ndu.edu.lb

Mexico

Universidad de Puebla
info.pue.udlap.mx

Indonesia

Jakarta Institute of Arts
Kompleks Tamam Ismail Marzuki
Jalan Cikini Raya 73
Jakarta 10330
Indonesia
fon +62 21 32 48 07

Universitas Pelita Harapan
UPH Tower - Lippo Karawaci
P.O. Box 453
Tangerang
15811 Indonesia
fon +62 21 5460901
fax +62 21 5460910
www.ph.edu

Russia

Higher Academic School of Graphic Design Moscow

Switzerland

Höhere Schule für Gestaltung, Basel
Vogelsangstrasse 15
Postfach 472
4021 Basel
fon +41 (0)61 6 95 67 70
fax +41 (0)61 6 95 68 80

Höhere Schule für Gestaltung, Zürich
Ausstellungsstr. 60
8005 Zürich
fon +41 (0)1 4 46 21 11

Taiwan

Shih Chien University
fon +886 02 2533 8151
www.scc.edu.tw

Turkey

Mimar Sinar Üniversitesi
Grafik Bölümü
Findikli, Istanbul
Turkey
fon +90 212 252 16 00
www.msu.edu.tr

USA

California Institute of Arts
24700 McBean Parkway
Valencia CA
91355 USA
fon +1 661 255 1050
www.calarts.edu

Cranbrook Academy of Art
P.O. Box 801
39221 Woodward Avenue
Bloomfield Hills MI
48303 USA
fon +1 248 645 3300
fax +1 248 646 0046
www.cranbrookart.edu

Minneapolis College of Art and Design
2501 Stevens Ave. S
Minneapolis MN
55404 USA
fon +1 612 874 3700
fax +1 612 874 3704
www.mcad.edu

School of Visual Arts
209 East 23 Street
New York NY
10010 USA
fon +1 212 592 2000
fax +1 212 725 3587
www.schoolofvisualarts.edu

University of Arts
320 South Broad Street
Philadelphia PA
19102 USA
fon +1 215 875 4800
www.uarts.edu

Rhode Island School of Design
2 College St.
Providence RI
02903 USA
fon +1 401 454 6171
fax +1 401 454 6117
www.risd.edu

Yale School of Art
1156 Chapel St
New Haven CT
06520 USA
fon +1 203 432 2600
fax +1 203 432 7158
www.yale.edu/art/

output 03
International Yearbook for awarded works of Graphic Design Students
Internationales Jahrbuch für prämierte Arbeiten von Grafik-Design Student/innen

Editors / Herausgeber

Florian Pfeffer
+
Dieter Kretschmann
for the German Design Council
für den Rat für Formgebung

Contributing Editors

Polly Bertram	Steven Heller	Peter Rea
Sheila de Bretteville	Ken Hiebert	Louise Sandhaus
Irma Boom	Werner Jeker	Ahn Sang-Soo
Hans van Dijk	Eckhard Jung	Robyn Stacey
Richard Doust	William Longhauser	Kan Tai-keung
Debra Drodvillo	Sadik Karamustafa	Chris Treweek
Gert Dumbar	Hanny Kardinata	Teal Triggs
Neil Grant	John Kortbawi	Hans-Dieter Reichert
David Grossman	Leila Musfy	Chris Vermaas
	Kali Nikitas	Omar Vulpinari

:output partners

Vormgevingsinstituut-Netherlands Design Institute, Amsterdam

Design

jung und pfeffer
visual communication, Bremen

Michael J Godfrey (CD-ROM)
jung und pfeffer

Translation / Übersetzung

Michael J Godfrey
Christopher Livings

Publishing and Distribution / Verlag und Vertrieb

Verlag Hermann Schmidt Mainz
Robert-Koch-Straße 8
55129 Mainz
Germany

Copyright

Florian Pfeffer, Bremen

Friederike

Thank you / Danke

Helge Aszmoneit, Anne Bracklow, Stef van Breugel, Lutz Dietzold, Anne Dombrowski,
Gabriele Eggers, Eric (aus Amsterdam), Ute Follmann, Michael J Godfrey, Svenja Hofert,
Friederike Lambers, Kay Michalak, Wolfram Sprunck, Frauke Stamerjohanns, Erna Theys

Deutsche Städte Medien GmbH, Bremen/Erfurt

ISBN

3-87439-542-1
Printed in Germany

All rights reserved. No part of this publication may be reproduced or transmitted
in any form or by any means electronical or mechanical, including photography or any
information storage and retrieval system.
Das Werk einschließlich aller seiner Teile ist urheberrechtlich geschützt. Jede
Verwertung außerhalb der engen Grenzen des Urheberrechts ist ohne Zustimmung
des Herausgebers unzulässig und strafbar. Das gilt insbesondere für
Vervielfältigungen, Übersetzungen und Verarbeitung in elektronischen Systemen.